A COLLECTION OF

CHINESE PROVERBS

By the late Rev. W. SCARBOROUGH

Revised and enlarged by the addition of some

Six Hundred Proverbs

By the

Rev. C. WILFRID ALLAN

Union Theological School, Changsha.

(Author of The Makers of Cathay)

Second Edition
PARAGON BOOK REPRINT
New York
1964

An unaltered and unabridged edition
of the revised and enlarged edition
first published in 1926 in Changsha, China

Second Edition
by Paragon Book Reprint Corp. New York, N.Y.

Printed in the United States of America

A COLLECTION OF CHINESE PROVERBS

PREFACE

This collection of Chinese Proverbs was issued by the Rev. W. Scarborough in 1875. At that time there was little literature on the subject, and the collections of proverbs that existed were meagre and unsatisfactory. The book met with a hearty reception, and was recognised as a valuable contribution to the knowledge of Chinese life and character.

The present reviser, having heard many expressions of regret that the collection of proverbs had run out of print, decided to revise Mr. Scarborough's work, and this book is the result. It is issued in the firm belief that the collection will, to use Mr. Scarborough's own words, prove both useful and interesting ; useful as a study of Chinese idiom and phraseology, and interesting as showing light on many phases of Chinese character and life.

Mr. Scarborough took great pains with the classification of the proverbs, but was conscious when the book was issued that the arrangement was defective, and it was criticised in the press. Many may have felt that the classification was not a real help, but on the whole it proved valuable, and this present volume has retained the results of Mr. Scarborough's careful work, though the alphabetical arrangement which he made has been discarded. It is hoped the present method of compilation will commend itself.

When the original volume was issued, many of the proverbs had rhymed translations, in accordance with a principle which Mr. Scarborough adhered to, that proverbs rhyming in the original should do so in translation. This was criticised in the foreign press as a doubtful principle, and said to detract somewhat from the value of the book to students of Chinese, because it failed to give the exact meaning of many of the proverbs. In the present volume a straightforward translation has been given. Some of these renderings may be considered as verbose, and therefore not in keeping with proverbial pithiness, but it is hoped that by this means things will be made easier not merely for the student of Chinese but also for the Chinese student of English. In the cases where Mr. Scarborough's translations were not in rhyme, his own words have been largely retained, only altered when the reviser felt that accuracy was at stake, or that ambiguity might lead to misunderstanding.

In order to give a fair conception of Chinese proverbial phraseology Mr. Scarborough allowed a certain number of coarse and vulgar sayings to appear, but in the opinion of many this was a mistake, as the expressions served no good purpose. In this volume these proverbs are omitted. Other omissions have also taken place, such as classic phrases which could hardly be called proverbs, and certain descriptive sentences of comparative little value. To replace these a number of sayings have been added from Mr. Scarborough's own manuscripts, and in order to make the compilation a little more comprehensive the present reviser has added some six hundred extra proverbs culled from various sources.

This book is primarily for the student of Chinese, and a few notes have been added in the hope that his labour might be lightened. One of the criticisms of the original volume was that the notes were too meagre and that the meaning of certain proverbs was lost for want of a little help. The notes in the present volume are not numerous, and are only added to clear up difficulties which sometimes perplex students of this variable language. The romanisation is practically the system of Sir Thomas Wade.

For any one who wishes to sound the depths of Chinese proverbial philosophy, and to gain a thorough knowledge of the workings of the Chinese mind, Dr. Arthur Smith's delightful book on Chinese Proverbs is available; but it is felt that this present volume will meet a need, especially that of a busy man who likes to turn up references with a minimum of labour and research. As the whole subject of proverbial philosophy is thoroughly discussed in Dr. Smith's book, the long essay or introduction of Mr. Scarborough's original volume has been omitted.

CHANGSHA, 1926.

SECTION I. ON MAN.

Chapter 1. Mankind.

人 生 一 百, 種 種 色 色

Jên shéng i pai, chung chung sê sê.

> Amongst a hundred men you'll find all sorts.

人 是 樹 椿, 全 靠 衣 裳

Jên shih shu chuang, ch'üan k'ao i shang.

> Man is like a tree trunk; entirely dependent on clothing.

人 同 此 心, 心 同 此 理

Jên t'ung tz'ǔ hsin, hsin t'ung tz'ǔ li.

> Men are one in heart, and their hearts one in principle.

人 非 聖 賢 就 能 無 過

Jên fei sheng hsien shu neng wu kuo?

> Who but the sages are free from faults?

人 有 好 歹, 貨 有 高 低

Jên yu hao tai, huo yu kao ti.

> There are good and bad men, as there are valuable and
> worthless goods.

人 爲 萬 物 之 靈

Jên wei wan wu chih ling.

> Man is the most intelligent of all creatures.

人 不 求 人 一 般 大, 水 不 流 來 一 般 平

Jên pu ch'iu jên i pan ta, shui pu liu lai i pan p'ing.

> When no favour is sought men are equal : where water
> does not flow, it remains at the same level.

坐 轎 子 也 是 人, 擡 轎 子 也 是 人

Tso chiao tzǔ yeh shih jên, t'ai chiao tzǔ yeh shih jên.

> He who sits in the chair is a man : he who carries the
> chair is a man also.

人 人 有 臉, 樹 樹 有 皮

Jên jên yu lien, shu shu yu p'i.

> All men have faces as all trees have bark.

人 身 一 小 天 地

Jên shên i hsiao t'ien ti.

Man is heaven and earth in miniature.

人 生 知 足 何 時 足，人 老 偸 閒・且 自 閒

Jên shêng chih tsu ho shih tsu, jên lao t'ou hsien ch'ieh tzu hsien.

When in their lives are men satisfied ; seeking leisure in old age, when are they at leisure ?

四 海 之 內 皆 兄 弟 也

Ssü hai chih nei chieh hsiung ti yeh.

All within the Four Seas are brothers.

相 識 滿 天 下，知 心 無 幾 人

Hsiang shih man t'ien hsia, chih hsin wu chi jên.

One may be acquainted with everybody in the empire, but know the hearts of only a few.

人 是 地 上 仙，十 天 不 見 走 一 千

Jên shih ti shang hsien, shih t'ien pu chien tsou i ch'ien.

Man is an Immortal of the earth, if he is not seen for ten days he will have travelled a thousand li.

一 母 生 百 般，一 龍 生 九 種

I mu sheng pai pan, i lung sheng chiu chung.

One mother gives birth to many kinds ; one dragon gives birth to nine sorts.

人 是 衣 裳，馬 是 鞍

Jên shih i shang, ma shih an.

Man is judged by his clothes ; a horse by its saddle.

遠 逛 衣 裳，近 逛 人

Yuan kuang i shang, chin kuang jên.

Abroad, a man's clothes are looked at ; at home, the man himself.

天 下 只 有 兩 人 忙

T'ien hsia chih yu liang jên mang.

In the empire there are only two busy men. i.e. Messrs. 利 Gain and 名 Reputation.

男 子 有 德 便 是 才, 女 子 無 才 便 是 德

Nan tzǔ yu tê pien shih ts'ai, nü tzǔ wu ts'ai pien shih tê.

A man's virtue is considered an endowment; a woman's
want of endowment is considered a virtu:.

人 無 百 年 身, 常 懷 千 年 憂

Jên wu pai nien shen, ch'ang huai ch'ien nien yu.

Man does not live a hundred years, yet he worries himself
enough for a thousand.

Chapter 2. Human Nature.

無 求 到 處 人 情 好, 不 飲 任 他 酒 價 高

Wu ch'iu tao ch'u jên ch'ing hao, pu yin jên t'a chiu chia kao.

Ask no favours and every where men are affable; if you
dont drink it doesnt matter what price wine is.

凡 人 不 可 貌 相, 海 水 不 可 斗 量

Fan jên pu k'o mao hsiang, hai shui pu k'o tou liang.

You cannot judge men by their looks; you cannot measure
the sea with a peck measure.

人 往 高 處 走, 水 往 低 處 流

Jên wang kao ch'u tsou, shui wang ti ch'u liu.

Man is naturally ambitious, but water flows downwards.

天 可 度, 地 可 量, 惟 有 人 心 不 可 防

T'ien k'o to, ti k'o liang, wei yu jên hsin po k'o fang.

You may measure heaven and earth, but you are not a
match for the heart of man. i.e. you cannot guard
yourself against its devices.

人 心 不 足, 得 隴 望 蜀

Jên hsin pu tsu, tê Lung wang Shu.

Man's heart is never satisfied; after obtaining Lung he
looks for Shu. (Lung and Shu were two states
during the period of the Three Kingdoms. The
words are attributed to 劉 秀 Liu Hsiu, founder of
the Eastern Han Dynasty.

堪 嘆 人 心 毒 似 蛇, 誰 知 天 眼 轉 如 車

K'an t'an jên hsin tu ssǔ shê, shui chih t'ien yen chuan ju c'hê.

Alas! man's heart is like a poisonous snake; but all unknown the eyes of heaven revolve as carriage wheels.

天高不見高，人心第一高，井水做酒賣，還說豬無糟

T'ien kao pu chien kao, jên hsin ti i kao, ching shui tso chiu mai, huan shuo chu wu tsao.

> Heaven is high though not appearing so, but man's desires rise higher; he makes wine out of well water, to sell and then complains because the pigs have no distillers' grains to eat.

天 下 無 難 處 之 人，只 須 三 个 必 自 反

T'ien hsia wu nan ch'u chih jên, chih hsü san ko pi tzŭ fan.

> Nobody on earth is difficult to manage; all that is necessary is to examine oneself thoroughly. Note. The last clause refers to the three passages in Mencius. See Book 4. Part 2. Chap. 28.

公 道 自 在 人 心

Kung tao tzŭ tsai jên hsin.

> Man's heart is naturally just.

百 年 成 之 不 足，一 旦 壞 之 有 餘

Pai nien ch'eng chih pu tsu, i tan huai chih yu yü.

> It is hard to build up, but easy to tear down. *Lit.* To complete a thing, a hundred years is not enough; to destroy, one day is more than sufficient.

學 好 千 日 不 足，學 歹 一 時 有 餘

Hsüeh hao ch'ien jih pu tsu, hsüeh tai i shih yu yü.

> To learn what is good, a thousand days are not sufficient; to learn what is evil, an hour is too long.

不 曉 得 他 葫 蘆 裏 裝 什 麼 藥

Pu hsiao tê t'a hu lu li chuang shih mo yao.

> I cannot fathom his devices. *Lit.* I do not know what sort of medicine he has in his calabash. Said of 鐵 拐 先 生 Ti'eh Kuai Hsien Sheng, one of the 八 仙 Pa Hsien, Eight Immortals of Taoism.

眼 不 見 心 不 怒

Yen pu chieh hsin pu nu.

> What the eye sees not, the heart does not vex itself over.

水 能 載 舟 亦 能 覆 舟

Shui neng tsai chou i neng fu chou.

> Water can both sustain and upset a ship. Note. This refers to the power men have for good or evil.

江 山 易 改 本 性 難 移

Chiang shan i kai, pen hsing nan i.

Rivers and hills may be easily altered; man's natural
disposition is difficult to change.

心 有 天 高 命 如 紙 薄

Hsin yu t'ien kao ming ju chih po.

His heart is as lofty as heaven; his fate is as thin as paper.
i.e. his ambition is great but he has no success.

老 馬 不 死，舊 性 還 在

Lao ma pu ssǔ, chiu hsing huan tsai.

So long as the old horse is alive, he retains his nature.

人 心 不 足，蛇 吞 象

Jên hsin pu tsu shê t'un hsiang.

Man's heart is never satisfied; the snake would swallow
the elephant.

人 心 隔 肚 皮，飯 飯 隔 炊 箄

Jên hsin kê tu p'i, fan tsêng kê ch'ui pei.

The heart is concealed in the body; as the rice steamer is
hidden in the cooking pot.

醫 得 身 醫 不 得 心

I tê shên i pu tê hsin.

The body may be healed but not the mind.

酒 色 人 人 愛，財 帛 動 人 心

Chiu sê jên jên ai, ts'ai pai tung jên hsin.

Men love wine and women; riches influence men's hearts.

難 中 好 試 人，難 中 好 救 人

Nan chung hao shih jên, nan chung hao chiu jên.

The time to test men and to save men is when they are
in difficulties.

路 遙 知 馬 力，事 久 見 人 心

Lu yao chih ma li, shih chiu chien jên hsin.

Distance tests a horse's strength; long service reveals a
man's character.

人 心 難 測

Jên hsin nan ts'ê.

The human heart is difficult to fathom. Comp. Jer. 17. 9.

畫 虎 畫 皮 難 畫 骨, 知 人 知 面 不 知 心

Hua hu hua p'i nan hua ku, chih jên chih mien pu chih hsin.

> You may sketch a tiger's skin, but you cannot sketch his bones; you may know a man's face, but you cannot know his heart.

人 情 似 紙 張 張 薄, 世 事 如 棋 局 局 新

Jên ch'ing ssu chih chang chang po, shih shih ju ch'i chü chü hsin.

> Man's nature is as thin as shee's of tissue paper; the world's affairs are like a game of chess varying at every move.

人 情 似 水 分 高 下, 世 事 如 雲 任 捲 舒

Jên ch'ing ssu shui fen kao hsia, shih shih ju yün jên chüan shu.

> Man's disposition, like water, distinguishes between high and low; the world is ever changing, like a cloud. *Lit.* Rolling up and unrolling.

生 不 認 魂, 死 不 認 屍

Shêng pu jên hun, ssŭ pu jên shih.

> Living, man knows not his soul; dead, he knows not his corpse. Note. Soul here, means his disembodied spirit.

入 山 不 怕 傷 人 虎, 只 怕 人 間 兩 面 刀

Ju shan pu p'a shang jên hu, chih p'a jên chien liang mien tao.

> Rather fear the man whose disposition is a two-edged sword, than the savage tiger of the mountains.

你 急, 他 未 急, 人 閒, 心 未 閒

Ni chi t'a wei chi, jên hsien hsin wei hsien.

> One is anxious when another is not; one may seem to be at leisure when his heart is not so.

人 老 心 未 老, 人 窮 志 不 窮

Jên lao hsin wei lao, jên ch'iung chih pu ch'iung.

> A man may be old and yet have a youthful heart; a man may be poor and yet his will be undaunted.

人 無 千 日 好, 花 無 百 日 紅

Jên wu ch'ien jih hao, hua wu pai jih hung.

> Man isn't always fortunate, flowers don't last for ever.

人 各 有 心·心 各 有 見

Jên ko yu hsin, hsin ko yu chien.

Each man has his own mind, and each mind its own
particular idea.

心 裏 光 明 是 天 堂,心 裏 黑 暗 是 地 獄

Hsin li kuang ming shih ti'en tang, hsin li hei an shih ti yü.

A mind enlightened is like heaven; a mind in darkness
is like hell.

爲 人 誰 無 個 錯 處

Wei jên shui wu ko ts'o ch'u?

Amongst men who is there without a fault? Comp.
Psalm 14. 1.

一 差 半 錯·那 個 沒 有

I ch'a pan ts'o, na ko mu yu.

What man is not guilty of slight errors?

蛇 入 竹 筒·曲 性 難 改

Shê ju chu t'ung, ch'u hsing nan kai.

Though a snake get into a bamboo tube it is hard to
change its wriggling disposition. i e. its straightness
is only temporary, owing to circumstances.

點 石 化 爲 金·人 心 猶 未 足

Tien shih hua wei chin, jên hsin yu wei tsu.

Though stones should be transformed into gold, men
would not be satisfied. Note 點化, to act upon. To
influence.

火 要 空 心,人 要 實 心

Huo yao k'ung hsin, jên yao shih hsin.

Fire should be hollow-hearted; man true-hearted. Note.
A fire in the stove is supposed to burn better if the
centre is hollow.

心 爲 一 身 之 主

Hsin wei i shên chih chu.

The mind is the master of man.

人 憐 溫 存·狗 憐 食

Jên lien wen ts'un kou lien shih.

Men love gentleness; dogs like food. Note. 憐 love does
not convey the idea of pity.

看 透 人 情 總 是 空

K'an t'ou jên ch'ing tsung shih k'ung.

> When you see into man's disposition, you perceive that all is false. Comp. Jer. 17. 9.

人 雖 至 愚 責 人 則 明，人 雖 至 明 責 已 則 昏

Jên sui chih yü tsê jên tsê ming, jên sui chih ming tsê chi tsê hun.

> However stupid a man may be, he is clever when blaming others; however wise, he is a dolt when blaming himself.

人 不 知 己 過，牛 不 知 力 大

Jên pu chih chi kuo, niu pu chih li ta.

> Men know not their own faults; oxen know not their own strength.

入 山 擒 虎 易，開 口 告 人 難

Ju shan ch'in hu i, k'ai k'ou kao jên nan.

> It is easier to seize the tiger in the hills than to appeal to man for support. Note. 告 means to request, to appeal to.

知 己 知 彼，將 心 比 心

Chih chi chih pi, chiang hsin pi hsin.

> Who knows himself knows others; for heart can be compared with heart.

人 有 失 錯，馬 有 漏 蹄

Jên yu shih ts'o, ma yu lou t'i.

> Man makes mistakes as a horse makes mis-steps.

谿 壑 易 塡，人 心 難 滿

Ch'i ho i t'ien jên hsin nan man.

> It is easier to fill up a ravine than to satisfy the heart of man.

相 隨 心 生，相 隨 心 滅

Hsiang sui hsin sheng, hsiang sui hsin mieh.

> A man's face is the reflex of his state of mind.

眼 不 見 肚 不 煩

Yen pu chien tu pu fan.

> What the eye doesn't see, the heart doesn't grieve over.

明 明 白 白 天 堂 路，千 千 萬 萬 不 肯 修

Ming ming pai pai t'ien t'ang lu, ch'ien ch'ien wan wan pu k'en hsiu.

> The road to Heaven is easy to find, but myriads of people refuse to follow it.

天 高 勿 算 高，人 心 節 節 高

T'ien kao wu suan kao, jên hsin chieh chieh kao.

> Heaven is not really high; the heart of man aspires higher and higher.

人 心 難 料 鴨 肫 難 破

Jên hsin nan liao ya chun nan p'o.

> It is as difficult to gauge a man's heart as it is to chop a duck's gizzard.

當 今 世 界 目 頭 淺，只 重 衣 裳 不 重 人

Tang chin shih kai mu t'ou ch'ien, chih chung i shang pu chung jên.

> The world's view is a shallow one; clothes are more respected than persons.

世 間 只 有 人 心 惡

Shih chien chih yu jên hsin wo.

> In the world it is only the heart of man that is evil.

心 之 本 體 有 正 不 邪，苟 有 主 持 自 然 不 惑

Hsin chih pen t'i yu cheng pu hsieh, kou yu chu ch'ih tzǔ jan pu huo.

> Man's nature is originally good and not evil; if self-control is exercised there will be no going astray.

水 底 魚，天 邊 鷹，高 可 射 低 可 釣。惟 有 人 心 不 可 料

Shui ti yü, t'ien pien ying, kao k'o shê, ti k'o tiao, wei yu jên hsin pu k'o liao.

> Fish though deep in the water may be hooked; birds though high in the air may be shot; but the depths of man's heart cannot be reached.

心 似 平 原 走 馬 易 放 難 收

Hsin ssǔ p'ing yüan tsou ma, i fang nan shou.

> The heart is like a horse on a level plain; easily started but not easily stopped.

人 心 主 宰 萬 事

Jên hsin chu tsai wan shih.

> Man's heart controls everything.

Chapter 3. Different Kinds of Men.

1. Young Men.

嘴 上 無 毛, 做 事 不 牢

Tsui shang wu mao, tso shih pu lao.

> He who has no hair on his lip can't be trusted to do anything well.

枯 木 逢 春 猶 再 發, 人 無 兩 度 再 少 年

K'u mu feng ch'un yu tsai fa, jên wu liang tu tsai shao nien

> Withered trees in spring burst forth afresh; but men cannot be young twice.

從 小 看 大

Ts'ung hsiao k'an ta.

> You may see the man in the boy.

細 娃 看 小 時

Hsi wa k'an hsiao shih.

> In judging of what a boy will be, notice what he is in infancy.

二 十 歲 入 孤 老 院, 享 福 太 早

Erh shih sui ju ku lao yuan, hsiang fu t'ai tsao.

> He who enters an asylum for the aged at twenty, enjoys happiness too soon.

年 紀 幼 嫩, 事 事 未 經 閱 歷

Nien chi yu nen, shih shih wei ching yueh li.

> In everything, youths are without experience.

少 壯 尙 不 如 人, 老 來 更 多 無 用

Shao chuang shang pu ju jên, lao lai kêng to wu yung.

> Inferior in youth, quite useless in old age.

必 定 少 年 高 發

Pi ting shao nien kao fa.

> Youth is the time to make one's mark.

2. Aged Men.

家 有 老, 是 個 寶

Chia yu lao, shih ko pao.

> A family that has an old person in it, has a jewel.

樹老半心空,人老事事通

Shu lao pan hsin k'ung, jên lao shih shih t'ung.

> Old trees are hollow inside; old men see things clearly.
> Note. Men of experience and perception are said
> to be 心空

八十歲老砍黃蒿,一日不死要柴燒

Pa shih sui lao k'an huang hao, i jih pu ssŭ yao ch'ai shao.

> Industry is necessary. *Lit.* An old man of eighty still
> cuts dried reeds; every day he lives he needs fuel
> to burn.

衣莫若新,人莫若故

I mo jo hsin, jên mo jo ku.

> There is nothing like newness in clothes; nothing like
> age in man. Note. 故 here means age.

人老無人情,天乾無露水

Jên lao wu jên ch'ing, ti'en kan wu lu shui.

> Age lacks kindness, as dry weather dew.

小兒愛衣老愛食

Hsiao er ai i lao ai shih.

> The young like dress; the aged food.

願短十年壽,不可老來貧

Yüan tuan shih nien shou, pu k'o lao lai p'ing.

> Better die ten years too soon, than spend those years in
> poverty.

下山坡日頭

Hsia shan p'o jih t'ou.

> An old man ready to depart. *Lit.* the sun descending
> the mountain side.

白髮不隨老人去,看看又上少年頭

Pai fa pu sui lao jên ch'ü, k'an k'an yu shang shao nien t'ou.

> White hairs are not only on old men; we see them also
> on the young.

莫笑他人老,終須還到我

Mo hsiao t'a jên lao, chung hsü huan tao wo.

> I wont laugh at another for having grown old, for that
> will assuredly happen to me.

記 得 少 年 騎 竹 馬，看 看 又 是 白 頭 翁

Chi tê shao nien ch'i chu ma, k'an k'an yu shih pai t'ou wêng.

> We remember riding on bamboos as boys, and lo! we are white-headed old men.

七 十 風 前 燭，八 十 瓦 上 霜

Ch'i shih fêng ch'ien chu, pa shih wa shang shuang.

> At seventy, a man is a candle in the wind; at eighty, hoar-frost on the tiles.

不 信 老 人 言，乞 兒 有 得 做

Pu hsin lao jên yen, ch'i êr yu tê tso.

> He who wont take an old man's advice, will one day become a beggar.

不 聽 老 人 言，必 有 心 慌 事

Pu t'ing lao jên yen, pi yu hsin huang shih.

> He who wont listen to aged men will do foolish things.

年 高 有 德

Nien kao yu tê.

> Aged men are virtuous.

公 道 世 間 惟 白 髮，貴 人 頭 上 不 曾 饒

Kung tao shih chien wei pai fa, kuei jên t'ou shang pu tsêng jao.

> On earth impartial justice is with the aged, they wont forgive even men of high estate.

薑 桂 之 性 愈 老 愈 辣

Chiang kuei chih hsing yü lao yü la.

> The older ginger and cinnamon are, the more pungent their flavour.

屈 志 老 成 急 則 可 相 倚

Ch'ü chih lao ch'eng chi tsê k'o hsiang i.

> If deferential to experienced old men, in trouble you can rely on them.

人 老 心 不 老，家 窮 行 不 窮

Jên lao hsin pu lao, chia ch'iung hsing pu ch'iung.

> Man grows old but his heart doesn't; a family may be poor but still do noble acts.

人 老 珠 黃 不 值 錢

Jên lao chu huang pu chih ch'ien.

> Man when he is old; the pearl when it is yellow, are worthless.

老 人 家 拜 世, 一 年 勿 及 如 一 年

Lao jên chia pai shih, i nien wu chi ju i nien.

> The aged come for new year congratulations, but each succeeding year is worse than the former.

後 生 不 信 老 人 言

Hou sheng pu hsin lao jên yen.

> Young people do not believe the words of the aged.

人 生 七 十 古 來 稀

Jên sheng ch'i shih ku lai hsi.

> From ancient times till now men of seventy years have been rare.

七 十 不 打, 八 十 不 罵

Ch'i shih pu ta, pa shih pu ma.

> Do not beat men of seventy, nor curse those of eighty years.

3. WOMEN.

一 等 官, 二 等 客, 三 等 寡 婦 惹 不 得

I teng kuan êrh teng k'o, san teng kua fu jê pu tê.

> There are three classes of people one must not provoke; officials, customers and widows. Note 客 equals 客 商 merchants customers.

十 個 婦 人 九 個 妒

Shih ko fu jên chiu ko tu.

> Nine women in ten are jealous.

幼 嫁 從 親, 再 嫁 由 身

Yu chia ts'ung ch'in, tsai chia yu shên.

> A maid marries to please her parents: a widow pleases herself. Note 從 equals 順 從

醜 了 梅 香 醜 了 小 姐

Ch'ou liao mei hsiang ch'ou liao hsiao chieh.

To defame the servant is to defame the mistress. Note 梅 香 *Lit.* plum-perfume is a common name for a maid-servant.

天 要 下 雨，娘 要 嫁 人，無 法 可 制

Ti'en yao hsia yü, niang yao chia jên, wu fa k'o chih.

If heaven wants to rain, or your mother marry again, nothing can prevent them.

懶 婆 娘 做 事 一 担 挑

Lan p'o niang tso shih i tan t'iao.

A lazy woman tries to carry everything at once.

在 家 由 父，出 嫁 從 夫

Tsai chia yu fu, ch'u chia ts'ung fu.

Unmarried, a woman obeys her father: married, her husband.

紅 顏 女 子 多 薄 命，聰 明 子 弟 少 容 顏

Hung yen nü tzŭ to po ming, ts'ung ming tzŭ ti shao yung yen.

Fair maidens are mostly unlucky, clever young men are seldom good-looking.

竹 青 蛇 兒 口．黃 蜂 尾 上 針
兩 般 不 算 毒，最 毒 婦 人 心

Chu ch'ing shê êrh k'ou, huang fêng wei shang chên.
Liang pan pu suan tu, tsui tu fu jên hsin.

There is no such poison in the green snake's mouth or the hornet's sting, as in a woman's heart.

情 人 眼 內 出 西 施

Ch'ing jên yen nei ch'u Hsi Shih.

The lover's eye sees a Hsi Shih in his mistress. (*Hsi Shih* is the *ne plus ultra* of loveliness in Chinese tradition.) She was the concubine of Fu Ch'a 夫 差 King of the ancient state of Wu. 吳

少 是 觀 音，老 是 猴

Shao Shih Kuan Yin, lao shih hou.

Young, she's a *Kuan Yin;* old, she's a monkey. (*Kuan Yin* is the popular Goddess of Mercy.)

嫫 姆 有 所 美，西 施 有 所 醜

Mo Mu yu so mei, Hsi Shih yu so ch'ou.

> Even Mo Mu had some beauty, and Hsi Shih some defect. Note. Mo Mu was one of the wives of the Emperor Huang Ti, a wise but ill-favoured woman.

一 笑 傾 人 城，再 笑 傾 人 國

I hsiao ch'ing jên ch'eng, tsai hsiao ch'ing jên kuo.

> With one smile she overthrows a city, with another, a kingdom. Note. The lady to whom this refers is Hsi Shih. See above.

大 抵 還 他 肌 骨 好，不 搽 紅 粉 也 風 流

Ta ti huan t'a chi ku hao, pu t'sa hung fen yeh fêng liu.

> Generally speaking women are good-looking, they don't need rouge to make them pretty.

女 德 無 極，婦 怨 無 終

Nü tê wu chi, fu yüan wu chung.

> A maid's virtue is unlimited; a wife's resentment without end.

三 姑 六 婆 實 淫 盜 之 媒

San ku lu p'o shih yin tao chih mei.

> The three classes of nuns and the six classes of dames are the go-betweens of adultery and robbery.

> Note. The ladies referred to are 尼姑 The Buddhist Nun, 道姑 The Taoist Nun, 覡姑 The Sorceress, 媒婆 The Go-between, 賣花婆 The Flower Seller, 收生婆 The Midwife, 優婆 The Singing Girl or Prostitute, 師婆 The Spiritual, 醫藥婆 The Doctoress.

一 笑 值 千 金

I hsiao chih ch'ien chin.

> A smile of her's was worth a thousand taels of gold. Note. This has reference to Pao Ssu 褒似 a famous concubine of Yu Wang 幽王 of the Chou 周 Dynasty. She was a great beauty but very sedate.

紅 粉 佳 人 休 便 老，風 流 浪 子 莫 敎 貧

Hung fen chia jên hsiu pien lao, fêng liu lang tzǔ mo chiao p'in.

> The rouged beauty repudiates age, the jolly profligate never speaks of poverty.

紅 紛 佳 人 不 及 當 初

Hung fen chia jên pu chi tang ch'u.

The rouged beauty cannot regain the bloom of youth.

好 女 于 室，醜 女 之 仇

Hao nü yü shih ch'ou nü chih ch'ou.

A good-looking woman in a house is the foe of all the plain ones.

婦 德 者 不 必 才 名 絕 異，婦 容 者 不 必 顏 色 美 麗，
婦 言 者 不 必 利 口 辨 詞，婦 工 者 不 必 技 巧 過 人

Fu tê chê pu pi ts'ai ming chüeh i, fu yung chê pu pi yen sê mei li,
Fu yen chê pu pi li k'ou pien t'zǔ, fu kung chê pu pi chi ch'iaokuo jên.

A woman's virtues need not be of the famous or un-common kind; her face need not be very beautiful, her conversation need not be very eloquent; and her work need not be surpassingly exquisite.

三 分 人 才 七 分 打 扮

San fen jên ts'ai ch'i fen ta pan.

Three tenths of her good looks are due to nature, seven tenths to dress.

婦 人 可 以 共 患 難，不 可 以 共 富 貴

Fu jên k'o i kung huan nau, pu k'o i kung fu kuei.

Women are able to share adversity, but not prosperity. i.e. in the latter their character deteriorates.

婦 人 短 見

Fu jên tuan chien.

Women are very short-sighted i.e. they only appreciate what is before their eyes.

婦 人 之 仁，匹 夫 之 勇

Fu jên chih jên, p'i fu chih yung.

A thing of little value. *Lit.* A woman's benevolence, a low fellow's courage.

男 怕 穿 靴，女 怕 帶 帽

Nan p'a ch'uan hsüeh, nü p'a tai mao.

Men fear to wear boots, women fear to wear hats.

婦 人 長 舌 維 厲 之 階

Fu jên ch'ang shê wei li chih chieh.

> A wife's long tongue is the flight of steps by which misfortune comes (to the house)

婦 人 無 德 有 三，曰 獨 妒·毒

Fu jên wu tê yu san, yüeh tu, tu, tu.

> A woman without virtue is one of three things; selfish, jealous or malicious.

一 朵 鮮 花 插 在 驢 頭 上

I to hsien hua ch'a tsai lü t'ou shang.

> A fresh-cut flower stuck in a donkey's head, i.e., a pretty woman married to an ugly man.

騍 馬 上 不 得 陣

K'o ma shang pu tê chen.

> A mare is not fit to go into battle. i.e. Woman cannot take man's place.

4. GOOD MEN.

一 正 壓 百 邪

I chêng ya·pai hsieh.

> One good man represses a hundred bad ones.

好 人 多 磨 難

Hao jên to mo nan.

> Good men suffer much.

賢 爲 國 家 之 寶

Hsien wei kuo chia chih pao.

> Virtuous men are a kingdom's treasure.

山 中 有 直 樹，世 上 無 直 人

Shan chung yu chih shu, shih shang wu chih jên.

> There are straight trees on the mountains, but no upright men in the world.

人 善 被 人 欺，馬 善 被 人 騎

Jên shan pei jên ch'i, ma shan pei jên ch'i.

> Good men get imposed upon, as good horses get ridden.

好 看 難 做·好 漢 難 做
Hao k'an nan tso, hao han nan tso.
> Pretty things and good men are difficult to make.

好 人 相 逢,惡 人 相 離
Hao jên hsiang fêng, o jên hsiang li
> Men join themselves to the good; but separate from the bad.

吃 得 虧,是 好 漢
Ch'ih tê k'uei, shih hao han.
> He is a good man who can endure wrong.

眞 金 不 怕 火
Chên chin pu p'a huo.
> True gold fears not the fire.

算 老 實 命 的 人
Suan lao shih ming ti jên.
> An honest man. *Lit.* One who tells true fortunes.

本 色 人
Pen sê jên.
> The same. *Lit.* An uncoloured man.

世 上 好 人 百 中 選 一
Shih shang hao jên pai chung hsien i.
> Good men are one in a hundred.

有 兩 個 好 人,一 個 死 了,一 個 未 生
Yu liang ko hao jên, i ko ssǔ liao, i ko wei sheng.
> There are only two good men.—one dead, the other unborn.

熬 苦 受 難,纔 爲 好 漢
Ao k'u shou nan, ts'ai wei hao han.
> He is a good man who can endure much.

心 裡 無 冷 病,那 怕 吃 西 瓜
Hsin li wu leng ping, na p'a ch'ih hsi kua.
> An innocent man fears nothing. *Lit.* He who is free from fever fears not to eat water melons.

水 退 石 出

Shui t'ui shih ch'u.

His bad qualities will appear by and by. *Lit.* As the water recedes the stones appear.

孝 廉 方 正，人 人 奉 敬

Hsiao lien fang cheng, jên jên fêng ching.

Filial, disinterested, and upright men, are honoured by all

巷 裡 趕 豬，直 來 直 去

Hsiang li kan chu, chih lai chih ch'u.

A straightforward man. *Lit.* Pursuing a pig in a passage; going and coming in a straight course.

行 得 正，坐 得 穩，出 言 人 皆 準

Hsing tê chêng, tso tê wen, ch'u yen jên chieh chun.

His words command general assent whose conduct is upright and unwavering.

靛 缸 裏 拉 不 出 白 布 來

Tien kang li la pu ch'u pai pu lai.

Good men not found amongst bad ones. *Lit.* Out of an indigo vat you can't draw white calico.

好 漢 做 事 好 漢 當

Hao han tso shih hao han tang.

A good fellow will stick to his bargain Note. 當 is equal to 擔 當 to bear, sustain.

神 仙 亦 有 遺 失 劍

Shen hsien i yu i shih chien.

The best will err. *Lit.* Gods and Genii sometimes lose their swords.

士 爲 知 己 者 死，女 爲 悅 己 者 容

Shih wei chih chi chê ssŭ, nü wei yüeh chi chê jung.

A good man will die for his friend; a woman will dress for those who appreciate her.

皇 天 不 負 有 心 人

Huang t'ien pu fu yu hsin jên.

High Heaven will not forget the man with good intent.

大 丈 夫 豈 肯 屈 膝

Ta chang fu ch'i k'en ch'u hsi.

> Will a hero easily bend his knee?

忠 厚 是 無 用 之 別 名

Chung hou shih wu yung chih pieh ming.

> Worthiness is only another name for uselessness. i.e.
> good men are often considered simple and therefore
> useless.

好 人 頭 上 三 尺 火

Hao jên t'ou shang san ch'ih huo.

> Good men have three feet of fire over their heads (to
> protect them from evil influences.)

5. SUPERIOR AND MEAN MEN.

君 子 之 交 淡 如 水, 小 人 之 交 嘴 換 嘴

Chun tzŭ chih chiao tan ju shui, hsiao jên chih chiao tsui huan tsui.

> The friendship of superior men is flavourless as water:
> the friendship of mean men needs constant interchange
> of feasts. Note. "Flavourless as water" indicates
> a wise restraint in mutual intercourse.

君 子 一 言, 快 馬 一 鞭

Chun tzŭ i yen, k'uai ma i pien.

> The superior man needs but one word; the swift horse
> needs but one lash.

君 子 安 貧, 達 人 知 命

Chun tzŭ an p'in, ta jên chih ming.

> The superior man is content in a state of poverty; the
> intelligent man submits himself to his destiny.

人 多 君 子 稀

Jên to chun tzŭ hsi.

> There are plenty of men, but few superior men.

君 子 雖 寒 而 不 顫

Chun tzŭ sui han erh pu chan.

> The superior man, though cold does not shiver. Note.
> Is not willing to betray his poverty.

共 君 一 夜 話 · 勝 讀 十 年 書

Kung chun i yeh hua, sheng tu shih nien shu.

One evening's conversation with a superior man, is better than ten years of study.

君 子 言 前 不 言 後

Chun tzŭ yen ch'ien pu yen hou.

The superior man speaks beforehand, not when all is finished.

大 丈 夫 性 命 交 於 天

Ta chang fu hsing ming chiao yü t'ien.

The superior man's life is at the service of Heaven.

文 質 彬 彬 君 子 樣

Wen chih pin pin chun tzŭ yang.

An equal combination of elegance and plainness is the fashion of the superior man.

君 子 絕 交 不 出 惡 聲

Chun tzŭ chüeh chiao pu ch'u o sheng.

A superior man breaks off a friendship without any unpleasantness.

君 子 避 酒 客

Chun tzŭ pi chiu k'o.

The superior man avoids intoxicated people.

君 子 愛 財 取 之 有 道

Chun tzŭ ai ts'ai, ch'ü chih yu tao.

If the superior man desires wealth, he gets it in a proper fashion.

君 子 羞 身 不 羞 口

Chun tzŭ hsiu shên pu hsiu k'ou.

The superior man cultivates himself, not his appetite.

茫 茫 四 海 人 無 數 · 那 個 男 兒 是 丈 夫

Mang mang ssŭ hai jên wu shu, na ko nan erh shih chang fu.

In the wide world men are numberless, but who is the great man?

酒 中 不 語 眞 君 子, 財 上 分 明 大 丈 夫

Chiu chung pu yü chên chun tzŭ, ts'ai shang fen ming ta chang fu.

> Not to be loquacious in liquor marks the true superior man; to be just in the administration of wealth shows the great man.

過 後 思 君 子

Kuo hou ssŭ chun tzŭ.

> When an affair is finished, men recognise the superior man.

義 動 君 子, 利 動 小 人

I tung chun tzŭ, li tung hsiao jên.

> Right influences the superior man; profit, the inferior man.

君 子 之 交 淡 如 水·小 人 之 交 甜 如 蜜

Chun tzŭ chih chiao tan ju shui, hsiao jên chih chiao t'ien ju mi.

> The friendship of superior men is as flavourless as water; the friendship of mean men, sweet as honey.

雪 裡 送 炭 眞 君 子, 錦 上 添 花 是 小 人

Hsüeh li sung t'an chên chun tzŭ, chin shang t'ien hua shih hsiao jên.

> He is a true superior man who gives charcoal in snowy weather; the mean man adds flowers to embroidery i.e. gives where not needed.

頭 大 是 君 子, 脚 大 是 小 人

T'ou ta shih chun tzŭ, chiao ta shih hsiao jên.

> A man with a big head is a superior man; a man with big feet is a mean man. Note. This is one of the sayings of physiognomical fortune tellers.

君 子 有 容 人 之 量, 小 人 存 忌 妒 之 心

Chun tzŭ yu yung jên chih liang hsiao jên ts'un chi tu chih hsin.

> The superior man is able to bear with others; the mean man cherishes an envious spirit.

君 子 吃 滋 味, 小 人 脹 死 不 足

Chun tzŭ ch'ih tzŭ wei, hsiao jên chang ssŭ pu tsu.

> The superior man eats but to taste flavours; the mean man gorges himself to death and is not satisfied.

禮治君子,法治小人

Li chih chun tzǔ, fa chih hsiao jên.

Propriety rules the superior man; law rules the mean man.

德勝才爲君子,才勝德爲小人

Tê sheng ts'ai wei chun tzǔ, ts'ai sheng tê wei hsiao jên.

He whose virtues exceed his talents is the superior man; he whose talents exceed his virtues is the mean man.

君子之心公而恕·小人之心私而刻

Chun tzǔ chih hsin kung erh shu, hsiao jên chih hsin ssǔ erh k'o.

The superior man's heart is liberal and indulgent; the mean man's heart is selfish and stingy.

賊是小人·智過君子

Tsei shih hsiao jên, chih kuo chun tzǔ.

A thief is a mean man, but in cleverness surpasses the superior man.

易漲易退山溪水易反易覆小人心

I chang i tu'i shan ch'i shui, i fan i fu hsiao jên hsin.

Easily swollen, easily exhausted is a mountain stream; easily moved to and fro is the heart of the mean man.

君子敬之則不勝·小人遠之則怨

Chun tzǔ ching chih tsê pu sheng hsiao jên yüan chih tsê yüan.

The superior man commands respect and yet keeps humble; the mean man resents being avoided.

君子愛人以德,小人之愛以姑息

Chün tzǔ ai jên i tê, hsiao jên chih ai i ku hsi.

The superior man loves men with a desire for their good; the mean man simply indulges their weaknesses.

君子喻於義,小人喻於利

Chün tzǔ yü yü i, hsiao jên yü yü li.

The superior man is conversant with his duty towards his neighbour; the mean man is conversant with self-interest.

君子小人之澤,五世而絕

Chün tzǔ hsiao jên chih tsê, wu shih erh chüeh.

After five generations the fame of both superior and mean men disappears.

君子雖貧存人義，小人藉富便欺人

Chün tzǔ sui p'in ts'un jên i, hsiao jên chieh fu pien ch'i jên.

> The superior man though poor still entertains benevolence;
> the mean man uses his wealth to oppress others.

大人不見小人過

Ta jên pu chien hsiao jên kuo.

> The superior man doesn't remember the faults of mean
> men.

君子淡如水，交久情益深

Chün tzǔ tan ju shui, chiao chiu ch'ing i shen.

> The superior man is flavourless as water (i.e., reserved)
> but his friendship is strengthened by time.

小人甘似蜜，轉眼成仇人

Hsiao jên kan ssǔ mi, chuan yen ch'eng ch'ou jên.

> The mean man is sweet as honey (demonstrative) but in
> a moment may become an enemy.

君子上達，小人下達

Chün tzǔ shang ta, hsiao jên hsia ta.

> The superior man improves, the mean man deteriorates.

6. BAD MEN.

捨得一身剮，皇帝老子挪下馬

Shê tê i shên kua, huang ti lao tzǔ no hsia ma.

> He who dare risk being cut to pieces, may drag the
> emperor's father down from his horse.

行凶打架，開口就罵

Hsing hsiung ta chia, k'ai k'ou chiu ma.

> His conduct is cruel and he always fights; when he opens
> his mouth he curses.

臉兒一皮，百事大吉

Lien erh i p'i, pai shih ta chi.

> To a shameless man all things are auspicious.   Note.
> One who does not consider his 'face' or reputation,
> is said to have a face of hide or leather.

面 黃 牙 齒 黑，必 定 鴉 片 客

Mien huang ya ch'ih hei, pi ting ya p'ien k'o.

A man with a yellow face and black teeth is sure to be
an opium smoker.

走 了 路 不 生 草

Tsou liao lu pu sheng ts'ao.

Where he has trodden no grass will grow.

光 棍 軟 如 綿，痴 漢 硬 似 鐵

Kuang kun yuan ju mien, ch'ih han yin ssǔ t'ieh.

A rogue is as soft as cotton; a fool as hard as iron.

光 棍 怕 眼 子，眼 子 怕 綿 纏

Kuang kun p'a yen tzǔ, yen tzǔ p'a mien ch'an.

A rogue fears a simpleton; and a simpleton fears importunity. Note. A simpleton may spoil a rogue's
plan; importunity will result in the simpleton's being
taken in.

一 個 老 鼠 打 壞 一 窠 洞

I ko lao shu ta huai i ch'ao tung.

One rat may spoil the nest.

眼 斜 心 不 正

Yen hsieh hsin pu cheng.

His heart is not upright whose eye looks askance.

強 中 更 有 強 中 手 惡 人 須 用 惡 人 磨

Ch'iang chung kêng yu ch'iang chung shou, ê jên hsü yung ê jên mo.

Amongst bullies there is always one more overbearing
than the rest; and bad men must be by bad men
ground down.

狐 羣 狗 黨

Hu ch'ün kou tang.

A tribe of foxes and a pack of dogs.

黑 心 爛 肝

Hei hsin lan kan.

A vicious rascal. *Lit.* One with a black heart and
rotten liver.

人 無 廉 恥, 百 事 可 爲

Jên wu lien ch'ih, pai shih k'o wei.

A shameless man is ready for anything.

靸 半 頭 鞋

Sa pan t'ou hsieh.

A lazy good-for-nothing. *Lit.* One who goes slipshod.

過 街 老 鼠 齊 叫 打

Kuo chieh lao shu ch'i chiao ta.

A bad man hated by everybody. *Lit.* A rat crossing the street, everybody cries "Hit him."

男 兒 無 信 鈍 鐵 無 鋼, 女 兒 無 信 爛 草 麻 蔃

Nan erh wu hsin tun t'ieh wu kang, nü erh wu hsin lan ts'ao ma jang.

An untruthful man is like untempered steel; an untruthful woman is like rotten grass and tangled hemp.

扯 謊 架 子

Ch'ê huang chia tzŭ.

A lying machine, i.e., a confirmed liar.

扯 謊 架 子, 進 不 得 城 門

Ch'ê huang chia tzŭ chin pu tê ch'eng men.

A lying machine ought not to enter a city gate.
Note. City dwellers are not so easily taken in as rustics.

臉 有 城 墙 厚

Lien yu ch'eng ch'iang hou.

The skin of his face is as thick as a city wall. i.e., he is shameless.

邪 不 敵 正

Hsieh pu ti cheng.

A bad man will not confront a good man.

乾 柴 傍 烈 火

Kan ch'ai p'ang lieh huo.

Quarrelsome men. *Lit.* Dry fuel near a blazing fire.

降 人 多 討 打

Chiang jên to t'ao ta.

The disobedient provoke many stripes.

十 個 禿 子 ; 九 個 詐 ; 那 個 不 詐 是 啞 叭

Shih ko t'u tzŭ chiu ko cha na ko pu cha shih ya pa.

Of ten bald men nine are deceitful, and the tenth is dumb.

禿 子 詐 瞎 子 乖 ; 一 個 眼 的 更 發 壞

T'u tzŭ cha hsia tzŭ kuai i ko yen ti kêng fa huai.

The bald are deceitful, the blind are perverse, and the one-eyed are even more wicked.

能 交 花 子 ; 不 交 瞎 子

Nêng chiao hua tzŭ pu chiao hsia tzŭ.

Associate with beggars but not with the blind.

不 見 棺 材 不 下 淚

Pu chien kuan ts'ai pu hsia lei.

Recklessly wicked. *Lit.* So long as he sees not the coffin he doesn't weep.

遠 賊 必 有 近 脚

Yuan tsê pi yu chin chiao.

The distant thief has a near foot i.e. an accomplice.

光 棍 不 吃 眼 前 虧

Kuang kun pu ch'i yen ch'ien k'uei.

A bully will not risk defeat.

7.   HYPOCRITES.

屬 燈 臺 的 ; 照 別 人 不 照 自 己

Shu teng t'ai ti, chao pieh jên pu chao tzŭ chi.

Like a lamp-stand; he lights others but not himself.

裝 聾 作 啞 無 眞 有 假

Chuang lung tso ya wu chên yu chia.

Pretending to be deaf and dumb; no truth but falsehood.

叫 化 子 走 夜 路 都 是 假 忙

Chiao hua tzŭ tsou yeh lu, tu shih chia mang.

When a beggar is out at night, it is all a pretence of being busy.

腰 裏 撇 一 個 死 老 鼠，假 充 打 獵 的

Yao li p'ieh i ko ssŭ lao shu, chia ch'ung ta lieh ti.

> He is a mock sportsman who slings a dead rat in his girdle.

明 爲 君 子，暗 爲 小 人

Ming wei chün tzŭ, an wei hsiao jên.

> Before people, a superior man; in secret, a mean man.

一 口 仁 義 道 德，肚 裏 男 盜 女 娼

I k'ou jên i tao tê, tu li nan tao nü ch'ang.

> A real hypocrite. *Lit.* To have the mouth full of Benevolence, Righteousness, Reason and Virtue, but in heart a thief or prostitute.

見 人 冷 眼 笑 一 面 心 中 暗 藏 殺 人 刀

Chien jên leng yen hsiao i mien, hsin chung an ts'ang sha jên tao.

> A man who gives a furtive glance and has a laughing face, hides in his heart a murderous sword.

笑 面 孔 曹 操

Hsiao mien k'ung ts'ao ts'ao.

> A laughing Ts'ao Ts'ao. (Ts'ao Ts'ao was a famous general during the wars of the Three Kingdoms; a pleasant but crafty fellow.)

僞 君 子，眞 小 人

Wei chün tzŭ chên hsiao jên.

> A false superior man, but a truly mean man.

外 披 羊 皮，內 藏 狼 心

Wai p'i yang p'i, nei ts'ang lang hsin.

> Outside he wears a sheep-skin; inside he hides a wolf's heart. Comp. Matt. 7. 15.

口 裏 甜 如 蜜，心 裏 毒 似 蛇

K'ou li t'ien ju mi, hsin li tu ssŭ shê.

> His mouth is as sweet as honey; his heart as venomous as a snake.

一 嘴 兩 舌 頭

I tsui liang shê t'ou.

> One mouth with two tongues.

狐 假 虎 威

Hu chia hu wei.

A fox assuming a tiger's ferocity.

甜 瓜 兒 嘴 苦 瓜 兒 心

T'ien kua erh tsui, k'u kua erh hsin.

A mouth like a sweet melon; a heart like a bitter gourd.

佛 口 蛇 心

Fu k'ou shê hsin.

The mouth of a Buddha; the heart of a snake.

東 頭 吃 羊 肉 西 頭 吃 狗 肉

Tung t'ou ch'ih yang jou hsi t'ou ch'ih kou jou.

當 面 親 家 母 背 後 老 虔 婆

Tang mien ch'in chia mu pei hou lao ch'ien p'o.

Two-faced. *Lit.* He eats mutton in the East and dog's-flesh in the West. In her presence he says "Mother," behind her back says "Old Hag."

8 STUPID MEN.

痴 痴 呆 呆 討 個 飽，刁 刁 掘 掘 餓 得 好

Ch'ih ch'ih tai tai t'ao ko pao, tiao tiao chüeh chüeh ô tê hao.

The fool is generally able to get a good meal but the cunning rogue is rightly left hungry.

懵 裏 懵 懂 挑 擔 水 桶，落 了 一 隻 又 往 前 踵

Mêng li mêng tung t'iao tan shui t'ung, lo liao i chih yu wang ch'ien chung.

A silly fellow carrying his water buckets; he lets one of them fall and goes on as though nothing had happened.

糊 塗 成 羹

Hu t'u ch'eng kêng.

Thick enough for soup. A dullard.

擀 麪 棍 吹 火 一 竅 不 通

Kan mien kun ch'ui huo i ch'iao pu t'ung.

An ignoramus. *Lit.* You can't blow up a fire through a rolling pin.

使 鑽 子 鑽 不 動

Shih tsuan tzǔ tsuan pu tung.

> Bore as one will, the gimlet will not enter. Note. Said
> of an intensely stupid man.

糊 塗 一 包 渣

Hu t'u i pao cha.

> A stupid bundle of dregs.

牛 皮 的 燈 籠

Niu p'i ti teng lung.

> An ox-leather lantern.

木 頭 人

Mu t'ou jên.

> **A wooden man.**

二 百 五

Erh pai wu.

> A simpleton. *Lit.* Two hundred and fifty.
> Note. Said to originate in Peking where 5 cash are
> counted as 20, and therefore 250 is an impossible
> number.

一 串 錢 四 開

I ch'uan ch'ien ssǔ k'ai.

> A simpleton. *Lit.* A thousand cash divided into fours.
> Same as above.

烏 漆 墨 黑

Wu ch'i mo hei. '

> Black as pitch and ink. Note. Said of a dark⁷mind.
> Also of a dark night.

有 眼 不 識 金 鑲 玉

Yu yen pu shih chin hsiang yü.

> He has eyes but can't recognise gold inlaid with jade.

男 笑 三 痴 女 笑 三 丟

Nan hsiao san ch'ih nǔ hsiao san tiu.

> A snickering man is a fool; a giggling woman a castaway.
> Note. 三 equals 再三, repeatedly, indicating a
> permanent trait of character.

沒有開過眼孔來的

Mu yu k'ai kuo yen k'ung lai ti.

> One who has not yet opened his eyes. *Note.* Said of a
> stupid clown who wonders at everything he sees.

光眼瞎子

Kuang yen hsia tzǔ.

> One who looks brighter than he is. *Lit.* A bright-eyed
> blind man.

坐井觀天所見不大

Tso chin kuan t'ien so chien pu ta.

> Who sits in a well to observe the sky does not see very
> much. Note. Said of an ignorant man whose sphere
> of observation is limited.

狗肉上不得正席

Kou jou shang pu tê chêng hsi.

> Fools are unequal to great undertakings. *Lit.* You can't
> serve dog's flesh at a banquet.

習文不成習武不就

Hsi wen pu ch'eng hsi wu pu chiu.

> A good-for-nothing. *Lit.* He can make nothing out
> either in literature or soldiery.

越不聰明反快活

Yüeh pu ts'ung ming fan k'uai huo.

> The more stupid the more happy.

水太清則無魚·人太謹則無智

Shui t'ai ch'ing tsê wu yü, jên t'ai chin tsê wu chih.

> If water be too clear it will contain no fish; if men are
> too cautious they will not be clever.

饒人不是癡漢·癡漢不會饒人

Jao jên pu shih ch'ih han, ch'ih han pu hui jao jên.

> An indulgent man is not a fool; a fool can't make
> allowances for others.

肉 眼 無 珠

Jou yen wu chu.

> Stupid, dull of apprehension. *Lit*. A fleshy pupil-less
> eye.

打 醋 的 錢 不 買 醬 油

Ta ts'u ti ch'ien pu mai chiang yu.

> He wont buy soy with money intended for vinegar.
>> Note. This is also used with reference to men of
>> integrity who scrupulously differentiate in the use of
>> public funds.

他 是 個 駱 駝 形 駄 重 不 駄 輕

T'a shih ko lo t'o hsing t'o chung pu t'o ch'ing.

> He is like a camel, preferring heavy weights to light
> ones.

才 智 無 有 爲 人 走 狗

Ts'ai chih wu yu wei jên tsou kou.

> A stupid man will be somebody's lap-dog.

逢 到 和 尙 喊 姐 夫

Fêng tao ho shang han chieh fu.

> A silly fellow. *Lit*. One who meeting a Bonze cries
> out "Brother-in-Law."

讀 書 讀 得 悵，只 爲 上 上 帳

Tu shu tu tê chang, chih wei shang shang chang.

> He studies to no purpose, all he can do is to keep accounts.

9. Clever Men.

大 才 必 有 大 用

Ta ts'ai pi yu ta yung.

> For one of great talents there is a sphere of great useful-
> ness.

八 仙 過 海 各 顯 神 通

Pa hsien kuo hai ko hsien shên t'ung.

> When the Eight Genii cross the sea, each displays his
> own supernatural powers. Note. The Eight Genii
> are immortalized beings of the Taoist religion.

有 本 事 好 省 事，省 得 事 來 有 本 事，
沒 本 事 好 生 事 生 得 事 來 沒 本 事

Yu pen shih hao shên shih, shen tê shih lai yu pen shih,
mu pen shih hao sheng shih, sheng tê shih lai mu pen shih.

> An able man can diminish work, and when diminished,
> it proves him able; one lacking ability likes to
> provoke trouble, and when it is provoked it shews
> he has no ability.

桅 子 上 掛 剪 子，高 裁

Wei tzŭ shang kua chien tzŭ, kao ts'ai.

> He who supends his shears on a mast is a tailor of high
> pretensions. Note. There is a pun on the last
> character which has the same sound as 才 Ts'ai
> talent. This proverb is used to compliment clever
> people.

尖 嘴 先 出 頭

Chien tsui hsien ch'u t'ou.

> Smart men are the first to rise in life. *Lit.* The lantern-
> jawed shew up first.

精 明 強 幹，絲 毫 不 亂

Ching ming ch'iang kan, ssŭ hao pu luan.

> Clever and strong people never make mistakes.

生 成 一 半，學 成 一 半

Sheng ch'eng i pan, hsüeh ch'eng i pan.

> Half his talents are natural ; the other half acquired.

是 明 白 人 說 得 就 知

Shih ming pai jên shuo tê chiu chih.

> A word is enough to an intelligent man.

聰 明 人 是 糊 塗 人 的 用 人

Ts'ung ming jên shih hu t'u jên ti yung jên.

> Clever men are often the servants of fools.

明 人 不 用 細 講 響 鼓 不 用 重 搥

Ming jên pu yung hsi chiang, hsiang ku pu yung chung ch'ui.

> An intelligent man needs but few words ; a good drum
> doesn't require hard beating.

三 個 愚 人 當 個 明 人 三 個 明 人 當 個 知 縣

San ko yü jên tang ko ming jên, san ko ming jên tang ko chih hsien.

Three fools are equal to one clever man; three clever men equal one District Magistrate.

聰 明 一 生 糊 塗 一 時

Ts'ung ming i sheng hu t'u i shih.

Clever for a lifetime; foolish for a moment.

有 智 養 千 口, 無 智 養 一 人

Yu chih yang ch'ien k'ou, wu chih yang i jên.

A wise man can nourish a thousand people; a fool can only keep himself.

知 者 減 半, 省 者 全 無

Chih chê chien pan, hsin chê ch'üan wu.

The sages are diminished by half; self-scrutinizing men are all gone.

巧 者 有 餘, 拙 者 不 足

Ch'iao chê yu yü, chüeh chê pu tsu.

The clever have a superabundance, the stupid have not enough.

好 漢 耍 三 個 幫 手

Hao han yao san ko pang shou.

A wise man needs three assistants.

明 人 點 頭 就 知

Ming jên tien t'ou chiu chih.

A nod of the head is enough for an intelligent man.

聰 明 反 被 聰 明 誤

Ts'ung ming fan pei ts'ung ming wu.

Clever men are sometimes the dupes of their own cleverness.

凡 事 閱 歷 過 一 回, 見 識 總 不 同 人

Fan shih yüeh li kuo i hui, chien shih tsung pu t'ung jên.

Let him do a thing once, and he will surpass all others.

明 人 不 作 暗 事

Ming jên pu tso an shih.

Enlightened men do no dark deeds.

螺 螄 頂 寶 塔 尖 過 頂

Lo shih ting pao t'a chien kuo ting.

A very cunning man. *Lit.* A pagoda on the end of a murex; too many points.

好 鼓 不 用 勤 搥 打

Hao ku pu yung ch'in chui ta.

A good drum does not require hard beating.

棋 逢 敵 手 將 遇 良 材

Ch'i fêng ti shou, chiang yü liang ts'ai.

He has met with his match. *Lit.* The chess-player has met with a sturdy opponent; the general has encountered a worthy foe.

明 人 自 斷

Ming jên tzŭ tuan.

Enlightened men pronounce sentence on themselves.

能 人 背 後 有 能 人

Neng jên pei hou yu neng jên.

There are always plenty of other able men.

聰 明 莫 過 於 帝 王，伶 俐 莫 過 於 宰 相

T'sung ming mo kuo yü ti wang, ling li mo kuo yü tsai hsiang.

There is none wiser than the Emperor; none more shrewd than the Premier.

鏡 明 則 塵 埃 不 染，智 明 則 邪 惡 不 生

Ching ming tsê ch'en ai pu jan, chih ming tsê hsieh ê pu sheng.

Dust never stains a polished mirror; nor does vice generate in an enlightened mind.

知 者 樂 水 仁 者 樂 山

Chih chê yao shui, jên chê yao shan.

The wise find pleasure in water; the virtuous find pleasure in hills.

寧 與 智 人 同 死, 不 與 愚 人 同 生

Ning yü chih jên t'ung ssŭ, pu yü yü jên t'ung sheng.

> It is better to die with a wise man than to live with
> a fool.

智 人 自 斷, 愚 人 公 斷

Chih jên tzŭ tuan, yü jên kung tuan.

> A wise man decides for himself; an ignorant man accord-
> ing to public opinion.

伶 俐 莫 如 光 棍

Ling li mo ju kuang kun.

> A clever man is not equal to a sharper.

有 計 不 在 年 紀 多

Yu chi pu tsai nien chi to.

> Ability to plan does not depend on old age.

敏 而 好 學 不 耻 下 問

Min erh hao hsüeh pu ch'ih hsia wen.

> He who is clever and willing to learn, is not ashamed to
> ask of his inferiors.

10. EXCITABLE MEN.

朝 也 忙 暮 也 忙, 那 見 忙 人 得 久 長

Chao yeh mang, mu yeh mang, na chien mang jên tê chiu ch'ang.

> Men in a flurry from morning to evening, seldom live
> long.

忙 人 無 智

Mang jên wu chih.

> Flurried men lack wisdom.

貓 頭 鼠 眼

Mao t'ou shu yen.

> He has the head of a cat, the eyes of a rat.

想 到 南 京 買 馬, 又 想 北 京 做 官

Hsiang tao nan ching mai ma, yu hsiang pei ching tso kuan.

> An unsettled person. *Lit.* One who wishes to go to
> Nanking to buy horses and at the same time wishes
> hold office in Peking.

火 裏 燒 粑 等 不 得 熱

Huo li shao pa teng pu tê jo.

He cannot wait till his cake is heated.

11. ANXIOUS MEN.

人 還 未 有 死 怕 爛 了 骨 頭

Jên huan wei yu ssŭ p'a lan liao ku t'ou.

An anxious individual. *Lit.* One who is afraid that his
bones will decay before he is dead.

人 未 死 怕 先 爛 眼 睛

Jên wei ssŭ p'a hsien lan yen ching.

Same as above. *Lit.* One who is afraid that his eyes
will decay before he is dead.

樹 葉 掉 了 怕 打 破 頭

Shu yeh tiao liao p'a ta p'o t'ou.

One who fears the falling leaves will break his head.

揚 塵 掉 下 來 怕 打 破 腦 磕

Yang ch'en tiao hsia lai p'a ta p'o nao k'o.

One who fears the falling dust will break his skull.

早 起 精 神 爽, 思 多 血 氣 衰

Tsao ch'i ching shên shuang, ssŭ to hsüeh ch'i shuai.

Early risers are robust; anxious people have poor health.

心 多 過 慮 如 杞 人 憂 天

Hsin to kuo lü ju ch'i jên yu t'ien.

Too anxious, as the Men of Ch'i who feared the heavens
might fall. Note. This refers to a passage in Lieh
Tzu 列 子.

12. CONCEITED MEN.

目 空 一 世, 眼 內 無 人

Mu k'ung i shih, yen nei wu jên.

His eye beholds an empty world; within its range no man
appears.

旁 若 無 人

P'ang jo wu jên.

He looks on others as nonentities.

少 了 你 這 個 紅 蘿 蔔 做 不 上 齋 來 麼

Shao liao ni chê ko hung lo po tso pu shang chai lai mo.

Can't we prepare a meal without your carrot?
Note. Said to one who takes too much upon himself.

三 分 不 像 人 七 分 不 像 鬼

San fen pu hsiang jên ch'i fen pu hsiang kuei.

Little like men, less like devils.   Note.   Said in contempt
of a proud pretentious knave.

好 耍 牌 子

Hao shua p'ai tzŭ

Very fond of bragging.   *Lit.*   Fond of hanging out a
signboard.

老 鼠 爬 秤 鈎 自 稱 自

Lao shu p'a ch'eng kou tzŭ ch'eng tzŭ.

A braggart.   *Lit.*   A rat climbing the steel-yard to
weigh itself.

愛 戴 高 帽 子

Ai tai kao mao tzŭ.

One fond of wearing a lofty hat.   i.e. One who desires
the praise of men.

目 無 長 上

Mu wu chang shang.

In his eye he has no superiors.

癩 蝦 蟆 打 呵 欠 大 口 大 氣

Lai hsia ma ta ho ch'ien ta k'ou ta ch'i.

Boastful talk.   *Lit.*   When a toad gapes, what a mouth,
and what breath !

謙 受 益, 滿 招 損

Ch'ien shou i, man chao sun.

The humble receive advantage; the self-sufficient provoke
loss.

自大是個臭字

Tzŭ ta shih ko ch'ou tzŭ.

Proud men are disgusting. *Lit.* The characters for "self" and "great" compose the character for "evil-smelling."

一丈八尺高的燈檯照遠不照近

I chang pa ch'ih kao ti teng t'ai chao yüan pu chao chin.

An eighteen feet lamp-post lights what is distant, not what is near. Note. Said of one blind to his own, but not to the faults of others.

乖僻自是悔懊必多

Kuai p'i tzŭ shih, hui wu pi to.

An evil, conceited man must make many mistakes.

自滿者敗,自矜者愚

Tzŭ man chê pai, tzŭ ching chê yü.

The self-conceited come to grief; the boastful are but fools.

愛戴鱔魚簍子

Ai tai shan yü lou tzŭ.

A braggart. *Lit.* One fond of wearing an eel-basket.

自損者益,自益者殃

Tzŭ sun chê i, tzŭ i chê yang.

The humble reap advantage; the haughty meet misfortune.

虛心竹有低頭葉

Hsu hsin chu yu ti t'ou yeh.

The hollow bamboo has drooping leaves.

天道虧盈而益謙

T'ien tao k'uei ying erh i ch'ien.

According to the principles of Right the proud are reduced and the humble enriched.

天地人神俱欣謙而不喜盈謙者賜之福盈者賜之禍

T'ien ti jên shên chü hsin ch'ien erh pu hsi ying, ch'ien chê tz'u chih fu ying chê tz'ŭ chih huo.

Heaven, earth, men and spirits delight in humility and dislike pride; the humble are blessed and the proud suffer calamity. Comp. Psalm 138. 6.

貧 寒 休 要 怨，富 厚 不 須 驕
P'in han hsiu yao yüan, fu hou pu hsü chiao.

> The poor should not repine; the rich should not be arrogant.

紙 糊 頭 老 虎
Chih hu t'ou lao hu.

> A braggart. *Lit.* A paper-headed tiger.

13. DEFORMED MEN.

聾 子 愛 打 刹，啞 叭 愛 說 話
Lung tzǔ ai ta ch'a, ya pa ai shuo hua.

> Deaf people like to pry into other people's affairs; dumb people love to talk. Note. 打 刹 is a colloquialism meaning to pry into, to be curious.

瞎 子 心 思 像 一 把 刀
Hsia tzǔ hsin ssǔ hsiang i pa tao.

> The thoughts of the blind are like a murderous knife.

瞎 子 有 人 牽 跛 子 有 人 扶
Hsia tzǔ yu jên ch'ien, po tzǔ yu jên fu.

> The blind get led and the lame supported.

啞 叭 好 做 顧 點
Ya pa hao tso ku tien.

> Dumb men are fond of making signs.

啞 叭 見 娘 有 話 說 不 出
Ya pa chien niang yu hua shuo pu ch'u.

> When a dumb man sees his mother he wants to speak but cannot.

矮 子 矮 一 肚 怪
Ai tzǔ ai i tu kuai.

> A dwarf among dwarfs is full of strange things.

眼 斜 心 不 正 鼻 歪 意 不 端
Yen hsieh hsin pu chêng, pi wai i pu tuan.

> If the eyes look askance the heart is not correct; if the nose is crooked the intentions are not upright.

一 盲 引 衆 盲 相 將 入 火 坑

I mang yin tsung mang hsiang chiang ju huo k'eng.

> When one blind man leads several blind men, they will
> soon fall into a fire pit.

瞎 子 攙 扶 瞎 子，未 必 不 掉 下 坑 去

Hsia tzŭ ch'an fu hsia tzŭ wei pi pu tiao hsia k'eng ch'u.

> When the blind help the blind they will certainly fall
> into the ditch.   Comp.   Matt. 15. 14.

瞽 者 善 聽，聾 者 善 視

Ku chê shan t'ing, lung chê shan shih.

> The blind are quick at hearing; the deaf are quick at
> sight.

矮 子 上 樓 梯，步 步 高 陞

Ai tzŭ shang lou t'i, pu pu kao sheng.

> A dwarf ascending a ladder.   He gets higher every step.

SECTION II. ON DOMESTIC CONCERNS.

Chapter 1. Food and Clothing.

熱 油 苦 菜 各 隨 人 愛

Jo yu k'u ts'ai ko sui jên ai.

> Hot oil or bitter cabbage; every man to his taste.

吃 飯 不 撐 腰，必 定 是 喉 包

Ch'ih fan pu ch'eng yao, pi ting shih hou pao.

> If you don't stretch yourself after a meal you will certainly have a tumour in your throat. Note. Men of sedentary lives are supposed to develop such.

吃 盡 天 下 鹽 好，用 盡 天 下 錢 好

Ch'ih chin t'ien hsia yen hao, yung chin t'ien hsia ch'ien hao.

> Anywhere in the world salt is good to eat; anywhere in the world money is good to use.

豬 不 可 吃 肝 血，魚 不 可 吃 蝦 鱉

Chu pu k'o ch'ih kan hsüeh, yü pu k'o ch'ih hsia pieh.

> Of pigs, don't eat the liver or the blood; of fishes, do not eat either shrimps or turtles. Note. These latter we generally classified under the finny tribe.

行 不 計 路，食 不 計 數

Hsing pu chi lu, shih pu chi shu.

> Whilst travelling don't reckon the distance; whilst eating don't reckon the quantity.

飯 有 三 餐 不 餓 衣 有 三 件 不 破

Fan yu san ts'an pu ô, i yu san chien pu p'o.

> A man wont pine on three meals a day; or go in rags if he has three suits.

顧 嘴 不 顧 身，衣 破 難 對 人

Ku tsui pu ku shên, i p'o nan tui jên.

> He who cares for his mouth and not for his person, will find that he has to appear before people in rags.

衣 不 長 寸. 鞋 不 差 分

I pu ch'ang ts'un, hsieh pu ch'a fen.

> Clothes must not be made an inch too long; boots must not be a fraction too small.

穿 衣 吃 飯 不 犯 條 律

Ch'uan i ch'ih fan pu fan ti'ao lü.

> In dress and food do not break rules.

牢 字 從 牛. 獄 字 從 犬, 不 食 牛 犬. 牢 獄 可 兇

Lao tzŭ ts'ung niu, yü tzŭ ts'ung ch'üan, pu shih niu ch'üan, lao yü k'o mien.

> The two characters for "prison" are under the radicals "ox" and "dog." If you refuse to eat these animals you will avoid imprisonment. Note. The slaughter of oxen and dogs is not considered permissible.

先 顧 食. 後 顧 衣

Hsien ku shih, hou ku i.

> First think of food, then of clothing.

魚 喫 新 鮮, 米 吃 熟

Yü ch'ih hsin hsien, mi ch'ih shu.

> Only eat fresh fish and ripened rice.

物 無 定 味 適 口 者 珍

Wu wu ting wei, shih k'ou chê chên.

> Viands have various flavours; what pleases the palate is good.

飯 不 熟, 氣 不 勻

Fan pu shu, ch'i pu yün.

> When rice is not well cooked it is because the steam has been unequally distributed.

鄉 裏 人 一 年 兩 回 葷 吃 了 年 飯 望 吃 新

Hsiang li jên i nien liang hui hun, ch'ih liao nien fan wang ch'ih hsin.

> Rustics feast twice a year; after the New year's meal they look for the harvest home.

吃 飯 靠 天

Ch'ih fan k'ao t'ien.

> Our daily bread depends on Heaven.

衣 飯 逐 日 生

I fan sui jih sheng.

Clothes and food are daily mercies.

肚 饑 好 吃 麥 米 飯

Tu chi hao ch'ih mai mi fan.

A hungry man is glad to get boiled wheat. Note. Wheat
is not a popular article of diet in Central China, hence
this comparatively local proverb.

閉 眼 吃 毛 蟲

Pi yen ch'ih mao ch'ung.

Eyes must be closed to swallow maggots in one's food.
Note. This is used to complain of the dirtiness of
any sort of food.

一 根 草 有 一 根 草 的 露 水 養

I ken ts'ao yu i ken ts'ao ti lu shui yang.

Each blade of grass has its own drop of dew to nourish it.

野 雀 無 糧 天 地 寬

Yeh ch'iao wu liang ti'en ti k'uan.

When the wild bird lacks food, all the world is before it.
Comp. Psalm 147. 9.

新 是 香 陳 是 臭

Hsin shih hsiang, ch'en shih ch'ou.

Always wishing for new things. *Lit.* What is fresh is
fragrant; what is stale is evil-smelling.

多 吃 少 滋 味，少 吃 多 滋 味

To ch'ih shao tzŭ wei, shao ch'ih to tzŭ wei.

The more you eat, the less flavour; the less you eat, the
more flavour.

物 可 充 腸 皆 美 食

Wu k'o ch'ung ch'ang chieh mei shih.

Whatever will satisfy hunger is good food.

日 圖 三 餐 夜 圖 一 宿

Jih t'u san ts'an yeh t'u i hsiu.

We plan for three meals per day, and for one sleep by
night.

口 是 無 量 斗

K'ou shih wu liang tou.

The mouth is an unlimited measure.

有 衣 打 扮 便 成 人

Yu i ta pan pien ch'eng jên.

Dress makes the gentleman or lady.

頂 冠 束 帶 人 人 愛

Ting kuan shu tai jên jên ai.

To wear the hat and the girdle is what everybody likes.

一 搖 三 擺 實 排 塲

I yao san pai shih p'ai ch'ang.

Those who go swinging and strutting are only dressed out for show.

屋 要 人 襯，人 要 衣 襯

Wu yao jên ch'ên, jên yao i ch'ên.

A house needs man to show it off; man needs clothes to adorn him.

鷄 叫 早 肚 之 飽，鷄 叫 中 肚 子 空

Chi chiao tsao tu tzǔ pao, chi chiao chung tu tzǔ k'ung.

When the cock crows in the morning my stomach wants food; when he crows at noon my stomach is empty. Note. 要 is to be understood before 飽.

侵 晨 飯 好 算 不 得 午 後 飽

Ch'in ch'ên fan hao suan pu tê wu hou pao.

A good breakfast doesn't take the place of a good dinner. Note. 侵 晨 equals 清 晨

飲 貪 約 而 精，園 蔬 逾 珍 饈

Yin shih yo erh ching, yüan su yü chen hsiu.

Feed moderately on wholesome food; garden herbs surpass rich viands.

勿 貪 口 腹 而 恣 殺 生 禽

Wu t'an k'ou fu êrh tzǔ sha sheng ch'in.

Don't think immoderately of food and so slay living things without restraint.

寧 可 清 飢 不 可 濁 飽

Ning k'o ch'ing chi, pu k'o cho pao.

Better be hungry and pure than well-filled and corrupt.

敲 船 三 日 坐，敲 碗 三 日 餓

Ch'iao ch'uan san jih tso, ch'iao wan san jih o.

If you drum on a boat you will have three days delay;
if you drum on a rice-bowl you will be hungry for
three days.

喫 了 早 起，無 那 晚 夕

Ch'ih liao tsao ch'i, wu na wan hsi.

Living from hand to mouth. *Lit.* Having eaten in the
morning there is nothing in the evening.

寧 人 等 粥，毋 粥 等 人

Ning jên teng chou, wu chou teng jên.

Better that a man should wait for his gruel than that the
gruel should wait for him.

北 船 不 到，米 如 珠

Pei ch'uan pu tao, mi ju chu.

When the northern-bound boats do not arrive, rice is as
dear as pearls.

寧 可 食 無 肉，不 可 居 無 竹

Ning k'o shih wu jou, pu k'o chü wu chu.

Better have meals without meat than a home without
the bamboo.

飢 不 擇 食，寒 不 擇 衣

Chi pu tsê shih, han pu tsê i.

He who is hungry doesn't select his food; he who is cold,
his clothes.

佛 是 金 裝，人 是 衣 裝

Fu shih chin chuang, jên shih i chuang.

Buddha has gold for a covering; men have clothes.
Note. This indicates these things are mere externals
and not the real person.

換 了 衣 裳 未 換 人

Huan liao i shang wei huan jên.

When you have changed the clothes you haven't changed
the man.

Chapter 2. Wine, and its effects.

點 酒 不 嘗,吃 荣 老 王

Tien chiu pu ch'ang, ch'ih ts'ai lao wang.

>He doesn't take a drop of wine, but he's an old hand at a feast.

有 花 方 酌 酒,無 月 不 登 樓

Yu hua fang cho chiu, wu yüeh pu teng lou.

>When flowers are blooming, pour out the wine; when there is no moon, do not go into the pavilion.
>Note. Pavilions, Kiosks, etc., are much frequented on moonlight nights by pleasure seekers.

莫 吃 卯 時 酒·昏 昏 醉 到 酉

Mo ch'ih mao shih chiu, hun hun tsui tao yu.

>Don't drink early in the morning, or you will be muddled all day.

若 要 斷 酒 法·醒 眼 看 醉 人

Jo yao tuan chiu fa, hsing yen k'an tsui jên.

>If you want to leave off drink, look when sober, at a drunken man.

渴 時 一 滴 如 甘 露 醉 後 添 杯 不 如 無

K'o shih i ti ju kan lu, tsui hou t'ien pei pu ju wu.

>To a thirsty man a drop of water is as refreshing as dew; to a man already drunk an extra cup is worse than none at all.

藥 能 醫 假 病,酒 不 解 眞 愁

Yao neng i chia ping, chiu pu chieh chên ch'ou.

>Medicine may heal imagined sickness, but wine cannot dispel real sorrow.

三 杯 通 大 道,一 醉 解 千 愁

San pei tung ta tao, i tsui chieh ch'ien ch'ou.

>Three glasses of wine fulfil the principles of true politeness; to get drunk banishes a thousand worries.

酒債尋常行處有

Chiu chai hsin ch'ang hsing ch'u yu.

> He got into debt for wine wherever he could.　Note.　Said
> of Li T'ai Po the great poet of the T'ang Dynasty,
> who because he saw that life was short, determined
> to enjoy in it as much pleasure as possible.

醉後乾坤大,閑中日月長

Tsui hou ch'ien k'un ta, hsien chung jih yueh ch'ang.

> To a drunken man everything is on a big scale; to a man
> of leisure days and months are long.

好酒紅人面,財帛動人心

Hao chiu hung jên mien, ts'ai pai tung jên hsin.

> Good wine reddens the face; riches excite the mind.

酒逢知己千杯少,話不投機半句多

Chiu fêng chih chi ch'ien pei shao, hua pu t'ou chi pan chü to.

> With a dear friend, a thousand cups of wine are too few;
> when opinions disagree, even half a sentence is too
> much.

三杯和萬事

San pei ho wan shih.

> Three glasses of wine can set everything to rights.

酒能成事,酒能敗事

Chiu neng ch'eng shih, chiu neng pai shih.

> Wine can both help and hinder business.

酒發心腹之言

Chiu fa hsin fu chih yen.

> Wine is a discoverer of secrets.

酒是人喝的,糟是豬吃的

Chiu shih jên ho ti, tsao shih chu ch'ih ti.

> Wine is for men to drink, the distillers grains are for the
> pigs.　Note.　This is said to deter men from drinking
> too much.

發酒瘋

Fa chiu fêng.

> To be mad with wine.

滿 面 春 風

Man mien ch'un fêng.

> A face reddened with wine. *Lit.* Spring breeze.
> Note. This expression is not confined to denoting the effects of wine.

莫 飲 過 量 之 酒

Mo yin kuo liang chih chiu.

> Do not drink more wine than you are able to carry.

酒 不 醉 人，人 自 醉

Chiu pu tsui jên, jên tzǔ tsui.

> Intoxication is not the wine's fault, but the man's.

酒 醉 心 明 白

Chiu tsui hsin ming pai.

> Drunk, but clear in intellect.

成 不 成 十 八 瓶

Ch'eng pu ch'eng shih pa p'ing.

> Whether the affair be settled or not, we must have our eighteen bottles of wine.

吃 酒 念 家 貧

Ch'ih chiu nien chia p'in.

> When drinking wine, remember the poverty of your family.

無 酒 不 會，無 酒 不 議

Wu chiu pu hui, wu chiu pu i.

> No wine, no company; no wine, no conversation.

酒 杯 說 話 輕

Chiu pei shuo hua ch'ing.

> Over the wine cup conversation is light.

美 不 美 鄉 中 酒

Mei pu mei hsiang chung chiu.

> Choice or not it is the wine of our country-side.

樂 極 則 悲, 酒 極 則 亂

Lo chi tsê pei, chiu chi tsê luan.

> Excessive joy breeds sorrow; excess of wine, disorder.

吃 不 盡 沽 來 的 酒

Ch'ih pu chin ku lai ti chiu.

> One can never drink all the wine there is for sale.

萬 事 不 如 杯 在 手

Wan shih pu ju pei tsai shou.

> A cup in the hand is worth all else.

朝 朝 出 去 酒 隨 後, 夜 夜 歸 來 花 滿 頭

Chao chao ch'u ch'ü chiu sui hou, yeh yeh kuei lai hua man t'ou.

> Every morning he goes out there is wine for him; every evening on his return there is joviality.

清 清 之 水 為 土 所 防, 濟 濟 之 士 為 酒 所 傷

Ch'ing ch'ing chih shui wei t'u so fang, chi chi chih shih wei chiu so shang.

> Limpid streams are bound within earthen banks; multitudes of scholars are injured by wine.

英 雄 多 困 於 酒 色

Yin hsiung to k'un yü chiu sê.

> Wine and Women have entangled many brave men.

戒 酒 三 年 也 無 錢, 吃 酒 三 年 也 無 錢

Chieh chiu san nien yeh wu ch'ien, ch'i chiu san nien yeh wu ch'ien

> If for three years I drink wine I have no money; if for three years I dont drink wine I still have no money.

酒 能 亂 性

Chiu neng luan hsing.

> Wine disorders man's nature.

紹 興 為 名 士, 燒 酒 為 光 棍

Shao hsing wei ming shih, shao chiu wei kuang kun.

> Shao Hsing wine is a gentleman; samshoo a disreputable fellow. Note. This refers to the effects produced by each kind. 燒 酒 is sometime called 三 燒 thrice fired or distilled. This has been corrupted by Europeans into samshoo.

酒 在 肚 裏, 事 在 心 裏

Chiu tsai tu li, shih tsai hsin li.

When inspired by wine that is the time for business.

酒 話 不 在 心 上

Chiu hua pu tsai hsin shang.

Drunken talk doesn't remain in the mind.

Chapter. 3. Household Affairs.

興 家 猶 如 針 挑 土, 敗 家 猶 如 水 推 洲

Hsing chia yu ju chên t'iao t'u, pai chia yu ju shui t'ui chou.

To make a family prosper is like digging clay with a needle; to ruin a family is like water removing a sandbank. Note. 挑 equals 挑挖 to dig out.

人 大 分 家, 樹 大 分 椏

Jên ta fên chia, shu ta fên ya.

When children are grown up the family is divided, when a tree is mature its branches are widespread.

堂 前 無 古 畫·不 是 舊 人 家

T'ang ch'ien wu ku hua, pu shih chiu jên chia.

If there are no ancient pictures in the hall, the family cannot be old.

一 家 不 彀, 百 家 相 助

I chia pu kou, pai chia hsiang ts'u.

When one family runs short, a hundred families combine to help. Note. This is often said by beggars.

早 起 三 日 當 一 工, 免 得 求 人 落 下 風

Tsao ch'i san jih tang i kung, mien tê ch'iu jên lo hsia fêng.

Three days early rising equals one day's work; thus may you avoid asking any one for a favour. Note. 落 下 風 means to be regarded with disfavour.

家 醜 不 可 外 揚

Chia ch'ou pu k'o wai yang.

Domestic foibles must not be spread abroad.

家 裏 不 和 外 人 欺

Chia li pu ho wai jên ch'i.

When families quarrel, outsiders deride.

盜 可 成 一 房, 不 可 敗 一 戶

Ning k'o ch'eng i fang, pu k'o pai i hu.

Better establish a branch than cut off a line. Note. You must perpetuate yourself in some way or other, either through your own or an adopted child.

一 團 和 氣 百 無 禁 忌

I t'uan ho ch'i pai wu chin chi.

With perfect harmony in the family, no evil influences can injure.

做 得 辱 門 敗 戶

Tso tê ju men pai hu.

To bring disgrace on the family.

當 家 纔 知 鹽 米 貴

Tang chia ts'ai chih yen mi kuei.

It is the householder that knows when salt and rice are dear.

相 論 逞 英 豪, 家 計 漸 漸 退

Hsiang lun ch'eng ying hao, chia chi chien chien t'ui.

Quarrelling for superiority will gradually destroy the affairs of a family.

婢 美 妾 嬌 非 閨 房 之 福

Pi mei ch'ieh chiao fei kuei fang chih fu.

Fair maid-servants and pretty concubines endanger family happiness.

家 人 犯 法, 罪 在 家 主

Chia jên fan fa, tsui tsai chia chu.

When any one in a family breaks the law, the head of the family is to blame.

家 鬼 弄 家 神

Chia kuei lung chia shên.

Family quarrels. *Lit.* One domestic demon mocks another domestic sprite.

會 說 說 都 市，不 會 說 屋 裡

Hui shuo shuo tu shih, pu hui shuo wu li.

> One who can speak, speaks of the city ; one who can't, speaks merely of household affairs.

國 易 治 ∶ 家 難 齊

Kuo i chih, chia nan ch'i.

> It is easier to rule a kingdom than to regulate a family.

房 屋 不 在 高 堂·不 漏 便 好，
衣 服 不 在 綾 羅，和 煖 便 好，
飲 食 不 在 珍 饈，一 飽 便 好，
婆 妻 不 在 顏 色，賢 德 便 好

Fang wu pu tsai kao t'ang, pu lou pien hao, i fu pu tsai ling lo, ho nuan pien hao, yin shih pu tsai chên hsiu, i pao pien hao, ch'ü ch'i pu tsai yen sê, hsien tê pien hao.

> The goodness of a house does not consist in its lofty halls, but in its excluding the weather ; the usefulness of clothes does not consist in their costliness but in their warmth ; the value of food is not in its rarity, but in its satisfying the appetite ; the excellence of a wife consists not in her beauty, but in her virtue.

蠢 妻 逆 子 無 法 可 治

Ch'un ch'i ni tzŭ wu fa k'o chih.

> There is no method of managing stupid wives and disobedient children.

錢 出 急 家 門

Ch'ien ch'u chi chia mên.

> When the family is in difficulties away goes the cash.

家 和 萬 事 興，事 不 由 人 算

Chia ho wan shih hsing, shih pu yu jên suan.

> Everything prospers in a united family ; though events do not happen according to men's calculations.

家 和 福 自 生

Chia ho fu tzŭ shêng.

> In a united family happiness springs up of itself.

怠 惰 自 甘 家 道 必 索

Tai to tzŭ kan chia tao pi so.

> The family affairs of a lazy self-satisfied man are sure
> to be in disorder.

天 亮 不 起 睡 不 多 時

T'ien liang pu ch'i shui pu to shih.

> He gets little more time for sleep who does not rise with
> the dawn.

一 夜 不 眠 十 日 不 安

I yeh pu mien shih jih pu an.

> The loss of one night's sleep entails ten days of discomfort.

一 家 之 計 在 於 和, 一 生 之 計 在 於 勤

I chia chih chi tsai yü ho, i sheng chih chi tsai yü ch'ing.

> Harmony should be the policy of the family; diligence
> that of the individual.

作 善 之 家 必 有 餘 慶, 作 不 善 之 家 必 有 餘 殃

Tso shan chih chia pi yu yü ch'iug, tso pu shan chih chia pi yu yü yang.

> A virtuous family is sure to have an abundance of felicity;
> an evil family, an abundance of misery.

清 官 難 斷 家 務 事

Ch'ing kuan nan tuan chia wu shih.

> Even an upright magistrate can hardly decide family
> disputes.

沒 有 馬 勺 不 磕 鍋 簷 的

Mu yu ma shao pu k'o kuo yen ti.

> There is no ladle which never strikes the edge of the
> cooking pot. i.e. There are little unpleasantnesses
> in the best of families.

家 有 家 法, 國 有 國 法

Chia yu chia fa, kuo yu kuo fa,

> The family has its rules and the country its laws.

Chapter 4. Masters and Servants.

你 不 來 我 不 怪, 你 要 來 受 我 戒

Ni pu lai wo pu kuai, ni yao lai shou wo chieh.

> If you don't come it makes no difference to me ; if you do come you must obey my orders.

起 心 人 難 留, 留 下 結 冤 仇

Ch'i hsin jên nan liu, liu hsia chieh yüan ch'ou.

> It is difficult to keep a servant if he is bent on leaving : if you keep him he will have a grudge against you.

捧 他 碗 服 他 管

P'êng t'a wan, fu t'a kuan.

> If you eat his rice you must obey him.

怕 你 不 嫁 你, 嫁 你 不 怕 你

P'a ni pu chia ni, chia ni pu p'a ni.

> If I were afraid of you I wouldn't have married you : as I have married you I am not afraid of you. Note. Having once engaged to serve he or she shrinks not from the responsibility.

長 短 是 根 棍, 大 小 是 個 人

Ch'ang tuan shih ken kun, ta hsiao shih ko jên.

> A stick's a stick whether long or short ; a man's a man whether great or small.

要 人 抱 在 懷 裏, 不 要 人 丟 在 崖 裏

Yao jên pao tsai huai li, pu yao jên tiu tsai ai li.

> If you want a man, you take him to your bosom ; if you don't want him you throw him down a precipice.

養 病 不 養 閑

Yang ping pu yang hsien.

> Nourish a sick, but never an idle servant.

催 工 莫 催 食

Ts'ui kung mo ts'ui shih.

> Hurry men at work, not at meat.

在 家 衛 家,在 國 衛 國

Tsai chia wei chia, tsai kuo wei kuo.

> In a family, defend the family ; in a country, defend the country.

抽 頭 扶 脚

Ch'ou t'ou fu chiao.

> To serve in a very attentive manner. *Lit.* To prop the head and support the foot.

在 家 靠 父 母,出 外 靠 主 人

Tsai chia k'ao fu mu, ch'u wai k'ao chu jên.

> At home—you are dependent on your parents; away from home you are dependent on your master.

除 了 尼 山 別 有 廟

Ch'u liao ni shan pieh yu miao.

> I can find employment elsewhere. *Lit.* There are temples elsewhere than on Mount Ni. Note. Mount Ni is the hill from which the names for Confucius were taken.

奴 僕 勿 用 俊 秀

Nu p'u wu yung chün hsiu.

> Do not employ handsome servants.

堂 中 無 俊 僕,必 是 好 人 家

T'ang chung wu chün p'u pi shih hao jên chia.

> Where no handsome servant is kept, the family must be virtuous.

明 珠 投 漆

Ming chu t'ou ch'i.

> A wise man in a fool's service. *Lit.* A clear pearl thrown into varnish.

打 照 面 過 日 子

Ta chao mien kuo jih tzŭ.

> Wasting his master's time. i.e., by pretence of work, etc. Note 打照面 indicates pretence.

站 到 三 百 兩 ; 坐 到 三 百 兩

Chan tao san pai liang tso tao san pai liang.

> Your income is certain whether you work or play. *Lit.*
> Whether you stand or sit you'll get three hundred
> taels.

狗 仗 人 勢 攔 路 咬 人

Kou chang jên shih lan lu ao jên.

> The dog takes his cue from the master, obstructs the way
> and bites.

直 木 先 伏 ; 甘 井 先 渴

Chih mu hsien fu kan ching hsien k'o.

> Able men are first employed. *Lit.* Straight trees are
> first felled : sweet wells are first drained.

東 方 不 亮 西 方 亮

Tung fang pu liang hsi fang liang.

> If you won't employ me, another will. *Lit.* If there
> be no light in the east, there will be in the west.

家 敗 奴 欺 主

Chia pai nu ch'i chu.

> When the family is ruined, the slave derides the master.

在 回 流 窩 裏 打 一 個 轉 身 的

Tsai hui liu wo li ta i ko chuan shên ti.

> You have turned round in a whirlpool. Note. Said in
> censure of a servant who has hurried through his
> work, doing it badly.

宰 相 門 下 七 品 官

Tsai hsiang men hsia ch'i p'in kuan.

> The Premier's underlings are seventh grade officials.

官 大 書 差 大

Kuan ta shu ch'ai ta..

> If the magistrate is great, so will be his secretaries and
> underlings. Note. This and the preceding proverb
> are used with the intention of extolling the position
> of servants under noted or wealthy masters.

一 人 挑 水 吃，二 人 抬 水 吃，三 人 沒 得 水 吃

I jên t'iao shui ch'ih erh jên t'ai shui ch'ih san jên mu tê shui ch'ih.

> The fewer servants, the better served. *Lit.* One man will carry two buckets of water for his own use: two will carry one for their joint use : three will carry none for anybody's use.

餓 夫 不 能 當 差

Ô fu pu neng tang ch'ai.

> No man will serve for starvation.

千 錯 萬 錯 來 人 不 錯

Ch'ien ts'o wan ts'o lai jên pu ts'o.

> Though the senders be ten thousand times wrong, it is not the messenger's fault.

打 我 來，罵 我 來，要 我 吃 虧 就 不 來

Ta wo lai ma wo lai yao wo ch'ih k'uei chiu pu lai.

> I'll come though you beat me ; I'll come though you curse me ; but not if I am to lose any pay.

冷 茶 冷 飯 吃 得 冷 言 冷 語 受 不 得

Leng ch'a leng fan ch'ih tê leng yen leng yü shou pu tê.

> Cold tea and cold rice are bearable, but to be "talked at" is unendurable.

狗 瘦 主 人 羞

Kou shou chu jên hsiu.

> A lean dog shames his master.

牡 丹 雖 好，必 要 綠 葉 扶 持

Mu tan sui hao pi yao lu yeh fu ch'ih.

> Though the peony be beautiful, its beauty is enhanced, by its green leaves.

茶 裡 不 尋，飯 裡 尋

Ch'a li pu hsin fan li hsin.

> If he doesn't quarrel with his cook for his tea, he does for his rice.

三分匠人七分主人

San fên chiang jên ch'i fên chu jên.

The workman may have three tenths of his own way, but the master has seven tenths of his.

大樹下好歇陰

Ta shu hsia hao hsien yin.

There is good shelter under great trees. (Patronage).

老虎不吃人惡像難看

Lao hu pu ch'ih jên ê hsiang nan k'an.

Though the tiger may not devour men, yet his dreadful appearance terrifies them.

千人上路，主事一人

Ch'ien jên shang lu chu shih i jên.

The affairs of a thousand men are under the control of one.

一國三公

I kuo san kung.

There is no master in the concern. *Lit.* One state, three rulers.

姜太公釣魚願者上鈎

Chiang T'ai Kung tiao yü yüan chê shang kou.

To employ volunteers only. *Lit.* Chiang T'ai Kung angling, catches only volunteers. Note. Chiang T'ai Kung or Chiang Tzu Ya, was a remarkable sage in the time of Wen Wang, who followed, in obscurity his favourite pursuit of angling. His hook had no barb, but many fishes, recognising his worth, allowed themselves to be caught. Most of the gods of China are popularly supposed to owe their deification to this powerful person, and to be under his control.

砧板上一塊肉，隨你橫砍直砍

Chên pan shang i k'uai jou sui ni heng k'an chih k'an.

You can treat an inferior any way you please. *Lit.* Meat on a block can be chopped any way to suit you.

含了屠戶難道連毛吃豬

Shê liao t'u hu nan tao lien mao ch'ih chu.

> Though the butcher is gone, do you think I'm going to eat pork with the bristles on.

主子管奴才，靴子裡摸襪子，

Chu tzǔ kuan nu ts'ai hsueh tzu li mo wa tzǔ.

> The master controls his slave as easily as one can feel the stocking in one's boot.

疑人莫用人，用人莫疑人

I jên mo yung jên yung jên mo i jên.

> If you suspect a man don't employ him ; if you employ him, don't suspect him.

不願柴頭破，只願斧頭脫

Pu yüan ch'ai t'ou p'o chih yüan fu t'ou t'o.

> I don't wish to split wood, I want to get rid of the axe.
> Note.　Said by a servant desiring dismissal.

人要頑得活，處處用得着

Jên yao wan tê huo ch'u ch'u yung tê cho.

> He who is willing to work will always find employment.

沒有硃砂，紅土之爲貴

Mu yu chu sha, hung t'u chih wei kuei.

> Where there is no cinnabar, red earth is considered valuable. Comp. "Among the blind a one-eyed man is king."

受人之託，必當忠人之事

Shou jên chih t'o pi tang chung jên chih shih.

> When you receive a trust from anyone, execute it with faithfulness.

天外有天，人外有人

T'ien wai yu t'ien, jên wai yu jên.

> There is no height but has another height above it ; no man but has his superior.

大旱三年餓不死厨子

Ta han san nien ê pu ssǔ ch'u tzǔ.

> A three years' drought will not starve a cook.

好 馬 不 背 雙 鞍

Hao ma pu pei shuang an.

A good horse cannot wear two saddles, i.e., does not serve two masters.

Chapter 5. Neighbours.

親 願 親 好, 鄰 願 鄰 好

Ch'in yuan ch'in hao lin yüan lin hao.

Relatives wish for good relatives ; neighbours wish for good neighbours.

居 街 坊 接 鄰 里

Chü chieh fang lin li.

Dwell in harmony with all your neighbours.

昔 孟 母 擇 鄰 處

Hsi Mêng mu tsê lin ch'u.

The mother of Mencius chose her dwelling place with reference to its neighbourhood. Note. This model mother considered the influences likely to be exerted upon her son.

良 禽 擇 木 而 棲

Liang ch'in tsê mu êrh ch'i.

A good bird selects the tree on which it wishes to rest.

遠 水 難 救 近 火, 遠 親 不 如 近 鄰

Yüan shui nan chiu chin huo, yüan ch'in pu ju chin lin.

Distant water will not quench a fire that is near ; distant relations are not so good as near neighbours. Comp. Proverbs 27.10.

分 家 三 年 成 鄰 舍

Fên chia san nien ch'eng lin shê.

Three years after a family has been divided, its members are mere neighbours.

察 實 莫 過 鄰 里

Ch'a shih mo kuo lin li.

If you want the truth about a man, the place to get it is his own neighbourhood.

行 要 好 伴, 住 要 好 鄰

Hsing yao hao pan chu yao hao lin.

> On a journey you need good company ; at home you
> need good neighbours.

得 好 鄉 鄰 勝 遠 親

Tê hao hsiang lin shêng yüan ch'in.

> Better good neighbours near, than relatives at a distance.

朝 廷 無 空 地, 鄰 舍 有 賢 人

Ch'ao t'ing wu k'ung ti lin shê yu hsien jên.

> The Court has no unoccupied places ; there are virtuous
> men among neighbours.

近 鄰 不 如 隔 壁, 隔 壁 不 如 對 門

Chin lin pu ju kê pi, kê pi pu ju tui men.

> Near neighbours are not equal to next-door neighbours ;
> next-door neighbours are not equal to those living
> opposite.

不 同 花 樹 同 花 園

pu t'ung hua shu t'ung hua yüan.

> Near neighbours. *Lit.* If we have not flowers and trees
> in common, we have the garden in common.

田 土 相 界, 屋 宇 相 連

T'ien t'u hsiang chieh wu yü hsiang lien.

> Fields are bounded by each other ; dwellings are joined
> together.

風 土 人 情 我 盡 知

Fêng t'u jên ch'ing wo chin chih.

> Possessed of a neighbour's knowledge. *Lit.* I know all
> about the place's customs, soil, and people.

輸 了 鄉 親 弱 了 己

Shu liao hsiang ch'in jao liao chi.

> If a countryman of mine gets beaten I am thereby
> weakened.

和 得 鄉 里 好，猶 如 檢 片 寶

Ho tê hsiang li hao, yu ju chien p'ien pao.

> To be on good terms with one's neighbour is as good as finding a treasure.

鄰 舍 做 官，大 家 喜 歡

Lin shê tso kuan, ta chia hsi huan.

> When our neighbour takes office we all rejoice.

打 不 斷 的 兒 女 親，罵 不 開 的 近 街 隣

Ta pu tuan ti erh nü ch'in, ma pu k'ai ti chin chieh lin.

> Incorrigible children are still one's own kin ; those you constantly curse in the same street are still neighbours.

SECTION III. ON EDUCATION.

Chapter I. Education Generally.

訓 子 嬰 孩 敎 婦 初 來

Hsün tzŭ ying hai chiao fu ch'u lai.

To instruct children and wives you must begin from the very first.

養 子 不 敎 如 養 驢, 養 女 不 敎 如 養 猪

Yang tzŭ pu chiao ju yang lü, yang nü pu chiao ju yang chu.

To rear a boy without educating him is to rear an ass; to rear a girl without educating her is to rear a pig.

有 田 不 耕 倉 廩 虛, 有 書 不 讀 子 孫 愚

Yu t'ien pu kêng ts'ang lin hsü, yu shu pu tu tzŭ sun yü.

If fields are left untilled the granaries will be empty; if your books are left unread your descendants will be ignorant.

桑 條 從 小 揉

Sang t'iao ts'ung hsiao jou.

The mulberry twig is bent, when it is young.

桑 條 從 小 屈, 長 大 屈 不 得

Sang t'iao ts'ung hsiao ch'ü, chang ta ch'ü pu tê.

The mulberry twig is bent when it is young; when mature, it can't be bent.

恨 鐵 不 成 鋼

Hen t'ieh pu ch'eng kang.

Angry because their iron does not become steel. Note. This refers to those who are angry because their dull sons do not become eminent.

敎 子 要 有 義 方

Chiao tzŭ yao yu i fang.

To educate children requires a proper method.

天 下 之 事 非 敎 無 成

T'ien hsia chih shih fei chiao wu ch'eng.

Nothing in all the world can be done without instruction.

堂 前 敎 子,枕 邊 敎 妻

T'ang ch'ien chiao tzŭ, chên pien chiao ch'i.

> Teach your son in the hall : your wife, on the pillow.

事 雖 小 不 作 不 成　子 雖 賢 不 敎 不 明

Shih sui hsiao pu tso pu ch'eng.　Tzŭ sui hsien pu chiao pu ming.

> Though an affair be small, it must be attended to, or it
> will not be completed ; though a son be good, he
> must be instructed or he will remain ignorant.

敎 子 孫 兩 條 正 路,惟 讀 惟 耕

Chiao tzŭ sun liang t'iao chêng lu, wei tu wei kêng.

> Teach your descendants the two proper roads,—literature
> and farming.

敎 子 敎 孫 須 敎 藝,栽 桑 栽 柘 少 栽 花

Chiao tzŭ chiao sun hsü chiao i, tsai sang tsai chê shao tsai hua.

> In the instruction of sons and grandsons be sure to
> teach them a trade ; plant the mulberry and the wild
> mulberry, but don't plant many flowers.

上 等 之 人 不 敎 而 善,中 等 之 人 一 敎 而 善,
　下 等 之 人 敎 亦 不 善

Shang têng chih jên pu chiao erh shan chung, têng chih jên i chiao
erh shan, hsia têng chih jên chiao i pu shan.

> Superior men are good without instruction : medium men
> are good with it ; but low fellows are bad even
> with it.

幼 小 讀 書 要 琢 磨,休 恨 嚴 師 敎 訓 多,
　黃 金 不 打 難 成 器,寶 劍 鈍 時 也 要 磨

Yu hsiao tu shu yao cho mo, hsiu hen yen shih chiao hsün to, huang
chin pu ta nan ch'eng ch'i, pao chien tun shih yeh yao mo.

> The youthful student must cut and grind ; he must not
> be grieved at the amount of instruction his strict
> teacher gives him : for nothing can be made of gold
> until it is hammered ; and when the trusty sword is
> blunt it must be sharpened.

大 家 禮 義 敎 子 弟,小 家 兇 惡 敎 兒 郎

Ta chia li i chiao tzŭ ti, hsiao chia hsiung wo chiao erh lang.

> Highborn children are taught to be polite and virtuous ;
> lowborn sons are taught violence and evil.

Chapter 2. Teachers.

教不嚴師之惰
Chiao pu yen shih chih to.

To educate without rigour shows the teacher's indolence.

惜錢莫教子,護短莫從師
Hsi ch'ien mo chiao tzǔ hu tuan mo ts'ung shih.

If you are a miser do not educate your son: if you wish to hide his faults, pay no heed to his teacher.

師嚴則道尊
Shih yen tsê tao tsun.

When the teacher is strict, his instruction will be respected.

燈盞無油枉費心
Têng chan wu yu wang fei hsin.

It there is no oil in the lamp the wick is wasted in vain. Note. The teacher wastes his strength on pupils of no ability.

財主敗落便教書
Ts'ai chu pai lo pien chiao shu.

When a rich man becomes poor he becomes a teacher.

課少主人嫌懶惰,功多弟子道難爲
K'o shao chu jên hsien lan to kung to ti tzǔ tao nan wei.

If he sets small tasks, his employers object to him because of his laziness; if the work is too much the scholars say they can't do it.

請師當請名人
Ch'ing shih tang ch'ing ming jên.

If you employ a teacher, employ one with a reputation.

一日之師,終身爲父
I jih chih shih chung shên wei fu.

Who teaches me a day is my father for life.

地 淨 塲 光 , 先 生 發 荒

Ti ching ch'ang kuang hsien shêng fa huang.

"When the ground is clean and the threshing floor bare,
The teacher's heart is filled with care". Note. This
indicates early winter when the teacher is uncertain
as to employment during the coming year.

冬 至 先 生 忙

Tung chih hsien sheng mang.

Near the end of the year the teacher is busy. i.e.
Looking out for employment. Note. *Lit*. The
Winter Solstice.

最 苦 不 過 的 是 敎 書 匠

Tsui k'u pu kuo ti shih chiao shu chiang.

It is impossible to be worse off than a teacher. *Lit*.
School-workman.

師 傅 不 明 徒 弟 拙

Shih fu pu ming t'u ti chüeh.

An inferior master makes a stupid pupil.

Chapter 3. Study.

布 衣 煖 , 菜 根 香 , 詩 書 滋 味 長

Pu i nuan, ts'ai ken hsiang, shih shu tzŭ wei ch'ang.

To one who is warm enough in cotton clothes, and who
likes his own ordinary food, the Book of Odes and
the Books of History are always full of flavour.

天 資 高 , 學 力 到

T'ien tzŭ kao, hsüeh li tao.

A man's natural gifts may be great, but it is application
that gives him success.

家 有 書 聲 家 必 興 , 家 有 歌 聲 家 必 傾

Chia yu shu sheng chia pi hsing, chia yu ko sheng chia pi ch'ing.

The home, in which there is the sound of study, will
prosper; the home where only singing is heard, will
be overthrown.

多 讀 書 方 能 免 俗

To tu shu fang neng mien su.

Study much' and you will avoid vulgarity.

只 要 用 心 讀，何 愁 書 不 熟

Chih yao yung hsin tu, ho ch'ou shu pu shu.

If you only apply your mind to study there will be no
need to worry about not knowing your subjects.

子 孫 雖 愚，經 書 不 可 不 讀

Tzǔ sun sui yü, ching shu pu k'o pu tu.

However stupid sons and grandsons may be, they must
study the Classics.

三 年 讀 書 不 如 聽 講

San nien tu shu pu ju t'ing chiang.

Three years' reading is not so good as hearing the
explanation. Note. This refers to the ordinary
method of first committing the books to memory,
and afterwards listening to the explanation of them.

人 不 學 古 今，馬 牛 而 襟 裾

Jên pu hsüeh ku chin ma niu erh chin chü.

Those who do not study the past and the present are only
horses and oxen in clothes.

幼 不 學，老 何 爲

Yu pu hsüeh lao ho wei.

If study be neglected in youth, what will you do in old
age ?

少 年 不 知 勤 學 早，白 頭 方 悔 讀 書 遲

Shao nien pu chih ch'in hsüeh tsao, pai t'ou fang hui tu shu ch'ih.

He who neglects to study diligently in youth, will, when
white-headed repent that he put it off until too late.

功 夫 不 日 進 則 日 退

Kung fu pu jih chin t-ê jih t'ui.

Learning which does not daily advance will daily decrease.

學 經 不 明，不 如 歸 耕

Hsüeh ching pu ming pu ju kuei kêng.

He who cannot understand the Classics had better return
to the plough.

千 般 易 學, 一 竅 難 得

Ch'ien pan i hsüeh i ch'iao nan tê.

> Most things are easy to learn, but hard to master.

開 卷 有 益

K'ai chüan yu i.

> In all learning there is profit. *Lit.* To open a book.

磨 穿 鐵 硯

Mo ch'uan t'ieh yen.

> Very studious. *Lit.* To rub away an iron ink-slab,

實 字 求 解, 虛 字 求 神

Shih tzŭ ch'iu chieh hsü tzŭ ch'iu shen.

> Seek the meaning of real words and the force of particles.
> Note. The Chinese loosely divide words into two
> classes 實 字 full or real, and 虛 字 empty words
> The latter are particles and abstract terms, which
> while hard to define and explain, are absolutely
> necessary to the right use of the language.

字 字 要 咬, 出 汁 漿 來

Tzŭ tzŭ yao ao ch'u chih chiang lai.

> Every character must be chewed to get out its juice.

熟 讀 深 思

Shu tu shen ssŭ.

> Study thoroughly and think deeply.

不 可 囫 圇 吞 棗

Pu k'o hu lun t'un tsao.

> You must assimilate what you learn. *Lit.* You can't
> swallow dates whole.

兩 耳 不 聽 窗 外 事, 一 心 只 讀 案 前 書

Liang êrh pu t'ing ch'uang wai shih, i hsin chih tu au ch'ien shu.

> Don't listen at all to the chatter outside the window, but
> apply yourself to the books immediately before you.

三 更 燈 火 五 更 鷄, 正 是 男 兒 立 志 時

San kêng têng huo wu kêng chi cheng shih nan êrh li chih shih.

> Burning the lamp into the third watch, and rising with
> the cock in the fifth ; these are the times when a
> student shows his resolution.

讀 書 如 流 水

Tu shu ju liu shui.

Study goes on like a flowing stream.

善 學 者 如 攻 堅 木

Shan hsüeh chê ju kung chien mu.

Good students resemble workers in hard wood.

讀 書 須 用 意，一 字 值 千 金

Tu shu hsü yung i i tzǔ chih ch'ien chin.

Be diligent in study, for every character is worth thousands of gold.

積 金 千 萬 兩 不 如 明 解 經 書

Chi chin ch'ien wan liang pu ju ming chieh ching shu.

It is better to understand the Classics than to amass riches.

人 學 始 知 道，不 學 亦 枉 然

Jên hsüeh shih chih tao, pu hsüeh i wang jan.

Knowledge comes by study, ignorance follows its neglect.

世 間 萬 般 皆 下 品，思 量 惟 有 讀 書 高

Shih chien wan pan chieh hsia p'in, ssǔ liang wei yu tu shu kao.

All pursuits are mean in comparison with that of learning.

學 然 後 知 不 足

Hsüeh jan hou chih pu tsu.

Some study shows the need of more.

三 日 不 讀 書 語 言 無 味

San jih pu tu shu yü yen wu wei.

Three day's neglect of study leaves one's conversation flavourless.

以 吃 愈 饑，以 學 愈 愚

I ch'ih yü chi i hsüeh yü yü.

By eating, we overcome hunger ; by study, ignorance.

讀 書 志 在 聖 賢，爲 官 心 存 君 國

Tu shu chih tsai sheng hsien, wei kuan hsin ts'un chün kuo.

In study, fix your mind on the sages ; in office, consider your prince and country.

做 到 老，學 不 了

Tso tao lao hsüeh pu liao.

You may study to old age and yet have things to learn.

讀 古 文 曉 得 做 時 文

Tu ku wen hsiao tê tso shih wen.

Read ancient essays and know how to compose modern ones.

學 之 染 人 勝 於 丹 青

Hsüeh chih jan jên shêng yü tan ch'ing.

Learning colours a man more than vermilion or black does.

書 乃 隨 身 之 寶

Shu nai sui shên chih pao.

Learning is a treasure which follows its owner everywhere.

學 無 老 少，達 者 爲 先

Hsüeh wu lao shao ta chê wei hsien.

Scholars are not classified by age, the intelligent take precedence.

學 無 前 後，達 者 爲 師

Hsüeh wu ch'ien hou ta chê wei shih.

In learning, length of study does not count ; the most intelligent becomes master.

古 今 之 事 理 無 窮，一 人 之 知 識 有 限

Ku chin chih shih li wu ch'iung i jên chih chih shih yu hsien.

Past and present times supply unlimited stores of knowledge ; but a man's capacity is limited.

書 到 用 時 方 恨 少，事 從 經 過 始 知 難

Shu tao yung shih fang hen shao, shih ts'ung ching kuo shih chih nan.

Having a chance to use one's reading, we regret that it is so meagre ; having accomplished a task, we begin to appreciate its difficulty.

最 樂 莫 如 讀 書 爲 善

Tsui lo mo ju tu shu wei shan.

No pleasure equals the pleasure of study.

富 家 不 用 買 良 田，書 中 自 有 千 鍾 粟

Fu chia pu yung mai liang t'ien, shu chung tzǔ yu ch'ien chung su.

Rich families have no need to buy fertile fields; and study is sure to yield its thousand measures of grain.

安 居 不 用 架 高 堂，書 中 自 有 黃 金 屋

An chü pu yung chia kao t'ang, shu chung tzǔ yu huang chin wu.

To live in peace there is no necessity to rear lofty halls; study naturally reveals its house of gold.

娶 妻 莫 恨 無 良 媒，書 中 有 女 顏 如 玉

Ch'ü ch'i mo hen wu liang mei, shu chung yu nü yen ju yü.

Don't grieve over the absence of a good go-between to arrange a marriage for you; study will provide you with a lady beautiful as jade.

讀 得 書 多 無 價 寶

Tu tê shu to wu chia pao.

Extensive reading is a priceless treasure.

莫 厭 經 史 煩，只 恐 工 夫 少

Mo yen ching shih fan, chih k'ung kung fu shao.

Don't complain of the trouble of having to master so many classics and histories; but fear lest your leisure should be too limited.

欲 知 天 下 事 須 讀 古 人 書

Yü chih t'ien hsia shih hsü tu ku jên shu.

Would you know the affairs of the empire, read the works of the ancients.

能 學 則 庶 民 之 子 爲 公 卿，不 學 則 公 卿 之 子 爲 庶 民

Neng hsüeh tsê shu min chih tzǔ wei kung ch'ing, pu hsüeh tsê kung ch'ing chih tzǔ wei shu min.

One who is studious, though a peasant's son may become a prince; a prince's son by neglecting study may become an ordinary person.

自 古 書 有 味, 硯 田 無 惡 歲

Tzŭ ku shu yu wei, yen t'ien wu ê sui.

> Books have always had a good flavour; the fields of
> literature have no poor harvests. Note. 味 indicates
> the intellectual relish or taste given. Literature;
> *Lit.* The ink-slab fields.

黃 金 有 價 書 無 價

Huang chin yu chia shu wu chia.

> Learning is far more precious than gold.

造 燭 救 明 讀 書 究 理

Chao chu chiu ming tu shu chiu li.

明 以 照 暗 室, 理 以 照 人 心

Ming i chao an shih, li i chao jên hsin.

> You make a candle to secure light; you study to
> understand right principles. The light illumines a
> dark room and right principles the heart of man.

人 不 學 不 知 義

Jên pu hsüeh pu chih i.

> If a man does not study, he will not know how to do
> what is right.

放 開 肚 皮 吃 飯, 頓 起 精 神 讀 書

Fang k'ai tu p'i ch'ih fan, tun ch'i ching shên tu shu.

> Do your best to make a full meal; exert your energies
> to the utmost for study.

Chapter 4. Literati.

學 者 如 禾 如 稻, 不 學 者 如 蒿 如 草

Hsüeh chê ju ho ju tao, pu hsüeh chê ju hao ju ts'ao.

> Studious men are like wheat and rice; non-studious men
> are like reeds and grass.

文 章 脹 齊 頸, 不 提 也 不 醒

Wen chang chang ch'i ching, pu t'i yeh pu hsing.

> A man full of learning up to his neck needs stirring up
> to impart it.

滿 嘴 裏 的 之 乎 也 者

Man tsui li ti chih hu yeh chê.

A pedant. · *Lit.* One whose mouth is full of particles.

秀 才 不 出 屋，能 知 天 下 事

Hsiu ts'ai pu ch'u wu, neng chih t'ien hsia shih.

Without leaving his study, a Bachelor of Arts may understand the affairs of the empire.

讀 書 不 成 方 作 吏

Tu shu pu ch'eng fang tso li.

He who fails to become a perfect scholar, may still be a magistrate's clerk.

求 不 到 官 有 秀 才

Ch'iu pu tao kuan yu hsiu ts'ai.

Though you cannot obtain office, you are still a Bachelor of Arts.

士 者 國 之 寶，儒 爲 席 上 珍

Shih chê kuo chih pao, ju wei hsi shang chên,

Scholars are their country's treasure : learned men are the richest ornaments of a feast.

秀 才 人 情 紙 半 張

Hsiu ts'ai jên ch'ing chih pan chang.

A Bachelor of Art's present is but half a sheet of paper, i.e., it may be something written by himself but not very costly.

讀 書 人 講 理，做 工 人 講 嘴

Tu shu jên chiang li, tso kung jên chiang tsui.

Scholars appeal to reason ; workmen simply talk and argue.

學 問 粗 疎，不 可 掛 讀 書 之 名

Hsüeh wen ts'u su, pu k'o kua tu shu chih ming.

He whose learning is rough and shallow, should not boast of scholarship.

寒 士 不 受 人 憐

Han shih pu shou jên lien.

A scholar though poor accepts no pity.

文 名 共 仰

Wen ming kung yang.

All look up to a famous scholar.

斯 文 同 骨 肉

Ssü wen t'ung ku jou.

All scholars are brethren.

秀 才 不 是 窮 家 子, 和 尙 不 是 富 家 兒

Hsiu ts'ai pu shih ch'iung chia tzŭ, ho shang pu shih fu chia êrh.

Bachelors of Arts are not the sons of poverty; Buddhist priest are not the sons of wealth.

旣 讀 孔 子 之 書, 必 知 周 公 之 禮

Chi tu K'ung Tzŭ chih shu, pi chih Chou Kung chih li.

As the student of the Confucian Canon; you must make yourself well acquainted with the Chou Ritual. Note. The Chou Li or Ritual of Chou consisting of rules for the guidance of Court officials is supposed to have been written by Chou Kung, 周 公 son of the famous Wen Wang 文 王.

學 在 一 人 之 下, 用 在 萬 人 之 上

Hsüeh tsai i jên chih hsia, yung tsai wan jên chih shang.

As a student—under one man; in office—over ten thousand.

士 爲 知 巳 用, 女 爲 悅 巳 容

Shih wei chih chi yung, nü wei yüeh chi jung.

A scholar will serve those who appreciate him; and a lady will be pleasant to those who please her.

手 拈 一 管 筆, 到 處 不 求 人

Shou nien i kuan pi, tao ch'u pu ch'iu jên.

He who can handle a pen, will have no need to beg.

腹 有 詩 書 氣 自 華

Fu yu shih shu ch'i tzŭ hua.

When the mind is stored with learning, the bearing will be elegant.

金 漆 棺 材 土 葬

Chin ch'i kuan ts'ai t'u tsang.

A gilt lacquer coffin buried in the earth, i.e., A good
scholar wasted on small or dull pupils.

Chapter 5. Literature.

讀 了 增 廣 會 說 話

Tu liao Tseng Kuang hui shou hua.

> Whoever has read the Tseng Kuang is able to converse.
> Note. The Tseng Kuang 增廣 is a very valuable
> little book of proverbs most of which are to be found
> in these pages.

讀 了 幼 學 會 設 罵

Tu liao Yu Hsüeh hui shê ma.

> He who has read the Yu Hsüeh well knows how to curse.
> Note. The Yu Hsüeh 幼學 is an encyclopedia, in
> four volumes, containing useful information. There
> seems to be no justification in the book itself for this
> proverb.

看 三 國 會 用 計

K'an san Suo Kui yung chi.

> He who reads the San Kuo will be able to use strategy.
> Note. The San Kuo Chih 三國志 is a history of
> the period immediately after the Later Han Dynasty,
> when China was divided into three kingdoms. The
> history abounds in stories of military tactics and
> strategy.

看 孫 子 知 用 兵

K'an Sun Tzŭ chih yung ping.

> He who reads the Sun Tzu will understand military
> tactics. Note. This book is a treatise on military
> tactics by Sun Wu 孫 武, an officer in the service of
> the State of Wu, during the sixth century B.C.

看 綱 鑑 可 以 知 古 人 事 蹟

K'an Kang Chien k'o i chih ku jên shih chi.

> He who reads the Histories knows the affairs of the
> ancients.

天 下 書 同 文

T'ien hsia shu t'ung wen.

All over the empire the written character is the same.

耕 讀 爲 本

Kêng tu wei pên.

Husbandry and letters are the two chief professions.

舌 織 而 衣, 筆 耕 而 食

Shê chih erh i, pi kêng erh shih.

The tongue weaves for clothes ; the pen tills for food.

詩 中 有 畫, 畫 中 有 詩

Shih chung yu hua, hua chung yu shih.

There are pictures in poems, and poems in pictures.

名 敎 中 自 有 樂 地

Ming chiao chung tzŭ yu lo ti.

In all famous sects there are fields of enjoyment. Note. This, though a general saying, is mostly used in reference to the enjoyments reaped in literary pursuits.

讀 書 不 負 三 代

Tu shu pu fu san tai.

The literary profession does not neglect three generations. i.e. they all benefit by it.

讀 孫 吳 之 書 可 以 知 戰

Tu Sun Wu chih shu k'o i chih chan.

He who has read the works of Sun and Wu, can understand the art of war. Note. Sun and Wu, bold military leaders of the 4th and 6th centuries B.C.

看 地 理 便 知 天 下 形 勢

K'an ti li pien chih t'ien hsia hsing shih.

Study geography and you will know the aspect of the empire.

四 書 五 經 通, 全 家 食 天 祿

Ssu shu wu ching t'ung, ch'üen chia shih t'ien lu.

If the Four Books and the Five Classics are thoroughly mastered ; your whole family will receive Imperial benefits.

SECTION IV. ON MANNERS.

Chapter 1. Bearing and Politeness.

人 無 禮 說 橫 話，牛 無 力 拉 橫 耙

Jên wu li shuo heng hua, niu wu li la heng pa.

> A man without manners speaks perversely; an ox without strength drags the harrow cross-wise.

鄉 裏 人 禮 行 大，先 罵 人 後 說 話

Hsiang li jên li hsing ta, hsien ma jên hou shua hua.

> Rustics are exceedingly polite ; after cursing each other they have a friendly chat.

秀 才 遇 刀 兵，有 禮 講 不 清

Hsiu ts'ai yü tao ping, yu li chiang pu ch'ing.

> A graduate encountering a soldier exercises his politeness in vain.

人 見 人 說 話，牛 見 牛 咿 呀

Jên chien jên shuo hua, niu chien niu i ya.

> When persons meet, they greet each other; when oxen see each other they low.

先 生 學 堂 女 子 繡 房

Hsien sheng hsüeh t'ang nü tzü hsiu fang.

> Privacy. *Lit.* A teacher's school, a lady's boudoir.

父 坐 子 立，禮 貌 整 齊

Fu tso tzŭ li, li mao cheng ch'i.

> It is proper politeness for the father to sit and the son to stand.

禮 多 人 不 怪

Li to jên pu kuai.

> No one is offended by too much politeness.

禮 多 人 必 詐

Li to jên pi cha.

> Excessive politeness must cover deceit.

有 禮 服 得 君 王 道

Yu li fu tê chün wang tao.

> Politeness gains the confidence of princes

怪 人 心 在 肚 相 見 又 何 妨

Kuai jên hsin tsai tu, hsiang chien yu ho fang.

> If you keep your offence in your bosom, what is there to hinder you meeting as before ?

不 知 好 歹,豈 識 高 低

Pu chih hao tai, ch'i shih kao ti.

> How can he discern good and bad manners who doesn't know right from wrong.

暑 天 無 君 子

Shu t'ien wu chün tzŭ.

> No one stands on ceremony in hot weather. *Lit.* There is no superior man in hot weather.

熟 不 拘 禮,富 而 多 文

Shu pu chü li, fu êrh tu wen.

> Familiar friends may waive etiquette, but with a rich man you must be very polite.

黑 地 下 作 揖

Hei ti hsia tso i.

> Ill-timed politeness. *Lit.* To make one's bow in the dark.

人 敬 我 一 尺,我 敬 人 一 丈

Jên ching wo i ch'ih, wo ching jên i chang.

> For every foot of honour shown me, I show ten.

蠻 人 無 藥 醫

Man jên wu yao i.

> No medicine can cure a vulgar man.

做 此 官 行 此 禮

Tso tz'ü kuan hsing tz'ü li.

> Follow the ceremonial of the rank to which you belong.

恭 敬 不 如 從 命

Kung ching pu ju ts'ung ming.

> Obedience is better than politeness.

人 惡 禮 不 惡

Jên ê li pu ê.

> The man may be bad whilst his manners are not.

奉 天 子 卽 天 子, 奉 諸 侯 卽 諸 侯

Fêng t'ien tzǔ chi t'ien tzǔ, fêng chu hou chi chu hou.

> He who acts for the emperor is emperor; he who acts for
> a prince is prince.

賣 糖 的 掉 鑼 搥 不 敢 當

Mai t'ang ti tiao lo chui pu kan tang.

> I am unworthy this favour. *Lit.* The sweetmeat seller,
> having lost his gong-stick dare not strike his gong.
> Note. This is a pun on the word ' tang ' which also
> indicates the sound of a gong.

輕 諾 必 寡 信

Ch'ing no pi kua hsin

> Too ready compliance is not to be trusted.

自 尊 自 貴 自 輕 自 賤

Tzǔ tsun tzǔ kuei, tzǔ ch'ing tzǔ chien.

> Self-respect. *Lit.* He who respects himself makes
> himself respected, he who lightly esteems himself
> makes himself base.

雅 不 好 鬥 雅 不 嗜 酒

Ya pu hao tou, ya pu shih chiu.

> Gentlemen do not quarrel neither do they take too much
> wine.

道 德 仁 義, 無 禮 不 成

Tao tê jen i, wu li pu ch'eng.

> Reason, virtue, benevolence and goodness are not brought
> to perfection without politeness.

怪 人 勿 知 禮, 知 禮 勿 怪 人

Kuai jên wu chih li. chih li wu kuai jên.

> If you suspect others you offend against propriety; he
> who observes propriety doesn't suspect others.

有 禮 走 遍 天 下 ,無 禮 寸 步 難 行

Yu li tsou p'ien t'ien hsia, wu li ts'un pu nan hsing.

> With politeness, one can go anywhere in the world ; without politeness it is difficult to take the smallest step.

寧 可 濕 衣 . 不 可 亂 步

Ning k'o shih i, pu k'o luan pu.

> It is better to get one's clothes wet than to hurry.

閉 門 造 車 ,出 門 合 轍

Pi mên chao ch'ê, ch'u mên ho ch'ê.

> You may make a cart indoors, but if you go out with it, it must follow the ordinary ruts. i.e. Do as you like at home, but in society observe its rules.

Chapter 2. Compliments.

恭 喜 賀 喜 元 寶 㯺 起

Kung hsi ho hsi yüan pao lo ch'i.

> Hearty congratulations. May your wealth increase.

易 長 易 成

I chang i ch'eng.

> May he easily grow up, and make a man of himself.

定 出 人 羣

Ting ch'u jên ch'ün.

> You certainly will outstrip the common herd.

出 人 頭 地

Ch'u jên t'ou ti.

> May you excel all others.

將 門 之 子

Chiang mên chih tzŭ.

> You are the son of a noble sire.

蘭 桂 騰 芳

Lan kuei te'ng fang.

> May all your descendants be famous. *Lit.* The rising perfumes of the orchid and cassia.

兄 弟 聯 芳

Hsiung ti lien fang.

May your brothers together grow famous.

你 的 好 造 化 兒 女 一 大 路

Ni ti hao tsao hua êrh nü i ta lu.

Your wonderful good fortune. A crowd of children.
Note. 造化 equals. 福氣.

五 福 臨 門

Wu fu lin mên.

May the Five Blessings descend on the dwelling. Note.
The Five Blessings are given in the Book of History
as Old Age, Wealth, Health, Love of Virtue, and A
Natural Death.

對 我 生 財

Tui wo sheng ts'ai.

May we also grow rich.

青 出 於 藍 而 勝 於 藍

Ch'ing ch'u yü lan êrh sheng yü lan.

The scholar has excelled his master. *Lit.* The black
dye succeeds the blue and is superior to it.

一 揮 而 就

I hui êrh chiu.

Yours is the pen of a ready writer *Lit.* One stroke and
it is done.

千 里 駒

Ch'ien li chü.

A wonderful child. *Lit.* A swift colt.

吉 祥 如 意

Chi hsiang ju i.

May you have the happiness you desire.

吉 星 拱 照

Chi hsing kung chao

May a lucky star shine upon you.

大 吉 利 市

Ta chi li shih.

May you have happiness and good profit.

Chapter 3. Presents.

莫 將 容 易 得 便 作 等 閒 看

Mo chiang jung i tê pien tso teng hsien k'au.

> Do not take anything easily obtained, and forthwith make it out to be unimportant. Comp. Prov. 20, 14.

千 里 送 毫 毛 寄 物 不 寄 失

Ch'ien li sung hao mao, chi wu pu chi shih.

> When the bearer of a trifling present to one at a great distance, be sure you do not lose it.

寶 劍 贈 於 烈 士, 紅 粉 贈 於 佳 人

Pao chien tsêng yü lieh shih, hung fên tsêng yü chia jên.

> Suit the present to the receiver. *Lit.* Present a sword to a warrior, a box of rouge to a pretty woman.

關 門 躱 債 主, 借 債 感 人 情

Kuan men to chai chu, chieh chai kan jên ch'ing.

> Though he has to shut his door against creditors he borrows money to make presents.

躭 得 猪 頭, 找 不 到 廟 門

Tan tê chu t'ou, chao pu tao miao men.

> To carry an offering of a pig's head, and be unable to find the door of the temple.

得 禮 還 禮, 總 不 得 意

Tê li huan li tsung pu tê i.

> To receive a gift; to make a suitable return: and still feel dissatisfied.

千 里 寄 毫 毛 禮 輕 人 意 重

Ch'ien li chi hao mao, li ch'ing jên i chung.

> When a trifling present is sent a long distance, the gift may be light but the intention is weighty.

供先生肉鮓魚蝦

Kung hsien sheng jou cha yü hsia.

> Present meat, minced fish and shrimps to a teacher.

以情還情

I ch'ing huan ch'ing.

> Return gift for gift.

得人一牛,還人一馬

Tê jên i niu, huan jêu i ma.

> If you receive an ox you must return a horse. Note.
> This is the rule in the giving and receiving of
> presents. i.e. Give more than you receive.

Chapter 4. Etiquette of Visiting.

寧添一斗莫添一口

Ning t'ien i tou mo t'ien i k'ou.

> Rather add a peck of rice than another mouth to eat it.

鴉鵲堂前叫,不久有客到

Ya ch'iao t'ang ch'ien chiao, pu chiu yu chiu yu k'o tao.

> When magpies chatter before the house, you will soon
> have callers.

請客莫請女客五十當一百

Ch'ing k'o mo ch'ing nü k'o wu shih tang i pai.

> When you invite guests don't invite ladies. If you do,
> fifty invited, may mean a hundred. Note. They
> will probably bring children.

請客不怕多,共吃一隻鵝

Ch'ing k'o pu p'a to, kung ch'ih i chih ê.

> Don't be afraid of inviting too many guests; one goose
> will be sufficient for them all.

寧可慢客不可餓客

Ning k'o man k'o pu k'o ô k'o

> Better slight a guest than starve him.

請客不催客,反以得罪客

Ch'ing k'o pu ts'ui k'o, fan i tê tsui k'o.

> If you do not press an invited guest you will offend him.

前 客 避 後 客, 粗 工 換 細 工

Ch'ien k'o pi hou k'o, ts'u kung huan hsi kung.

> First callers must retire before later callers : inferior workmen give place to skilled workmen.

上 屋 到 下 屋 是 一 個 客

Shang wu tao hsia wu shih i ko k'o.

> He who only comes from an upper to a lower storey is really a guest.

添 客 不 殺 雞

T'ien k'o pu sha chi.

> Though you add a guest you need not kill another fowl.

走 人 家 多 謝 煙 茶

Tsou jên chia to hsieh yen ch'a.

> Wherever you call, thank your host for tobacco and tea.

相 見 易 得 好, 久 住 難 爲 人

Hsiang chien i tê hao, chiu chu nan wei jên.

> It is easy to treat a guest well at first ; but if he stays too long it is hard.

在 家 不 會 迎 賓 客, 出 外 方 知 少 主 人

Tsai chia pu hui ying pin k'o, ch'u wai fang chih shao chu jên,

> He who cannot in his own house entertain a guest, when abroad will find few to enterta   him.

客 來 主 不 顧 應 恐 是 癡 人

K'o lai chu pu ku ying k'ung shih ch'ih jên.

> He who lacks hospitality to guests, is probably a fool.

良 賓 主 不 顧, 自 是 無 良 賓

Liang pin chu pu ku, tzŭ shih wu liang pin.

> He who is not hospitable to an excellent guest will soon have none.

久 住 令 人 賤, 貧 來 親 也 疎

Chiu chu ling jên chien, p'in lai ch'in yeh su.

> Long visits make hosts uncivil ; when a poor man visits his relatives they treat him coolly.

白 酒 釀 成 延 好 客, 黃 金 散 盡 爲 詩 書

Pai chiu niang ch'eng yen hao k'o, huang chin san chin wei shih shu.

> Having fermented your white wine you can invite a worthy guest ; having spent all your gold in studying you can enjoy the odes and histories.

道 院 迎 仙 客, 書 堂 隱 相 儒

Tao yüan ying hsien k'o, shu t'ang yin hsiang ju.

> Taoist monasteries entertain the genii ; colleges hide future premiers and scholars.

送 君 千 里 終 須 一 別

Sung chün ch'ien li chung hsü i pieh.

> Though we escort a guest a thousand miles, we still must part.

宴 客 切 勿 留 連

Yen k'o ch'ieh wu liu lien.

> Entertain guests, but do not detain them.

座 上 客 常 滿, 杯 中 酒 不 空

Tso shang k'o ch'ang man, pei chung chiu pu k'ung.

> His house is constantly full of guests, and the wine cup is never empty.

甚 麼 風 吹 了 你 來

Shen mo fêng ch'ui liao ni lai.

> What wind has blown you here ? Note. This is said to an infrequent guest.

居 家 不 可 不 儉, 請 客 不 可 不 豐

Chü chia pu k'o pu chien, ch'ing k'o pu k'o pu fêng.

> In ordinary life you must be economical ; when you invite guests you must be lavish in hospitality.

客 無 親 疎, 來 者 當 受

K'o wu ch'in su, lai chê tang shou.

> Receive all guests that come, making no difference betweeen relatives and strangers.

見 官 莫 向 前, 做 客 莫 向 後

Chien kuan mo hsiang ch'ien, tso k'o mo hsiang hou.

> Keep in the background before an official, but not before a host.

在 家 不 打 人·出 外 無 人 打

Tsai chia pu ta jên, ch'u wai wu jên ta.

> As you treat guests at home you will be treated abroad. *Lit.* At home do not beat men, then abroad, men will not beat you.

親 戚 要 走 得 稀·菜 園 要 去 得 勤

Ch'in ch'i yao tsou tê hsi, ts'ai yüan yao ch'u tê ch'in.

> Relations must be seldom visited; kitchen gardens, often.

仰 你 的 饅 頭 蜇 你 的 嘴

Yang ni ti man t'ou ch'ai ni ti tsui.

> I sting your lips with your own bread. Note. This is said in apology by a poor host who is obliged to serve up the gift just received for his guest to eat.

拭 棹 還 席

Shih cho huan hsi.

> Too much politeness. *Lit.* No sooner are the tables cleared than he invites me to a return feast.

一 客 不 擾 二 主

I k'o pu jao erh chu.

> One guest does not trouble two hosts.

衣 服 破 時 賓 客 少; 識 人 多 處 是 非 多

I fu p'o shih pin k'o shao, shih jên to ch'u shih fei to.

> When one's clothes are torn, he will have few guests; when one knows many people, there is sure to be much gossip.

客 去 主 人 安

K'o ch'ü chu jên an.

> When the guests are gone; the host is at rest.

SECTION V. PRUDENCE.

Chapter 1. Caution.

回頭再看,不得失散

Hui t'ou tsai k'an, pu tê shih san.

He who turns round to look again won't lose anything.

各照衣帽,小心爲要

Ko chao i mao, hsiao hsin wei yao.

Let each be careful to look after his own coat and hat.

照前照後衣食常彀

Chao ch'ien chao hou i shih ch'ang kou.

He who looks after what is in front and what is behind, will not lack food and clothing.

內要伶俐外要痴呆,聰明逞盡惹禍招災

Nei yao ling li wai yao ch'ih tai, ts'ung ming ch'eng chin jê huo chao tsai.

Be inwardly clever, but outwardly clownish : if you brag too much about your wisdom you are sure to come to grief.

下錯一步,滿盤都輸

Hsia ts'o i pu, man p'an tu shu.

Make one false move and you lose the game.

城牆高萬丈,內外要人輔

Ch'eng ch'iang kao wan chang, nei wai yao jên fu.

Though the city wall be exceedingly high, it must have guards stationed inside and out.

毒人的莫吃,犯法的莫做

Tu jên ti mo ch'ih, fan fa ti mo tso.

Don't eat anything poisonous, and don't break the law.

打得一塲開,免得百塲來

Ta tê i ch'ang k'ai, mien tê pai ch'ang lai.

Settle one, and avoid a hundred (difficulties).

醜 話 說 在 先
Ch'ou hua shuo tsai hsien.
> State all conditions first.

日 防 風 浪 之 險,夜 防 盜 賊 之 憂
Jih fang fêng lang chih hsien, yeh fang tao tsei chih yu.
> Beware of storms by day and thieves by night.

瓜 田 不 納 履,李 下 不 整 冠
Kua t'ien pu na li, li hsia pu chêng kuan.
> Avoid suspicion. *Lit.* Do not put on your shoes in a melon field ; nor adjust your hat under a plum tree.

瓜 田 李 下,各 避 嫌 疑
Kua t'ien li hsia, ko pi hsien i.
> Same as above. *Lit.* In a melon field and under a plum tree, avoid suspicion.

念 念 有 如 臨 敵 日,心 心 常 似 過 橋 時
Nien nien yu ju lin ti jih, hsin hsin ch'ang ssǔ kuo ch'iao shih.
> Be as careful as if you were entering on a contest : or crossing a bridge.

明 知 山 有 虎,莫 向 虎 山 行
Ming chih shan yu hu mo hsiang hu shan hsing.
> When you know there are tigers on the hills don't go there.

路 逢 狹 處 須 防 劍
Lu fêng hsia ch'u hsü fang chien.
> In a narrow passage be prepared for a dagger.

安 不 可 忘 危,治 不 可 忘 亂
An pu k'o wang wei, chih pu k'o wang luan.
> Always be provided against danger and rebellion.

吃 飯 防 哽 行 路 防 跌
Ch'ih fan fang kêng hsing lu fang tieh.
> In eating, avoid choking ; in walking, avoid stumbling.

走 一 步,打 個 樁
Tsou i pu, ta ko chuang.
> Proceed cautiously. *Lit.* Take a step, drive a pile.

不 見 所 欲，使 心 不 亂

Pu chien so yü, shih hsin pu luan.

> Look not on that which you desire and your mind will
> not be disturbed.

小 心 天 下 去 得，大 意 百 事 吃 虧

Hsiao hsin t'ien hsia ch'ü tê ta i pai shih ch'ih k'uei.

> With caution, one may go anywhere in the empire; if
> careless, everything will go wrong.

裝 聾 作 啞

Chuang lung tso ya.

> To act the part of one deaf and dumb. Note. That is
> for fear of becoming involved in danger or crime.

戴 氈 帽 安 繩

Tai chan mao an shêng.

> Over cautious. *Lit.* To wear strings on a felt hat.

有 柺 棍 兒 不 跌 倒，有 商 量 兒 不 失 錯

Yu kuai kun êrh pu tieh tao, yu shang liang êrh pu shih t'so.

> If you use a walking stick you will not fall; if you take
> counsel you will not err.

飛 不 高，跌 不 傷

Fei pu kao, tieh pu shang.

> A fall hurts not those who fly low.

隔 牆 須 有 耳，窗 外 豈 無 人

Kê ch'iang hsü yu êrh, ch'uang wai ch'i wu jên.

> Partition walls have ears; and are there not listeners
> under the window?.

無 事 時 要 提 防，有 事 時 要 鎮 定

Wu shih shih yao t'i fang, yu shih shih yao chên ting.

> When free from trouble be on your guard; when trouble
> comes keep calm.

勤 是 無 價 之 寶，慎 是 護 身 之 符

Ch'in shih wu chia chih pao shen shih hu shên chih fu.

> Diligence is an inestimable treasure, and prudence a
> defensive charm.

房 裏 無 人 莫 烘 衣,烘 衣 猶 恐 帶 頭 垂

Fang li wu jên mo hung i, hung i yu k'ung tai t'ou ch'ui.

> If there is no one at home, don't leave clothes before the fire to dry; in drying clothes take care that no sashes hang down.

執 燭 過 防 光 燥 物,吹 燈 要 看 火 星 飛

Chih chu kuo fang kuang tsao wu, ch'ui têng yao k'an huo hsing fei.

> Don't carry a candle near inflammable things ; when you blow a lamp out, watch the flying sparks.

家 中 縱 有 千 般 事,臨 睡 厨 房 走 一 回

Chia chung tsung yu ch'ien pan shih, lin shui ch'u fang tsou i hui.

> Though a thousand things may claim attention in your household, never go to bed without a look at the kitchen.

來 得 明,去 得 白

Lai tê ming, ch'ü tê pai.

> He comes publicly and goes openly.

行 船 要 辦 落 水 之 計

Hsing ch'uan yao pan lo shui chih chi.

> When you travel by boat be prepared for a ducking.

一 念 之 差,終 身 之 悔

I nien chih ch'a, chung shên chih hui.

> One miscalculation may cause a life-long regret.

差 之 毫 釐,失 之 千 里

Ch'a chih hao li, shih chih ch'ien li.

> Deviate a fraction and you lose a thousand miles.

風 平 浪 未 靜

Fêng p'ing lang wei ching.

> Though the wind has fallen, the waves have not ye settled.

廣 記 不 如 淡 墨

Kuang chi pu ju tan mo.

> A good memory is not equal to pale ink.

男 怕 輸 筆，女 怕 輸 身

Nau p'a shu pi, nü p'a shu shên.

> Men fear a slip of their pens, women a slip of their morals.

不 怕 人 不 請，就 怕 藝 不 真

Pu p'a jên pu ch'ing, chiu p'a i pu chên.

> Rather fear that you should not prove an adept, than that you should lack employment.

若 要 人 不 知，除 非 己 莫 爲

Ju yao jên pu chih, ch'u fei chi mo wei.

> Never do what you don't want to be known.

月 明 月 明，不 可 獨 行，實 要 獨 行，手 提 紅 燈

Yüeh ming yüeh ming, pu k'o tu hsing, shih yao tu hsing, shou t'i hung têng.

> The moon may be bright but don't walk alone ; if you must walk alone take a red lantern with you.

籬 牢 犬 不 入

Li lao ch'uan pu ju.

> If the fence is secure the dogs will not enter.

七 十 不 留 宿，八 十 不 留 坐

Ch'i shih pu liu su, pa shih pu liu tso.

> Don't keep people of seventy over-night ; don't invite those who are eighty to sit down, i.e., it might be awkward if they were taken ill, etc.

一 人 不 入 廟 二 人 不 看 井

I jên pu ju miao, êrh jên pu k'an ching.

> One person alone should not enter a temple ; two persons should not together look into a well.

老 虎 入 山 洞，顧 前 不 顧 後

Lao hu ju shan tung, ku ch'ien pu ku hou.

> Like a tiger entering into a cave ; looking ahead but not behind.

Chapter. 2. Discretion.

不 是 撑 船 手，休 拿 竹 篙 頭

Pu shih ch'eng ch'uan shou, hsiu na chu kao t'ou.

If you are not a sailor don't handle a boat-hook.

求 人 須 求 大 丈 夫，濟 人 須 濟 急 時 無

Ch'iu jên hsü ch'iu ta chang fu, chi jên hsü chi chi shih wu.

If you ask favours, ask them from worthy men ; if you
help people, help those who are in distress.

未 來 休 指 望，過 去 莫 思 量

Wei lai hsiu chih wang, kuo ch'ü mo ssü liang.

Don't set your mind on things that are still in the future ;
don't worry about affairs that are already past.

入 門 休 問 榮 枯 事，觀 看 容 顔 便 得 知

Ju mên hsiu wen jung k'u shih, kuan k'an jung yen pien tê chih.

When you enter a home don't ask whether things are
prosperous or otherwise ; you will be able to tell by
looking at the inmates' faces.

無 益 語 言 休 着 口，無 干 己 事 少 當 頭

Wu i yü yen hsiu cho k'ou, wu kan chi shih shao tang t'ou.

If you have nothing worth saying don't open your mouth ;
if it is no business of yours don't interfere too much.

要 飯 吃 莫 得 罪 火 頭

Yao fan ch'ih mo tê tsui huo t'ou.

If you want your dinner don't offend the cook.

扁 担 往 上 翹，犂 轅 往 下 翹，各 有 各 翹

Pien tan wang shang chiao, li yüan wang hsia chiao, ko yu ko chiao.

Mind your own business. *Lit.* The carrying pole curves
upwards ; the plough shaft curves downwards : each
has its own curve.

手 管 往 前 彎，脚 管 往 後 彎，各 有 各 彎

Shou kuan wang ch'ien wan, chiao kuan wang hou wan, ko yu ko wan.

The same. *Lit.* The arm bends toward the front ; the
leg bends toward the back, each has its own bend.

說 話 說 與 知 音：送 飯 送 與 饑 人
Shuo hua shuo yü chih yin, sung fan sung yü chi jên.

> Talk to those who understand, and give food to those who are hungry.

見 景 生 情
Chien ching sheng ch'ing.

> Suit self to circumstances.

力 微 休 負 重·言 輕 莫 勸 人
Li wei hsiu fu chung, yen ch'ing mo ch'üan jên.

> If your strength be small, don't carry heavy burdens ; if your words be worthless, don't give advice.

無 錢 休 入 衆,遭 難 莫 尋 親
Wu chien hsiu ju tsung, tsao nan mo hsin ch'in.

> If you are poor, keep out of the crowd ; if in difficulties, don't seek a relative.

人 很 不 攙,酒 很 不 吃
Jên hen pu ch'an, chiu hen pu ch'ih.

> Don't mix with violent men ; don't drink strong wine.

莫 信 直 中 直·須 防 仁 不 仁
Mo hsin chih chung chih, hsü fang jên pu jên.

> Do not trust in an excessive show of honesty ; beware of an excessive show of kindness.

見 事 莫 說·問 事 不 知·閒 事 莫 管,無 事 早 歸
Chien shih mo shuo, wen shih pu chih, hsien shih mo kuan, wu shih tsao kuei.

> Do not tell what you see ; do not know what you are asked ; do not meddle with other folk's business ; if you have nothing to do go home early.

不 是 才 人 莫 獻 詩
Pu shih ts'ai jên mo hsien shih.

> Do not present your verses to any but a clever man.

到 那 裏 說 那 裏 話
Tao na li shuo na li hua.

> Wherever you go ; speak as you find the people speak.

井 裡 蛙 蟆 井 裡 好。

Ching li wa mo ching li hao.

The frog that lives in the well is best where he is.

受 恩 深 處 宜 先 退，得 意 濃 時 便 好 休

Shou en shên ch'u i hsien t'ui, tê i nung shih pien hao hsiu

It is better to retire when you are in greatest favour ;
and to break off negotiations when you have gained
your object.

國 亂 思 良 將，家 貧 思 賢 妻

Kuo luan ssü liang chiang. chia p'in ssü hsien ch'i.

When the country is in confusion, look out for a good
general ; when a family is poor, for a virtuous wife.

風 大 隨 風，雨 大 隨 雨

Fêng ta sui fêng, yü ta sui yü.

Yield to circumstances. *Lit.* When the wind is strong,
yield to the wind ; if the rain be heavy, yield to the
rain.

草 裡 失 針，草 裏 尋

Ts'ao li shih chen, ts'ao li hsin.

If you lost your needle in the grass, look for it there.

各 人 自 掃 門 前 雪，休 管 他 人 瓦 上 霜

Ko jên tzǔ sao mên ch'ien hsüeh, hsiu kuan t'a jên wa shang
shuang.

Let every one sweep away the snow from his own front
door ; and not trouble about the hoar-frost on his
neighbour's tiles.

要 得 無 事，少 管 閑 事

Yao tê wu shih, shao kuan hsien shih.

If you want to be at peace, don't meddle with other
people's affairs.

只 管 自 己 門 戶，休 說 別 人 女 妻

Chih kuan tzǔ chi men hu, hsiu shuo pieh jên nü ch'i.

Look after your own family, and don't talk about other
men's daughters and wives.

錢 不 錯 用，工 無 枉 使

Ch'ien pu ts'o yung, kung wu wang shih.

> Neither spend foolishly, nor work fruitlessly.

事 不 可 做 盡，勢 不 可 倚 盡，言 不 可 道 盡，福 不 可 享 盡

Shih pu k'o tso chin, shih pu k'o i chin, yen pu k'o tao chin, fu pu k'o hsiang chin.

> In the transaction of business, in the use of power, in the use of speech, and in the enjoyment of happiness, don't go too far.

與 人 方 便，與 己 方 便

Yü jên fang pien, yü chi fang pien.

> If you are accommodating to others, you will find it an accommodation to yourself.

知 止 常 止，終 身 不 耻

Chih chih ch'ang chih, chung shen pu ch'ih.

> If you know where to stop, and always stop there, you will never be in disgrace.

合 理 可 作，小 利 莫 爭

Ho li k'o tso, hsiao li mo cheng.

> All that accords with reason may be done; but never quarrel over petty profits.

寧 向 直 中 取，不 可 曲 中 求

Ning hsiang chih chung ch'ü, pu k'o ch'ü chung ch'iu.

> Better straightforwardly seize a thing, than seek it in an underhand way.

懼 法 朝 朝 樂，欺 公 日 日 憂

Chu fa chao chao lê, ch'i kung jih jih yu.

> Fear the law, and you will daily live in happiness; cheat the public and you will daily be in trouble.

奴 才 不 可 逞，小 孩 不 可 哄

Nu ts'ai pu k'o ch'eng, hsiao hai pu k'o hung.

> Neither indulge a slave, nor deceive a child.

三 思 而 行，再 思 可 矣

San ssŭ êrh hsing, tsai ssŭ k'o i.

Act after reflection but one's second thoughts may be best.

有 勢 勿 可 盡 行，有 力 勿 可 盡 撐

Yü shih wu k'o chin hsing, yu li wu k'o chin ch'eng.

If you have influence don't be continually exerting it ; if you have strength don't use it to the utmost.

留 點 尾 巴 擔 擔 蒼 蠅

Liu tien wei pa tan tan ts'ang ying.

Leave a little of the tail to whisk off flies. i.e. Don't be too economical.

小 船 勿 宜 重 載

Hsiao ch'uan wu i chung tsai.

Don't put heavy cargo into a little boat.

養 狼 當 犬 看 家 難

Yang lang tang ch'uan k'an chia nan.

If you rear a wolf in place of a dog, it will be difficult to guard your house.

鹹 魚 船 上 莫 打 鹽

Hsien yü ch'uan shang mo ta yen.

Don't add salt to a boat-load of salt fish.

幾 長 人 穿 幾 長 衣 服

Chi ch'ang jên ch'uan chi ch'ang i fu.

Men of a certain height must wear clothes of a certain length.

輸 贏 無 悔

Chu ying wu hui.

Whether losing or winning don't regret.

見 怪 不 怪，其 怪 自 滅

Chien kuai pu kuai, ch'i kuai tzŭ mieh.

If you see an uncanny thing and do not regard it is such, its uncanniness will disappear. i.e. Ghosts, etc. only exist for those who believe in them.

使 口 不 如 自 走，求 人 不 如 求 己

Shih k'ou pu ju tzŭ tsou, ch'iu jên pu ju ch'iu chi.

> Better go yourself than send ; better do it yourself than ask any one to do it for you.

守 己 須 責 己，用 人 不 疑 人

Shou chi hsü tsê chi, yung jên pu i jên.

> If you would control yourself you must rebuke yourself ; if you would employ men, do not suspect them.

少 飲 不 亂 性，惜 氣 免 傷 財

Shao yin pu luan hsing, hsi ch'i mien shang ts'ai.

> Temperance in drinking, saves the mind from confusion : restraint of passion, preserves fortunes unimpaired.

Chapter 3. Economy.

家 有 一 萬，繚 補 一 半

Chia yu i wan, liao pu i pan.

> "Though you be a millionaire, mend one half the clothes you wear"

器 具 質 而 潔，瓦 缶 勝 金 玉

Ch'i chü chih êrh chieh, wa fou sheng chin yü.

> If your household articles are substantial and clean, earthenware will be found better than gold or jade.

莫 令 接 不 到 頭

Mo ling chieh pu tao t'ou.

> Don't fail to make ends meet.

十 兩 銀 子 莫 置 衣，百 兩 銀 子 不 娶 妻

Shih liang yin tzŭ mo chih i, pai liang yin tzŭ pu ch'ü ch'i.

> If you have only ten taels don't buy many clothes ; if you have only one hundred taels don't marry a wife.

冷 水 要 人 挑 熱 水 要 人 燒

Leng shui yao jên t'iao, jo shui yao jên shao.

> Cold water has to be carried; hot water has to be heated.
> Note. The implication is, Don't waste it.

上 屋 搬 下 屋 要 得 三 擔 糯 穀

Shang wu pan hsia wu, yao tê san tan no ku.

> It will cost you three piculs of the best rice to remove from the upper story to the ground floor.

勿 營 華 屋，勿 謀 良 田

Wu ying hua wu, wu mou liang t'ien.

> Don't build fine houses; don't covet rich fields.

一 文 錢 不 落 虛 空

I wen ch'ien pu lo hsü k'ung.

> Never spend one cash uselessly.

近 水 不 可 多 用 水

Chin shui pu k'o to yung shui.

> Though living near water don't waste it.

近 山 不 可 枉 燒 柴

Chin shan pu k'o wang shao ch'ai.

> Though living near mountains do not waste firewood.

惜 衣 得 衣，惜 食 得 食

Hsi i tê i, hsi shih tê shih.

> To be careful of clothes is to obtain clothes ; to be careful of food is to obtain food.

切 勿 奢 侈 過 度

Ch'ieh wu shê ch'ih kuo tu.

> By all means avoid extravagance.

破 破 皷 救 救 月

P'o p'o ku chiu chiu yüeh.

> A broken drum saves the moon. Note. This refers to the custom of using drums and gongs on the occasion of an eclipse of the moon.

烏 龜 吃 大 麥 蹧 蹋 糧 食

Wu kuei ch'ih ta mai tsao t'a liang shih.

> It is wanton waste to feed a tortoise with barley.

一 吊 錢 開 不 得 串

I tiao ch'ien k'ai pu tê ch'uan.

> Avoid breaking into a string of cash (i.e. it will soon be spent.)

買 馬 的 錢 沒 得 製 鞍 的 多
Mai ma ti ch'ien mu tê chih an ti to.

> The trappings cost more than the horse.

得 了 便 宜 柴，燒 了 夾 底 鍋
Tê liao pien i ch'ai, shao liao chia ti kuo.

> Cheapness may not be economy. *Lit.* Fuel has been so cheap that he has burnt the bottom out of his cooking pot.

從 儉 入 奢 易，從 奢 入 儉 難
Ts'ung chien ju shê i, ts'ung shê ju chien nan.

> From economy to extravagance is easy ; from extravagance to economy is difficult.

減 用 免 求 人
Chien yung mien ch'iu jên.

> Economy makes men independent.

量 體 裁 衣
Liang t'i ts'ai i.

> Cut your cloth according to your measure.

自 奉 必 須 儉 約
Tzŭ fêng pi hsü chien yo.

> In providing for self, practise rigid economy.

錢 糧 有 數，時 用 無 數
Ch'ien liang yu shu, shih yung wu shu.

> Taxes are fixed but expenses are not.

花 籃 提 水 難 存 留
Hua lou t'i shui nan ts'un liu.

> A basket cannot for long dam a stream.

一 個 錢 把 做 兩 個 用
I ko ch'ien pa tso liang ko yung.

> Make every cash serve two purposes.

牡 丹 花 大 空 入 目，棗 花 雖 小 結 實 成
Mu tan hua ta k'ung ju mu, tsao hua sui hsiao chieh shih ch'eng.

> The peony, though large is useless ; the date blossom, though small, yields fruit.

惜 人 得 人 用, 惜 衣 得 衣 穿
Hsi jên tê jên yung, hsi i tê i ch'uan.

> Who spare men, will always have men to use ; who spare their clothes, will always have clothes to wear.

用 錢 容 易 賺 錢 難
Yung ch'ien jung i, chuan ch'ien nan.

> It is easy to spend, but hard to earn money.

積 少 成 多
Chi shao ch'eng to.

> Little will grow to much.

飛 災 橫 禍 不 入 慎 家 之 門
Fei tsai heng huo pu ju shen chia chih men.

> Sudden calamity and unexpected misfortune cannot enter a careful family.

傳 家 惟 有 菜 根 香
Ch'uan chia wei yu ts'ai ken hsiang.

> The only way to keep a family in existence for generations is to think cabbage-stalks nice, i.e. to be economical in food.

Chapter 4. Experience.

近 水 知 魚 性, 近 山 識 鳥 音
Ch'in shui chih yü hsing, chin shan shih niao yin.

> Those who live near water know the nature of fishes ; those who live near hills discriminate the songs of birds.

一 回 着 蛇 咬, 二 回 不 趲 草
I hui cho shê yao, êrh hui pu tsan ts'ao.

> He who is once bitten by a snake, will not walk in the grass.

見 過 不 如 做 過, 做 過 不 如 錯 過 多
Chien kuo pu ju tso kuo, tso kuo pu ju ts'o kuo to.

> To have done a thing oneself is better than watching others do it ; to have made many mistakes in doing it is better than simply doing it once.

不 上 當 不 成 內 行

Pu shang tang pu ch'eng nei hang

> If you haven't been deceived by others you will never learn the trade.

初 吃 饅 頭 三 口 生

Ch'u ch'ih man t'ou san k'ou sheng.

> He who eats bread for the first time, feels strange over the first three mouthfuls. Note. This is a proverb of Central and Southern China where wheat is not so much eaten as rice.

口 說 不 如 身 逢

K'ou shuo pu ju shen feng.

> Hearsay is not equal to personal experience.

不 住 鄉 不 知 艱 難 辛 苦

Pu chu hsiang pu chih chien nan hsin k'u.

> If you have not lived in the country, you do not know what hardship means.

不 住 城 不 知 禮 義

Pu chu ch'eng pu chih li i.

> If you have not lived in the town, you do not know what is polite and proper.

當 時 若 不 登 高 望 誰 信 東 流 海 樣 深

Tang shih jo pu teng kao wang, shui hsin tung liu hai yang shen.

> Suppose no one ever ascended a mountain to see, who would believe that the water flowed down eastward from a height as great as depth of the sea.

飲 水 知 源

Yin shüi chih yüan.

> If you drink the water you will know the spring.

甘 苦 備 嘗

Kan k'u pei ch'ang.

> He has tasted both sweet and bitter.

耳 聞 不 如 眼 見

Erh wen pu ju yen chien.

> Hearsay is not equal to seeing for oneself.

耳 聽 是 虛，眼 見 是 實

Erh t'ing shih hsü, yen chien shih shih.

What one hears is doubtful ; what one sees is certain.

耗 子 纔 知 耗 子 路

Hao tzŭ ts'ai chih hao tzŭ lu.

Rats know the ways of rats. Comp. "Set a thief to catch a thief"

蛇 鑽 的 洞 蛇 曉 得

Shê tsuan ti tung shê hsiao tê.

The snake knows its own hole.

事 非 經 過 不 知 難

Shih fei ching kuo pu chih nan'

You don't know how difficult a thing is until you try to do it.

眼 瞎 路 熟

Yen hsia lu shu.

Though blind, the road is familiar to him.

不 到 黃 河 心 不 死

Pu tao huang ho hsin pu ssŭ.

He will not be satisfied until he gets to the Yellow River. Note. Said of any headstrong man who pursues his own course against the advice of others.

巢 居 知 風，穴 居 知 雨

Ch'ao chü chih feng, hsüeh chu chih yü.

They know what wind is who dwell in nests ; what rain is who dwell in caves.

前 事 之 不 忘，後 事 之 師 也

Ch'ien shih chih pu wang, hou shih chih shih yeh.

The remembrance of the deeds of past ages is our best guide in the future.

明 鏡 可 以 察 形，往 古 可 以 知 今

Ming ching k'o i ch'a hsing, wang ku k'o i chih chin.

As one sees a reflection in a polished mirror, so can one know the present by studying ancient times.

要 知 山 下 路 須 問 過 來 人

Yao chih shan hsia lu, hsü wen kou lai jên.

> If you want to know the road down the mountain, ask those who have trodden it.

千 學 不 如 一 見

Ch'ien hsüeh pu jn i chien.

> One sight is better than a thousand lessons.

一 年 吃 蛇 咬 三 年 怕 草 索

I nien ch'ih shê yao, san nien p'a ts'ao so.

> One year bitten by a snake; three years afraid of grass ropes.

強 龍 難 壓 地 頭 蛇

Ch'iang lung nan ya ti t'ou shê.

> The mighty dragon can't crush the local snake. i.e. It knows the locality.

––––––

Chapter 5. Forethought.

草 不 除 根，終 當 復 生

Ts'ao pu ch'u ken, chung tang fu sheng.

> Grass that is not taken up by the root will spring up again.

有 得 大 樹，何 愁 柴 燒

Yu tê ta shu, ho ch'ou ch'ai shao.

> Having a great tree, why be anxious about fuel.

留 得 五 湖 明 月 在，不 愁 無 處 下 金 鈎

Liu te wu hu ming yüeh tsai, pu ch'ou wu ch'ü hsia chin kou.

> Treat men from all parts well, and wherever you go you will be well treated. *Lit.* Make sure of a clear moon in all the five lakes, and you will not suffer the lack of an angling place. Note. The five lakes are Poyang in Kiangsi, the Tung Ti'ng and Chi'ng Ts'ao in Hunan, and the Tan Yang and Tai Hu in Kiangsu.

年 年 防 饑，夜 夜 防 盜

Nien nien fang chi, yeh yeh fang i. ?

> Yearly guard against famine ; nightly guard against thieves.

寧 可 信 其 有，不 可 信 其 無

Ning k'o hsin ch'i yu, pu k'o hsin ch'i wu.

> Better be too credulous than too sceptical.

有 備 無 患

Yu pei wu huan.

> Where there is previous preparation there will be no calamity. Note. These characters are often seen where water kangs or fire engines are established.

與 其 病 後 能 求 藥，不 如 病 前 能 自 防

Yü ch'i ping hou neng ch'iu yao, pu ju ping ch'ien neng tzŭ fang.

> It is better to ward off than to cure disease.

禦 病 不 如 却 病，多 事 不 如 省 事

Yü ping pu ju ch'üeh ping, to shih pu ju shen shih.

> Better prevent, than cure disease ; better diminish than add to trouble.

一 不 積 財 一 不 結 怨，睡 也 安 寧，走 也 方 便

I pu chi ts'ai, i pu chieh yüan, shui yeh an ning, tsou yeh fang pien.

> He who neither hoards up wealth, nor makes an enemy, may sleep in peace and travel in safety.

過 去 事 巳 過 去 了，未 來 不 必 預 思 量

Kuo ch'ü shih i kuo ch'ü liao, wei lai pu pi yü ssŭ liang.

> Let the past be past ; don't trouble about the future.

水 來 土 掩，兵 來 將 當

Shui lai t'u yen, ping lai chiang tang.

> Equal to all emergencies. *Lit.* If flood water comes, soil can dam it ; if rebels come, a general can oppose them.

思 前 容 易 悔 後 難

Ssŭ ch'ien jung i, hui hou nan.

> Forethought is easy, repentance difficult.

閒 時 置 下 忙 時 用

Hsien shih chih hsia mang shih yung.

> Collect at leisure to use in haste.

常 將 有 日 思 無 日，莫 把 無 時 作 有 時

Ch'ang chiang yu yih ssŭ wu jih, mo pa wu shih tso yu shih.

> In plenty, think of want, in want, do not presume on
> plenty

池 塘 積 水 須 防 旱，田 土 深 耕 足 養 家

Ch'ih t'ang chi shui hsü fang han, t'ien t'u shen keng tsu yang chia.

> Keep your ponds full of water and thus prepare against
> drought; cultivate well your fields and you will have
> enough to support your family.

庭 栽 棲 鳳 竹，池 養 化 龍 魚

T'ing tsai ch'i feng chu, ch'ih yang hua lung yü.

> Plant before the hall bamboos that the phoenix will roost
> on; rear in your ponds fish that will turn to dragons.

養 兒 防 老，積 穀 防 饑

Yang êrh fang lao, chi ku fang chi.

> Rear sons for old age; and store grain against famine.

晴 帶 雨 傘，飽 帶 饑 糧

Ch'ing tai yü san, pao tai chi liang.

> In fine weather carry an umbrella; though not hungry
> take provisions with you.

宜 未 雨 而 綢 繆，勿 臨 渴 而 掘 井

I wei yü êrh ch'ou miu, wu lin k'o êrh chüeh ching

> Thatch your roof before rainy weather; dig your well
> before you are parched with thirst.

一 年 之 計 在 於 春；一 日 之 計 在 於 寅

I nien chih chi tsai yü chün, i jih chih chi tsai yü yin.

> Make plans for the year in spring; make plans for the
> day in the early morning.

人 無 遠 慮·必 有 近 憂

Jên wu yuan lü, pi yu chin yu.

> He who has no anxious thoughts for the future will find
> trouble nigh at hand.

得 寵 思 辱，安 居 慮 危
Tê ch'ung ssǔ ju, an chü lü wei.

> He who enjoys favours should be prepared for reverses;
> he who lives in security should think of possible
> danger.

驗 其 前 便 知 其 後
Yen ch'i ch'ien pien chih ch'i hou.

> Consider the past and you will know the future.

花 子 預 備 下 雨 粮
Hua tzǔ yü pei hsia yü liang.

> The beggar provides for a rainy day.

Chapter 6. Imprudence.

靜 坐 閒 談 不 得 燭 頭 了
Ching tso hsien t'an pu tê chu t'ou liao.

> He who sits chatting about nothing loses his candle.
> Note. This is similar to the familiar saying "The
> game is not worth the candle".

麻 雀 跳 在 糠 籮 裏，一 塲 歡 喜 一 塲 空
Ma ch'iao t'iao tsai k'ang lo li, i ch'ang huan hsi i ch'ang k'ung.

> When the sparrow hops into the chaff basket, it's
> rejoicing is soon at an end. Moral. Dont rejoice
> too soon.

無 錢 方 斷 酒，臨 老 始 看 經
Wu ch'ien fang tuan chiu, lin lao shih k'an ching.

> When your money is spent, you cut off wine; when
> growing old, you turn to the Classics. i.e. it is too
> late.

只 顧 前 走 不 顧 後 退
Chih ku ch'ien tsou, pu ku hou t'ui.

> Think only of advance, and never of retreat.

紙 糊 燈 籠 指 穿 不 得

> Don't thrust your finger through your own paper lantern.
> Comp. "Don't give the show away."

混 水 捉 魚，大 小 難 分

Hun shui tso yü, ta hsiao nan fen.

> He who fishes in muddy water cannot distinguish the great from the small.

弄 巧 反 拙

Lung ch'iao fan cho.

> To pretend to be clever and show one's self to be a fool.

破 船 多 攬 載

P'o ch'uan to lan tsai.

> To overlade a leaking ship.

火 上 添 油

Huo shang t'ien yu.

> To pour oil on the flames.

信 人 哄 賣 了 鷄 婆 種

Hsin jên hung mai liao chi p'o chung.

> To be " taken in," selling one's sitting hens.

栽 林 養 虎，虎 大 傷 人

Tsai lin yang hu, hu ta shang jên.

> If you plant a grove to rear tigers in, when grown, the tigers will injure you.

惜 了 臉 皮，悞 了 肚 皮

Hsi liao lien p'i, wu liao tu p'i.

> Suffering hunger to spare one's face.

隨 風 倒 柁，順 水 推 船

Sui fêng tao to, shun shui t'ui ch'uan.

> To sail any way with wind and tide.

把 臥 着 的 老 虎 哄 起 來 了 自 找 吃 虧

Pa wo cho ti lao hu hung ch'i lai liao tzŭ chao ch'ih k'uei.

> He who rouses a sleeping tiger runs the risk of harm.

大 處 不 算 小 處 算

Ta ch'ü pu suan hsiao ch'u suan

> To be careless in great matters and careful in small ones

剮 肉 補 瘡

Kua jou pu chuang.

> To scrape off the flesh in one place to mend a sore in another.

送 腦 殼 接 石 頭

Sung nao k'o chieh shih t'ou.

> To present one's head to a shower of stones.

護 疱 成 膿

Hu p'ao ch'eng lung.

> To spare a swelling till it becomes ulcerous. Note. This is used with regard to petted and spoilt children.

晴 乾 不 肯 去，直 待 雨 淋 頭

Ch'ing kan pu k'en ch'ü chih tai yü lin t'ou.

> He won't go in fair weather, but waits till the rain soaks his head.

燕 巢 幕 上 棲 身 難 安

Yen ch'ao mu shang ch'i shen nan an.

> The swallow which builds its nest on a bamboo screen finds it difficult to rest.

作 舍 道 傍 三 年 不 成

Tso shê tao p'ang san nien pu ch'eng.

> Build a cottage by the roadside, and you will not get it finished in three years. Note. The passers by will have all sorts of objections.

這 隻 耳 朵 進，那 隻 耳 朵 出

Chê chih erh to chin, na chih erh to ch'u.

> Unheeded instruction. *Lit.* Goes in at this ear and out at the other.

露 出 馬 脚 來

Lu ch'u ma chiao lai.

> To divulge a secret. *Lit.* To disclose the horse's foot. Note. The horse's foot is the popular name for the process of exorcising demons in sickness.

騎 虎 難 下 背

Ch'i hu nan hsia pei.

> He who rides a tiger is afraid to dismount.

旗 桿 磴 下 倒 誤 了 操

Ch'i kan teng hsia tao wu liao ts'ao.

Though under the flagstaff, he misses his drill.

脚 踏 兩 邊 船

Chiao t'a liang pien ch'uan.

To stand on two boats at once.

舍 近 而 圖 遠

Shê chin erh t'u yuan.

To neglect the present and plan for the future.

因 小 失 大

Yin hsiao shih ta.

To lose the great for the small.

臨 上 轎，才 扎 耳 朶 眼 兒

Lin shang chiao, ts'ai cha erh to yen erh.

Too late. *Lit.* Piercing the ears of the bride when she has already got into the bridal chair.

當 斷 不 斷，反 受 其 亂

Tang tuan pu tuan, fan shou ch'i luan.

Trouble neglected becomes more troublesome.

SECTION VI. ON BUSINESS.

Chapter 1. Buying and Selling.

二 人 同 一 心，黃 土 變 成 金

Erh jên t'ung i hsin, huang t'u pien ch'eng chin.

> When two men are of one mind, clay may be turned into gold.

時 值 估 價，不 得 相 罵

Shih chih ku chia, pu tê hsiang ma.

> Do business at market prices and avoid reviling each other.

求 買 求 賣，生 意 不 快

Ch'iu mai ch'iu mai, sheng i pu k'uai.

> Where there is much soliciting trade is not very lively.

現 錢 不 抓，不 是 行 家

Hsien ch'ien pu chua, pu shih hang chia.

> He who does not clutch at ready money is no business man.

園 裡 選 瓜，越 選 越 差

Yüan li hsüan kua, yüeh hsüan yüeh ch'a.

> Picking out melons in a melon patch, the more one does it the more one gets confused.

人 無 利 息 誰 肯 早 起

Jên wu li hsi, shui k'en tsao ch'i.

> Who will rise early if no profit is to be made?

兩 足 忙 忙 走，只 爲 身 和 口

Liang tsu mang mang tsou, chih wei shên ho k'ou.

> One's feet hurry to and fro for nothing but clothes and food.

大 雪 粉 紛 下，柴 米 油 鹽 都 長 價

Ta hsüeh fen fen hsia, ch'ai mi yu yen tu chang chia.

> After a heavy fall of snow, fuel, rice, oil, and salt all go up in price.

賺 錢 少 用 錢 多，一 身 受 奔 波

Chuan ch'ien shao yung ch'ien to, i shen shou pen po.

> Small profits and heavy expenses mean a life of ceaseless activity.

成 千 累 萬，要 有 力 賺

Ch'eng ch'ien lei wan, yao yu li chuan.

> To amass an immense fortune, a man must know how to make profit.

三 個 錢 買 兩 個 錢 賣，不 圖 賺 錢 只 圖 快

San ko ch'ien mai liang ko ch'ien mai, pu t'u chuan ch'ien chih t'u k'uai.

> He plans less for profit than for quick returns, who will buy a thing for three cash and sell it for two.

出 外 做 客，不 要 露 白

Ch'u wai tso k'o, pu yao lu pai.

> If you go out to buy anything don't show your silver.

天 晴 不 出 門，天 濕 賣 涼 粉，六 月 賣 氈 帽，正 月 賣 門 神

T'ien ch'ing pu ch'u men, t'ien shih mai liang fen, lu yüeh mai chan mao, cheng yüeh mai men shên.

> An incompetent business man. *Lit.* In fine weather he doesn't go out; in damp weather he hawks cold jelly; in the sixth month he sells felt hats and in the first month, door gods. Note. Door Gods are sold for the New Year decorations, and as soon as the New Year comes in are not wanted.

撇 開 油 喝 湯，不 與 我 相 商

P'ieh k'ai yu ho t'ang, pu yü wo hsiang shang.

> You skim the oil and drink the soup without consulting me. Note. This signifies a partner complaining of his fellow-partner.

先 錢 後 酒，吃 了 就 走

Hsien ch'ien hou chiu, ch'ih liao chiu tsou.

> Pay your cash and take your wine; drink it and off you go.

賺 錢 公 分, 折 本 公 認

Chuan ch'ien kung fen, chê pen kung jên.

Share equally in profit and loss.

客 是 寶, 貨 是 草

K'o shih pao, huo shih ts'ao.

Customers are to be valued ; goods are mere grass.

隨 筆 登 賬 免 後 思 量

Sui pi teng chang mien hou ssǔ liang.

Careful book-keeping saves anxious afterthought.

吃 米 也 有 幾 顆 穀 稗

Ch'ih mi yeh yu chi k'o ku pai.

Even in the rice we eat there are a few husks and tares.
Note. This may be said in answer to any complaint
about mixing inferior goods.

有 錢 莫 買 臘 月 貨

Yu ch'ien mo mai la yüeh huo.

Though you have money do not spend it in the twelfth
month. Note. At the end of the year goods of all
kinds are dearer.

貨 買 三 家 不 上 當

Huo mai san chia pu shang tang.

If you would not be cheated ask the price at three shops.

小 錢 不 去, 大 錢 不 來

Hsiao ch'ien pu ch'ü ta ch'ien pu lai.

If a little cash does not go, much cash will not come.
Note. Money must be spent in the entertainment
of customers, or in advertising.

以 小 到 大

I hsiao tao ta.

Use the little to get the big.

拋 磚 引 玉

P'ao chuan yin yü.

Throw a brick to allure a gem. Compare "Throw a
sprat to catch a mackerel."

人 無 笑 臉 休 開 店

Jên wu hsiao lien hsiu k'ai tien.

> A man without a pleasant face had better not go into trade.

便 宜 不 是 貨，是 貨 不 便 宜

Pien I pu shih huo shih huo pu pien.

> Cheap things are not good; good things are not cheap.

賣 瓜 的 說 瓜 甜

Mai kua ti shuo kua t'ien.

> The melon seller declares his melons sweet.

見 快 莫 趕

Chien k'uai mo kan.

> If there is a rush dont you hurry.

十 日 灘 頭 坐，一 日 走 九 洲

Shih jih t'an t'ou tso I jih tsou chiu chou.

> After ten days waiting above the rapids you may traverse the nine districts in one day. Note. The nine districts are the divisions of the empire subsequent upon the engineering labours of Yü the Great. This and the preceding proverb point out the advantage to be gained by patient perseverance in trade.

打 綱 日 曬 綱 時

Ta wang jih shai wang shih.

> There is a time to fish and a time to dry nets.

林 中 不 賣 薪，湖 上 不 鬻 魚

Lin chung pu mai hsin hu shang pu yü yü.

> Fuel is not sold in a forest nor fish on a lake.

利 大 害 大

Li ta hai ta.

> Great profits, great risks.

貨 消 碼 頭，錢 用 地 頭

Huo hsiao ma t'ou ch'ien yung ti t'ou.

> Use both such goods and money as suit your market.

開 店 容 易, 守 店 難

K'ai tien jung I shou tien nan.

It is easy to open a shop but hard to keep it open.

數 錢 如 看 金, 不 差 半 毫 分

Shu ch'ien ju k'an chin pu ch'a pan hao fen.

Count cash as though it were gold, and so avoid the least mistake.

折 本 不 如 賤 賣 貨

Chê pen pu ju chien mai huo.

Better sell for small profits than fail in business.

內 行 不 上 當

Nei hang pu shang tang.

One who is in the trade can't be cheated.

秤 鈎 打 釘 兩 扯 直

Ch'eng kou ta ting liang ch'e chih.

When a steelyard hook is beaten into a nail, both its ends are drawn out straight. Note. The steelyard hook in question is formed by bending one straight piece of iron wire; straightened out again it assumes its former condition. Hence this proverb is applied to one who is neither richer nor poorer for his trading.

貨 有 好 歹, 價 有 高 低

Huo yu hao tai chia pu kao ti.

Wares are good and bad; prices high and low.

人 強 命 不 強, 人 硬 貨 不 硬

Jên ch'iang ming pu ch'iang jên ying huo pu ying.

A man may be more vigorous than his luck; more unyielding than his goods.

河 裏 無 魚 蝦 也 貴

Ho li wu yü hsia yeh kuei.

When there is no fish in the river shrimps are dear. Note. This saying is sometimes applied to children, showing that daughters are precious in the absence of sons.

生意有路人無路

Sheng I yu lu jen wu lu.

There may be trade to be done but no way found to do it.

買貨的客人怕上當

Mai huo ti k'o jên p'a shang tang.

What the customer fears is being taken in.

嘴要爭船要撐

Tsui yao cheng ch'uan yao ch'eng.

Bargaining is as necessary to trade as poling to a vessel.

現錢賣現貨

Hsien ch'ien mai hsien huo.

Ready money can buy anything in stock.

銅銀子買母豬肉

T'ung yin tzŭ mai mu chu jou.

Bad silver will only buy old sow's flesh. Note. Sow's flesh is considered poor eating.

得了便財唱雅調

Tê liao pien ts'ai ch'ang ya tiao.

He sings for joy who makes a profit easily.

瞞天講價，就地還錢

Man t'ien chiang chia chiu ti huan ch'ien.

When one cheats up to heaven in the price he asks; you come down to earth in the price you offer.

肥了騾子瘦了馬

Fei liao lo tzŭ shou liao ma.

To fatten the mule and starve the horse. Note. This refers to a partner in a firm enriching himself at the expense of the other.

不得魚也得蝦

Pu tê yü yeh tê hsia.

Who cannot catch fish must catch shrimps.

生意中要一團和氣

Sheng I chung yao I t'uan ho ch'i.

In business one must be perfectly affable.

生 意 各 有 道 路
Sheng I ko yu tao lu.

Every trade has its ways.

人 多 變 化 必 不 蠢, 貨 不 停 留 利 自 生
Jên to pien hua hsin pu ch'un huo pu t'ing liu li tzŭ sheng.

He who can turn his hand to anything is not a fool; stock which never lies dead, naturally yields a profit.

百 貨 中 百 客
Pai huo chung pai k'o.

There are customers for all sorts of goods.

三 天 賣 兩 條 黃 瓜
San t'ien mai liang t'iao huang kua.

Poor business. Lit. To sell a couple of cucumbers in three days.

水 漲 船 高, 高 抬 市 價
Shui chang ch'uan kao t'ai shih chia.

When water rises vessels rise; so rise market prices.

價 高 招 遠 客
Chia kao chao yuan k'o.

High prices attract sellers from afar.

目 下 一 言 爲 定, 早 晚 時 價 不 同
Mu hsia I yen wei ting tsao wan shih chia pu t'ung.

One word just now will settle a bargain, though prices vary from morning till night.

買 賣 爭 毫 釐
Mai mai cheng hao li.

Buyers and sellers dispute over a fraction of a cash.

爭 價 不 爭 平
Cheng chia pu cheng p'ing.

Dispute the price but don't dispute the weight.

鮮 魚 小 菜 提 籃 着 價
Hsien yä hsiao ts'ai t'i lan cho chia.

Buying fresh, fish and vegetables, examine them first then fix the price.

放 得 千 日 貨，自 有 賺 錢 時

Fang tê ch'ien jih huo tzŭ yu chuan ch'ien shih.

> Hold back your goods for a thousand days and you will be able to sell at a profit.

一 本 萬 利 滿 載 而 歸

I pen wan li man tsai erh kuei.

> Ten thousand per cent means a full cargo and return to one's home.

蠅 頭 小 利，奔 西 走 東

Ying t'ou hsiao li pen hsi tsou tung.

> To hurry east and west for profits no bigger than a fly's head.

秤 平 斗 滿 不 虧 人

Ch'eng p'ing tou man pu k'uei jên.

> Just scales and full measures injure no man.

買 不 盡 便 宜 上 不 盡 當

Mai pu chin pien I shang pu chin tang.

> Don't buy everything that is cheap, and you won't be greatly cheated.

耐 煩 等 得 羣 魚 到 大 魚 不 來 小 魚 來

Nai fan teng tê ch'ün yü tao ta yü pu lai hsiao yü lai.

> He who has patience to wait for a shoal of fish, will catch small ones if not large.

針 杪 上 削 鐵

Chen miao shang hsiao t'ieh.

> Scraping iron from a needle's point. Note. The opposite of a lucrative employment.

親 兄 弟 明 算 賬

Ch'in hsiung ti ming suan chang.

> Own brothers keep careful accounts.

親 家 不 親 家 蘿 葡 三 百 錢 一 擔

Ch'in chia pu ch'in chia, lo po san pai ch'ien I tan.

> Whether relations or not, my turnips are three hundred cash per picul.

小 生 意 賺 大 錢

Hsiao sheng I chuan ta ch'ien.

Small trades make great profits.

癡 漢 不 把 本 饒 人

Ch'ih han pu pa pen jao jên.

Even a dolt will not sell under cost price to favour anybody.

買 貨 買 得 眞，折 木 折 得 輕

Mai huo mai tê chên chê pen chê tê ch'ing.

When you buy, buy genuine articles; and if you must
lose, lose as little as possible.

賺 錢 不 費 力，費 力 不 賺 錢

Chuan ch'ien pu fei li fei li pu chuan chien.

Those who make money exert themselves little; those
who exert themselves don't make money.

好 客 三 年 不 換 店，好 店 三 年 不 換 客

Hao k'o san nien pu huan tien hao tien san nien pu huan k'o.

A good customer wont change his shop, or a good shop
lose its customer once in three years.

會 做 買 賣 不 爭 衙 稅

Hui tso mai mai pu cheng ya shui.

Those who do good trade don't wrangle over taxes.

關 老 爺 賣 豆 腐 人 強 貨 弱

Kuan lao yeh mai tou fu jên ch'iang huo jo.

Kuan Lao Ye selling bean-curd; the man is strong the
goods are weak. Note. Kuan Ti, the God of War,
is supposed to have been a bean-curd seller, and as
such he is represented on the stage. This proverb is
used in pointing out to a man that though he himself is a good salesman his goods are poor.

會 買 莫 買 怕 人 會 賣 莫 賣 怕 人

Hui mai mo mai p'a jên, hŭi mai mo mai p'a jên.

Able to buy, don't so buy as to frighten the seller; able
to sell, don't so sell as to frighten the buyer. 怕
here is used in its active sense. Some buyers and
sellers are so mean and grasping that they deter men
from doing business.

此處無魚別下鈎

Tz'u ch'ü wu yü pieh hsia kou.

> When there is no fish in one spot cast your hook in another.

未算買先算賣

Wei suan mai hsien suan mai.

> Before you calculate on buying, calculate on selling.

不圖今年竹,也圖來年筍

Pu t'u chin nien chu yeh t'u lai nien sun.

> If you can't reckon on this year's bamboo, you can on next year's bamboo-sprouts.

一串錢打起脚後跟

I ch'uan ch'ien ta ch'i chiao hou ken.

> A string of cash can but reach to the back of one's heel. Note. The meaning is, the sum is a mere trifle, said to any one who is sparing of his cash.

急水好捕魚

Chi shui hao pu yü.

> Swiftly running water is a good place to catch fish. i.e. Have your business on a busy street.

隔口袋買貓

Kê k'ou tai mai mao.

> To buy a cat in a bag.

東山老虎要拖人,西山老虎要拖人

Tung shan lao hu yao t'o jên hsi shan lao hu yao t'o jên.

> The tigers of the eastern hills catch men, so do the tigers of the western hills. i.e. You'll get no fairer price anywhere else.

見利思義

Chien li ssŭ I.

> When gain is in view, think of righteousness.

要價不嫌多,還價不嫌少

Yao chia pu hsien to huan chia pu hsien shao.

> Asking a price don't be afraid to ask a high one : offering a price don't be afraid to offer a low one.

不 見 兎 子 不 撒 鷹

Pu chien t'u tzǔ pu sa ying.

> Don't loose the falcon till you see the hare. i.e. Ask for ready money.

秤 不 離 砣, 客 不 離 貨

Ch'eng pu li t'o k'o pu li huo.

> The steel-yard cannot be separated from the weight, nor the merchant from his goods.

Chapter 2. Capital.

兩 人 一 般 心, 有 錢 堪 買 金,
一 人 一 般 心, 無 錢 堪 買 針

Liang jên I pan hsin yu ch'ien k'an mai chin,
I jên I pan hsin, wu ch'ien k'an mai chên.

> Two men of one mind will make enough money to buy gold ; each man for himself won't secure enough money to buy a needle.

本 大 利 小 還 是 大, 本 小 利 大 還 是 小

Pen ta li hsiao huan shih ta pen hsiao li ta huan shih hsiao.

> Small profits on large capital are after all great ; big profits on small capital are after all only small.

本 大 利 大

Pen ta li ta.

> Great capital great profits.

扠 雞 也 要 兩 顆 米

Ch'a chi yeh yao liang k'o mi.

> You cannot trade without capital. *Lit*. You must have a couple of grains of rice in order to catch fowls.

非 針 不 引 線, 無 水 不 渡 船

Fei chen pu yin hsien wu shoi pu tu ch'uan.

> Same as above. *Lit*. No one can sew without a needle, no one can row a boat without water.

打 濕 指 甲 黏 鹽

Ta shih chih chia nien yen.

> You must wet your finger to take up salt. Note. This is specially applicable to cases of bribery or gifts with a purpose.

肉 爛 了 在 鍋 裏

Jou lan liao tsai kuo li.

> Though boiled too much, the meat is still in the pan. Note. This is applicable to stock in trade or capital in hand.

同 夥 本 如 同 命

T'ung huo pen ju t'ung ming.

> Union of capital is like union of fate.

乾 指 甲 黏 不 起 鹽 來

Kan chih chia t'ien pu ch'i yen lai.

> A dry finger cannot pick up salt. See above.

庄 家 無 牛 客 無 本

Chuang chia wu niu k'o wu pen.

> A merchant without capital is like a farmer without an ox.

檢 到 麥 子 開 磨 坊

Chien tao mai tzŭ k'ai mo fang.

> To get on without capital. *Lit.* To pick up grain and open a mill.

手 上 沒 得 一 根 麻 線，心 裏 想 打 十 二 股 綱

Shou shang mu tê I ken ma hsien, hsin li hsiang ta shih erh ku wang.

> To attempt great trade without capital. *Lit.* With never a single hempen thread in his hand, he intends to make a dozen nets.

Chapter 3. Debts, Credit, Borrowing, etc.

本 小 利 窄，賒 欠 不 得

Pen hsiao li tsê shê ch'ien pu tê.

> With small capital and slender profits, credit cannot be given.

有 錢 將 錢，無 錢 將 言

Yu ch'ien chiang ch'ien wu ch'ien chiang yen.

> If you have money pay your debt, if not, offer apologies and explanations.

還 利 不 爲 欠，還 本 不 爲 騙

Huan li pu wei ch'ien huan pen pu wei p'ien.

> It's not considered debt if you have paid the interest; you can't be accused of fraud if you have paid the principal.

借 傘 勿 用 謝，只 要 晾 過 夜

Chieh san wu yung hsieh chih yao liang kuo yeh.

> You need not thank me for the loan of my umbrella; but please hang it up to dry during the night. i.e. Take care of things borrowed.

是 銅 是 鐵，腰 裏 -- 撇

Shih t'ung shih t'ieh yao li i pieh.

> Whether brass or iron, put it in your girdle. Note. This is advice to take whatever can be got of a debt.

千 賒 不 如 八 百 現

Ch'ien shê pu ju pa pai hsien.

> Eight hundred cash ready money is better than credit for a thousand.

有 錢 當 還 無 利 債，時 來 當 報 有 恩 人

Yu ch'ien tang huan wu li chai, shih lai tang pao yu ên jên.

> Loans without interest must be repaid as soon as possible; benefactors must be rewarded at the first opportunity.

賒 賬 斷 主 顧

Shê chang tuan chu ku.

> Credit cuts off customers.

現 錢 照 顧，賒 者 免 言

Hsien ch'ien chao ku shê chê mien yen.

> We attend to ready money customers; those who want credit needn't trouble to apply.

賖三不如現二

Shê san pu ju hsien erh.

> Better twenty per cent on ready money than thirty per cent on credit.

欠字壓人頭

Ch'ien tzǔ ya jên t'ou.

> Debt oppresses man. *Lit.* The character for "debt" presses on the head of the character for "man."

荒年易得過, 實收難見人

Huang nien i tê kuo shih shou nau chien jên.

> I shall easily get over this year's famine; but in my affluence it will be difficult for you to meet me. Note. This is said by one in financial straits who wishes to borrow money from one who refuses to lend.

世上若要人情好, 賖去貨物不取錢

Shih shang jo yao jên ch'ing hao, shê ch'ü huo wu pu ch'ü ch'ien.

> If one wishes to enjoy the good will of his fellows, let him sell on credit and never collect the money.

寅年支了卯年糧

Yin nien chih liao mao nien liang.

> One year borrows another year's food. Note. 寅卯 are the character representing two years of the Chinese cycle.

躭倒柱頭把磉礅借人

Tan tao chu t'ou pa sang tun chieh jên.

> Exceedingly generous. *Lit.* He will lift the pillars himself and lend the plinths to others.

忍嘴不欠債

Jên tsui pu ch'ien chai.

> He who checks his appetite avoids debt.

丟肉骨頭打狗子

Tiu jou ku t'ou ta kou tzǔ.

> To lend without prospect of payment. *Lit.* To throw a fleshy bone at a dog.

肉 餃 子 打 狗 子，有 去 無 來

Jou chiao tzŭ ta kou tzŭ yu ch'ü wu lai.

> The same. *Lit.* To pelt a dog with a meat dumpling. You lose all and get nothing.

逼 得 像 烏 龜

Pi te hsiang wu kuei.

> Urged to pay, he resembles a tortoise. Note. This indicates the difficulty of collecting debts. The one approached draws in his head and hides himself.

殺 他 無 肉，刮 他 無 皮

Sha t'a wu jou kua t'a wu p'i.

> He cannot pay his debts. *Lit.* If I kill him he has no flesh, if I scrape him he has no skin.

不 怕 奸 只 怕 沒 錢

Pu p'a chien chih p'a mu ch'ien.

> No fear of dishonesty; the only fear is of penury. Note. Payment may be compelled in the one case, not in the other.

放 賬 如 捨 賬，收 賬 如 撿 賬

Fang chang ju she chang shou chang ju chien chang.

> Lending is like throwing away; receiving payment is like finding something.

人 死 債 爛

Jên ssŭ chai lan.

> When the man dies the debt is lost. Note. This is if he leave no responsible persons behind, such as his sons.

父 欠 子 還，子 欠 父 不 知

Fu ch'ien tzŭ huan tzŭ ch'ien fu pu chih.

> A son pays his father's debts, but a father will not recognise a son's.

忍 口 莫 欠 債，無 錢 且 耐 煩

Jên k'ou mo ch'ien chai wu ch'ien ch'ieh nai fan.

> Check your appetite and don't run into debt; though penniless, be patient.

水 流 長 江 歸 大 海，原 物 交 還 舊 主 人

Shui liu ch'ang chiang kuei ta hai yüan wu chiao huan chiu chu jên.

> As the streams pour their waters into the Yangtse and thus return to the sea, so what a man has lent is returned to him again.

借 錢 不 還 反 招 怪

Chieh ch'ien pu huan fan chao kuai.

> Lend to one who won't repay and you provoke his dislike.

只 有 犯 罪 的 獄，那 有 該 債 的 牢

Chih yu fan tsui ti yü na yu kai chai ti lao.

> There are only prisons for criminals; where are there prisons for debtors?

欠 債 不 如 勤 見 面

Ch'ien chai pu ju ch'ing chien mien.

> If you owe a man anything there is nothing like seeing him often. Note. This assures the man of your presence and respectability, he is not afraid of your absconding.

山 上 捉 虎 易，開 口 借 錢 難

Shan shang cho hu i, k'ai k'ou chieh ch'ien nan.

> It is easier to capture a tiger on the mountains than to ask for a loan of money.

拆 東 墻，補 西 壁

Ch'e tung ch'iang pu hsi pi.

> To borrow of one to pay another. *Lit.* To tear down an eastern to repair a western wall.

挑 五 牛 換 六 馬

Ti'ao wu niu huan liu ma.

> To select five oxen and exchange six horses.

羞 恥 易 過，欠 債 難 還

Hsiu ch'ih i kuo ch'ien chai nan huan.

> The feeling of shame soon passes but the debt is difficult to pay.

許 人 一 物, 千 金 不 移

Hsü jên i wu ch'ien chin pu i.

> If you promise a thing don't break your promise even for a thousand pieces of gold.

撑 大 船, 負 大 債

Ch'eng ta ch'uan fu ta chai.

> If you ply a large boat you will have large debts.

欠 債 怨 財 主, 不 孝 怨 父 母

Ch'ien chai yüan ts'ai chu pu hsiao yüan fu mu.

> When you owe money you wrong your creditors ; if you are unfilial you wrong your parents.

欠 債 還 錢, 殺 人 償 命

Ch'ien chai huan ch'ien sha jên shang ming.

> If you owe money you pay money ; if you kill a man you pay with your life.

Chapter 4. Frauds.

家 家 賣 私 酒, 不 犯 是 好 手

Chia chia mai ssǔ chiu pu fan shih hao shou.

> Smuggled wine is sold by many ; the one who is not detected is a clever rogue.

上 當 莫 做 聲

Shang tang mo tso sheng.

> If you get taken in say nothing about it.

將 錢 不 買 輸

Chiang chien pu mai shu.

> With money in your hand don't be taken in.

賣 得 三 分 假, 買 不 得 一 担 眞

Mai tê san fen chia mai pu tê i tan chen.

> You may sell a small quantity of an adulterated article, but you cannot buy a picul of the genuine.

走 了 和 尙，走 不 了 廟

Tsou liao ho shang tsou pu liao miao.

> The priest may run away, the temple cannot. Note.
> Said of men, who trading in their native place,
> where their shops are situated, are not likely to run
> away.

吃 虧 只 這 一 回

Ch'ih k'uei chih chê i hui.

> I shall only be taken in this once.

假 顏 染 就 眞 紅 色，也 被 旁 人 說 是 非

Chia yen jan chiu chen hung sê yeh pei p'ang jên shuo shih fei.

> If you try to dye genuine red with spurious colouring,
> you must bear the unfavourable criticisms of by-
> standers.

站 得 樹 下 等 風

Chan tê shu hsia têng fêng.

> To stand under a tree waiting for the wind. Note.
> This is applicable to those who await opportunities
> of defrauding others.

碼 頭 未 找 到 就 挑 籮

Ma t'ou wei chao tao chiu t'iao lo.

> Ignorant of the jetties and pretending to be a porter.

借 屋 漏 騙 佃 錢

Chieh wu lou p'ien tien ch'ien.

> To pretend that the house leaks in order to defraud the
> landlord of his rent.

吃 虧 是 佔 便 宜

Ch'ih k'uei shih chan pien i.

> If you get a thing too cheaply you'll be taken in.

跟 到 龍 船 喊 號 子

Ken tao lung ch'uan han hao tzŭ.

> To follow the Dragon Boat shouting its cry. Note.
> This is said of anyone who makes a mere pretence
> of working. The Dragon Boat Festival occurs on
> the 5th day of the 5th month.

少 一 個 錢 短 一 歲 壽
Shao i ko ch'ien tuan i sui shou.

> If I have cheated you out of one cash, may I die a year before my time.

偷 得 利 而 後 有 害
T'ou tê li erh hou yu hai.

> Gain dishonestly acquired will injure a man.

現 放 着 鴨 子 不 拿, 要 拿 鵝
Hsien fang cho ya tzŭ pu na yao na ê.

> Allowing the duck to escape in order to get the goose, i.e., passing over a legitimate profit in order to get a larger amount.

Chapter 5. Pawning and Suretyship.

做 中 做 保, 就 代 不 小
Tso chung tso pao tan tai pu hsiao.

> Those who act as middlemen or sureties accept grave responsibilities.

官 不 保 人, 私 不 保 債
Kuan pu pao jên ssŭ pu pao chai.

> Don't act as surety in public for any man, or privately for any debts.   Comp. Prov. 11-15.

招 弓 如 招 箭
Chao kung ju chao chien.

> To hand over the bow is to hand over the arrow, i.e., you are responsible for any injury.

當 當 抵 當 當 還 在
Tang tang ti tang tang huan tsai.

> Redeem one pledge with another, still that other is in pawn.

當 當 取 當 當 抵 當
Tang tang ch'ü tang tang ti tang.

> To do nothing else but pawn. *Lit.* To pawn, and take out of pawn, and pawn again.

軍 犯 開 小 押，財 主 開 典 當

Chün fan k'ai hsiao ya ts'ai chu k'ai tien tang.

> Military offenders open small pawnshops; wealthy men
> open large ones.

斧 打 鑿，鑿 入 木

Fu ta tso tso ju mu.

> The axe strikes the chisel, and the chisel enters the
> wood. Note. The axe represents the creditor, the
> chisel the surety, and the wood the debtor.

只 有 添 錢 的 中 人，那 有 貼 錢 的 中 人

Chih yu t'ien ch'ien ti chung jen, na yu t'ieh ch'ien ti chung jen.

> All middle-men prompt you to increase your offer; where
> is the middle-man who will assist you with money.

薦 主 面 子 大

Chien chu mien tzŭ ta.

> He who can recommend another has great respectability.

當 人 不 當 物

Tang jên pu tang wu.

> "A man is better than a pledge."

中 人 不 挑 担，保 人 不 還 錢

Chung jên pu t'iao tan pao jen pu huan ch'ien.

> "Middle-men bear no responsibilities; sureties pay no
> debts."

話 落 中 人 口

Hua lo chung jên k'ou.

> The middle-man settles the bargain. *Lit*. The words
> drop from the middle-man's mouth.

硬 肩 的 保

Ying chien ti pao.

> A firm-shouldered surety.

保 得 將 軍 進，保 得 將 軍 出

Pao tê chiang chün chin pao tê chiang chün ch'u.

> Similar to above. *Lit*. To guarantee the general's
> entering into the battle, and also his coming out
> safely.

賣基賣窠,請中說合

Mai chi mai ch'ao ch'ing chung shuo ho.

Selling land, sell the house on it, and invite a middle-
man to settle your bargain.

Chapter 6. Trades, Professions, etc.

自己無能,反推物鈍

Tzŭ chi wu neng fan t'ui wu tun.

Bad workmen b'ame blunt tools.

打鑼賣餹,各有一行

Ta lo mai t'ang ko yu i hang.

Beat your gong and sell your candies; every man to his
trade.

秀才談書,屠戶談豬

Hsiu tsai t'an shu t'u hu t'an chu.

A bachelor of arts discusses books; a pork-butcher, pigs.

工字不出頭,只能養一口

Kung tzŭ pu ch'u t'ou chih neng yang i k'ou.

One like the character ''kung'' which cannot raise its
head, can only feed one mouth. Note. The
character ''kung'' has nothing above its horizontal
stroke, it cannot raise its head, any more than a
workman can aspire to a high position.

逢年遇節,百工都歇

Fêng nien yü chieh pai kung tu hsieh.

At the New Year and on feast days, work of all kinds
is given up.

世間只有三般醜,忘八戲子吹鼓手

Shih chien chih yu san pan ch'ou, wang pa hsi tzŭ ch'ui ku shou.

There are but three kinds of villains in the world,—the
keeper of a bad house, an actor, and a low musician.
Note. 忘八. *Lit.* Forgetter of the eight virtues
which are 孝弟忠信禮義廉恥 Filial Piety,
Brotherliness, Fidelity, Sincerity, Propriety, Righteousness, Honesty and Sense of Shame.

挑籮抬轎歇下就要

T'iao lo t'ai chiao hsieh hsia chiu yao.

When coolies and chair-bearers put down their burdens,
they immediately want payment.

鄉裏人收了穀，不打官事就做屋

Hsiang li jên shou liao ku, pu ta kuan shih chiu tso wu.

Country gentlemen who have stored their grain, either
go to law or begin to build.

爲人莫學吹鼓手，坐在階簷喝冷酒

Wei jên mo hsüeh ch'ui ku shou tso tsai chieh yen ho leng chiu.

Don't learn to play the fife or drum, and have to sit
under the eaves and drink cold wine.

敎學不離書，窮人不離豬

Chiao hsüeh pu li shu ch'iung jen pu li chu.

The teacher must stick to his books, and the poor man
to his pig.

百藝無如一藝精

Pai i wu ju i i ching.

Better be master of one than Jack of all trades.

隔行如隔山

Kê hang ju kê shan.

To be of separate trades is like being separated by
mountains. Note. The idea conveyed is that the
barrier between two different kinds of trade or profession is as difficult to cross as a range of mountains.

河水不犯井水

Ho shui pu fan ching shui.

Similar to above. *Lit.* The river does not cause the
well to overflow.

當行厭當行

Tang hang yen tang hang.

Two of a trade dislike each other.

同道者相愛，同藝者相娸

T'ung tao chê hsiang ai t'ung i chê hsiang chi.

There is mutual love between men of the same creed;
mutual jealousy between men of the same trade.

幫 人 一 日 爲 奴，肩 挑 四 兩 爲 客

Pang jên i jih wei nu chien t'iao ssŭ liang wei k'o.

> Serve but a day and you are a slave; deal in ever so small a way and you are a merchant. Note. Deal, etc. *Lit.* Carry four ounces of silver on the shoulder; alluding to the old custom of carrying strings of cash over the shoulder.

打 魚 的 不 離 船 邊

Ta yü ti pu li ch'uan pien.

> The fisherman must not leave his boat side.

船 多 不 碍 港，車 多 不 碍 路

Ch'uan to pu ai chiang ch'ê to pu ai lu.

> There is room for all sorts of traders. *Lit.* Many boats do not obstruct a channel; many vehicles do not block up the road.

和 尙 歸 寺，客 歸 店

Ho shang kuei ssŭ k'o kuei tien.

> Every one to his calling. *Lit.* The priest reverts to his monastery, and the merchant to his shop.

殺 豬 剝 狗，無 有 下 稍

Sha chu po kou wu yu hsiao shao.

> Pork-butchers and dog-slayers will come to no good end. Note. In this saying vegetarians predict the punishment of those who eat flesh. Note. 下 稍 equals 結 局 a conclusion, result.

買 賣 如 修 行

Mai mai ju hsiu hsing.

> To carry on trade is like being a priest. Note. Priests are "virtue cultivators," and trading is a school for the practise of virtue.

與 肩 挑 貿 易 無 佔 便 宜

Yü chien t'iao mao i wu chan pien i.

> Trading with petty hucksters, don't banter too much.

賣 布 的 不 怕 扁 担 量

Mai pu ti pa p'a pien tan liang.

> A cloth huckster doesn't fear your measure, though it is as long as a carrying pole. Note. You can't outdo him. If he uses your measure, he will charge a higher price.

開 飯 店 的 不 怕 你 的 肚 子 大

K'ai fan tien ti pu p'a ni ti tu tzǔ ta.

> An eating-house keeper doesn't care how big your appetite is.

三 生 趕 不 到 一 熟

San sheng kan pu tao i shu.

> Three raw hands are not equal to one good hand.

管 山 的 燒 柴，管 河 的 吃 水

Kuan shan ti shao ch'ai kuan ho ti ch'ih shui.

> Who keeps the hills, burns the wood; who keeps the stream, drinks the water.

田 家 自 有 樂

T'ien chia tzǔ yu lo.

> Farmers naturally realize enjoyment.

行 行 出 狀 元

Hang hang ch'u chuang yüan.

> There is a senior wrangler in every calling.

藝 多 不 養 家

I to pu yang chia.

> A man of many trades cannot support a family.

銀 匠 不 偷 銀，餓 死 一 家 人

Yin chiang pu t'ou yin o ssǔ i chia jên.

裁 縫 不 偷 布，婦 人 莫 得 褲

Ts'ai fêng pu t'ou pu fu jen mo tê k'u.

> If the silversmith doesn't purloin the silver, his family will starve to death; if the tailor doesn't purloin the cloth, his wife won't have any garments to wear.

船 中 老 鼠 艙 內 覓 食

Ch'uan chung lao shu ts'ang nei mi shih.

> Living on one's own business. *Lit.* The boat rats seek their food in the boat's compartments.

本 山 牛 只 食 本 山 草

Pen shan niu chih shih pen shan ts'ao.

> The ox of its native hills eats the grass on the hills.

SECTION VII. WEALTH AND POVERTY.

Chapter 1. Riches.

大 富 由 命，小 富 由 勤

Ta fu yu ming hsiao fu yu ch'in.

> Great possessions depend on fate ; small possessions come from diligence.

柴 米 油 鹽 醬 醋 茶，七 字 安 排 好 人 家

Ch'ai mi yu yen chiang ts'u ch'a ch'i tzǔ an p'ai hao jên chia.

> The house of a well-to-do man is indicated by the presence of the following,—fuel, rice, oil, salt, sauce, vinegar and tea.

老 鼠 拖 葫 蘆，大 頭 在 後 頭

Lao hu t'o hu lu ta t'ou tsai hou t'ou.

> When a rat runs off with a calabash, the thick end is always behind. Note. This proverb is applicable in the case of gradual acquisition of wealth.

貪 財 不 得 財，不 貪 財 自 來

T'an ts'ai pu tê tsai pu t'an ts'ai tzǔ lai.

> If you covet wealth you won't get it ; if you don't covet, it will come of itself.

弟 兄 雖 親，財 帛 分 明

Ti hsiung sui ch'in ts'ai pai fen ming.

> Though brothers are so closely related, they disseminate between their possessions.

先 苦 後 甜，富 貴 萬 年

Hsien k'u hou t'ien, fu kuei wan nien.

> The bitter comes first, then the sweet ; riches and honour for a myriad years.

求 財 點 卦，分 毫 不 差

Ch'iu ts'ai tien kua, fen hao pu ch'a.

> If you want to be wealthy consult a fortune-teller, and he will direct you without a mistake.

馬 上 銅 鈴 響，親 戚 都 來 往，
馬 上 銅 鈴 破，親 戚 無 半 個

Ma shang t'ung ling hsiang, ch'in ch'i tu lai wang, ma shang t'ung
ling p'o, ch'in ch'i wu pan ko.

> When the bells on one's horses sound, all one's relations
> soon gather; when the bells are broken, not even half
> a man is to be seen.   Note.   The possession of
> horses indicates wealth.

瞎 子 見 錢 眼 也 開，和 尚 見 錢 經 也 賣

Hsia tzŭ chien ch'ien yen yeh k'ai, ho shang chien ch'ien ching yeh
mai.

> Money will make a blind man to see ; will make a priest
> sell his breviary.

火 到 豬 頭 爛，錢 到 公 事 辦

Huo tao chu t'ou lan, ch'ien tao kung shih pan.

> When there is enough fire the pig's head is well boiled ;
> when there is enough money, you can get business
> done, i.e. at the Yamen or Government Office.

前 人 田 地 後 人 收，還 有 收 人 在 後 頭

Ch'ien jên t'ien ti hou jên shou, huan yu shou jen tsai hou t'ou.

> The estates of those who have gone before are inherited
> by their descendants ; but there are still others to
> come who will in their turn inherit them.

財 是 英 雄 酒 是 胆

Ts'ai shih ying hsiung chiu shih tan,

> Wealth serves for heroism ; wine for bravery.

財 多 累 己，食 飽 傷 心

Ts'ai to lei chi, shih pao shang hsin.

> Great wealth troubles its owner ; as too much food causes
> discomfort to the eater.

富 貴 沿 門 走，紗 帽 滿 天 飛

Fu kuei yen men tsou, sha mao man t'ien fei.

> Riches and honour pass near to each door; official positions
> are within reach of all.   Note.   The idea is that
> these things are of uncertain character, and are easily
> lost by one person and gained by another.   Official
> positions. *Lit.* The air full of flying gauze hats.
> These latter, worn in the Ming Dynasty signify office.

銀 錢 會 說 話，衣 服 會 打 恭

Yin ch'ien hui shuo hua, i fu hui ta kung.

> If you have money you are able to speak ; if you have clothing you can be polite.

刻 薄 成 家，理 無 久 享

K'o po ch'eng chia, li wu chiu hsiang.

> Those who make a fortune by being miserly, will not enjoy it long.

勸 人 不 必 苦 貪 財，貪 得 財 來 天 降 災

Ch'üan jên pu pi k'u t'an ts'ai, t'an tê ts'ai lai t'ien chiang tsai.

> Warn men against covetousness, for wealth thus coveted provokes the wrath of Heaven.

貴 自 勤 中 得，富 自 儉 裡 來

Kuei tzŭ ch'in chung tê, fu tzŭ chien li lai.

> Honour springs from diligence ; and riches from economy.

富 貴 有 根，聰 明 有 種

Fu kuei yu ken, ts'ung ming yu chung.

> Wealth and honour have their root, and cleverness its seed.

家 有 黃 金，外 有 戥 秤

Chia yu huang chin, wai yu têng ch'eng.

> When any family has gold, outsiders have money scales.

那 個 貓 兒 不 吃 老 鼠

Na ko mao êrh pu ch'ih lao shu.

> Who does not desire riches? *Lit*. What cat will not worry rats.

富 貴 不 過 沈 萬 山

Fu kuei pu kuo Shen Wan Shan.

> It is impossible to be richer than Shen Wan Shan. Note. This individual was a Chinese Croesus of Nanking, whose riches served towards the establishment of the Ming Dynasty.

沈 萬 山 打 死 人

Shen Wan Shan ta ssŭ jên.

> Shen Wan Shan killing a man. Note. This would be considered a small matter, seeing he had plenty of money to satisfy the relatives.

黃金無種，獨生勤儉人家

Huang chin wu chung, tu sheng ch'in chien jên chia.

    Gold is not grown from seed, but only springs up in diligent and economical families.

錢財如糞土，仁義值千金

Ch'ien ts'ai ju fen t'u, jen i chih ch'ien chin.

    Wealth is but dung; Benevolence and Righteousness are worth thousands of gold.

欲求生富貴，須下死工夫

Yü ch'iu sheng fu kuei, hsü hsia ssŭ kung fu.

    If you long for wealth and honour, you must work yourself to death for it.

磨刀恨不利，刀利傷人指，
求財恨不多，財多害人己

Mo tao hen pu li, tao li shang jên chih, ch'iu ts'ai hen pu to, ts'ai to hai jên chi.

    Men grind a knife because they dislike it blunt, but when they have sharpened it, it cuts their fingers; men seek wealth because they dislike poverty, but when they get much of it, it inflicts personal injury.

人無混財不富，馬無夜草不肥

Jên wu hun ts'ai pu fu, ma wu yeh ts'ao pu fei.

    A man doesn't get rich without ill-gotten gain; a horse doesn't get fat without feeding in the night.

不求金玉重重貴，但願兒孫個個賢

Pu ch'iu chin yü chung chung kuei, tan yüan erh sun ko ko hsien.

    Do not seek for gold, jade, and suchlike valuables; rather desire that each of your descendants be virtuous.

人為財死，鳥為食亡

Jên wei ts'ai ssŭ, niao wei shih wang.

    Men will die for wealth as birds for food.

良田萬頃日食一升，大廈千間夜眠八尺

Liang t'ien wan ch'ing jih shih i sheng, ta hsia ch'ien chien yeh mien pa ch'ih.

    Though your fields yield many bushels of rice, you can eat but a pint per day; though your house be never so large, you sleep on but eight feet by night.

廣 錢 通 神

Kuang ch'ien t'ung shen.

> Much money moves the gods, i.e. enables a man to do anything.

有 錢 蓋 百 醜

Yu ch'ien kai pai ch'ou.

> Money hides many deformities.

不 但 色 迷 人, 財 也 能 迷 人

Pu tan sê mi jên, ts'ai yeh neng mi jên.

> Wealth leads men astray as well as beauty.

會 使 不 在 家 豪 富, 風 流 不 用 着 衣 多

Hui shih pu tsai chia hao fu, fêng liu pu yung cho i to.

> Ability to command does not lie in being well off; elegance and grace do not depend on multitudes of dresses.

賺 錢 猶 如 針 挑 土, 用 錢 猶 如 水 冲 沙

Chuan ch'ien yu ju chen t'iao t'u, yung ch'ien yu ju shui ch'ung sha.

> Making money is like digging with a needle; spending it is like water soaking into sand.

聰 明 保 一 人, 富 貴 保 一 家

Ts'ung ming pao i jên, fu kuei pao i chia.

> Wit protects one man; wealth and honour protect a whole family.

珠 玉 非 寶 五 穀 爲 寶

Chu yü fei pao wu ku wei pao.

> The really precious things are not pearls and jade, but the Five Grains. i.e. Hemp, Millet, Rice, Wheat, Pulse.

和 氣 生 財

Ho ch'i sheng ts'ai.

> Amiability begets riches.

人 拗 損 財, 牛 拗 損 力

Jên yao sun ts'ai, niu yao sun li.

> Obstinate men waste wealth as obstinate oxen strength.

有 道 之 錢 方 可 取，無 道 之 財 莫 強 求

Yu tao chih ch'ien fang k'o ch'ü wu tao chih ts'ai mo ch'iang ch'iu.

> If riches can be acquired with propriety, then acquire them ; but let not unjust wealth be sought for with violence.

生 財 有 道

Sheng ts'ai yu tao.

> There is a proper method of gaining wealth.

無 故 而 得 千 金，不 有 大 福 必 有 大 禍

Wu ku erh tê ch'ien chin, pu yu ta fu pi yu ta huo.

> He who gets a large sum by chance, will either be made very happy, or very miserable by it.

無 義 錢 財 湯 潑 雪，儻 來 田 地 水 推 沙

Wu i ch'ien ts'ai t'ang p'o hsüeh, t'ang lai t'ien ti shui t'ui sha.

> Unjustly-gotten wealth is but snow sprinkled with hot water ; lands improperly obtained are but sand in a stream.

賢 人 多 財 則 損 其 智，愚 人 多 財 則 益 其 過

I sien jên to ts'ai tsê sun ch'i chih, yü jên to ts'ai tsê i ch'i kuo.

> When a virtuous man has much wealth, it diminishes his knowledge ; when a worthless man has much wealth, it increases his faults.

無 義 錢 財 休 着 想，不 干 己 事 莫 當 頭

Wu i ch'ien ts'ai hsiu cho hsiang, pu kan chi shih mo tang t'ou.

> Never desire unjustly-gotten wealth, nor undertake affairs that are not your business.

冤 枉 財 來 冤 枉 去

Yüan wang ts'ai lai yüan wang ch'ü.

> Wealth got by wrong-doing will go by wrong-doing.

張 門 田 李 門 屋，今 日 錢 家 明 日 陸

Chang men t'ien Li men wu, chin jih ch'ien chia ming jih lu.

> The fields of the Chang's, and the houses of the Li's, to day belong to the Chi'en's, and to-morrow will belong to the Lu's.

一 家 飽 煖 千 家 怨，半 世 功 名 百 世 冤

I chia pao nuan ch'ien chia yüan, pan shih kung ming pai shih yüan.

One family with plenty to eat and wear is the envy of a thousand other families, half a life-time's fame provokes the resentment of a hundred generations.

勿 貪 意 外 之 財

Wu t'an i wai chih ts'ai.

Do not covet wealth on which you have no claim.

白 手 成 家

Pai shou ch'eng chia.

To grow rich by one's own sole endeavours.

能 知 三 日 事，富 貴 幾 千 年

Neng chih san jih shih, fu kuei chi ch'ien nien.

Whoever can foresee the affairs of three days, will be rich for several thousand years.

易 得 來 易 得 去

I tê lai i tê ch'ü.

It comes easily and goes easily. i.e. Wealth.

掙 得 未 來 錢，發 蹟 在 眼 前

Tseng tê wei lai ch'ien, fa chi tsai yen ch'ien.

Thinking of money not yet obtained is as though it were before your eyes.

有 錢 佈 施 不 落 空

Yu ch'ien pu shih pu lo k'ung.

If you do good with your money it won't be used in vain.

銀 錢 二 字 雖 是 養 命 之 源，亦 是 害 人 之 物

Yin ch'ien erh tzǔ sui shih yang ming chih yüan, i shih hai jên chih wu.

The characters for gold and silver indicate the source of life's sustenance; also things harmful to man.

富 貴 人 間 夢，功 名 水 上 鷗

Fu kuei jên chien meng, kung ming shui shang ou.

Riches and honour are but the dreams of men; rank and degree are but gulls on the water.

金 用 火 試，人 用 財 試

Chin yung huo shih, jên yung ts'ai shih.

> Gold is tried by fire ; man is tested by wealth.

黃 金 何 足 貴，安 樂 值 錢 多

Huang chin ho tsu kuei, an lo chih ch'ieh to.

> Gold is worth nothing much ; peace and happiness are priceless.

金 也 空 銀 也 空，死 後 何 曾 在 手 中

Chin yeh k'ung yin yeh k'ung, ssǔ hou ho ts'eng tsai shou chung.

> Gold and silver are but vain things ; after death how can they remain in your hands.

橫 財 不 久 享

Heng ts'ai pu chiu hsiang.

> Unjust gain is not long enjoyed.

千 年 田 地 八 百 主

Ch'ien nien t'ien ti pa pai chu.

> Estates during a thousand years have eight hundred owners.

Chapter 2. Riches and Poverty.

有 錢 男 兒 漢 無 錢 漢 兒 難

Yu ch'ien nan êrh han wu ch'ien han êrh nan.

> With money, you are a brave son of Han ; without it, it is difficult to be even a son of Han.

喫 麵 檢 到 金 箍 子，洗 澡 又 掉 了，湯 裏 來 水 裏 去

Ch'ih mien chien tao chin ku tzǔ, hsi tsao yu tiao liao, t'ang li lai shui li ch'ü.

> Transient wealth. *Lit.* To find a gold ring whilst eating vermicelli and to lose it whilst bathing ; it comes in the soup and goes in the water.

富 從 升 合 起，貧 因 不 算 來

Fu ts'ung sheng ko ch'i, p'in yin pu suan lai.

> Riches spring from small beginnings ; poverty is the result of non-calculation. Note. 升合 means small amounts such as pints, gills, etc.

禮 義 生 於 富 足，盜 賊 出 於 貧 窮

Li i shen yü fu tsu, tao tsê chu yü p'in ch'iung.

Politeness and Righteousness are the children of Wealth
and Contentment ; Brigandage and Robbery are the
offspring of Poverty.

有 錢 使 得 鬼 動，無 錢 喚 不 人 來

Yu ch'ien shih tê kuei tung, wu ch'ien huan pu tê jên lai.

With money one may command devils ; without it, one
cannot even summon a man.

富 貴 皆 因 勤 儉 起，貧 窮 都 爲 手 頭 鬆

Fu kuei chieh yin ch'in chien ch'i, p'in ch'iung tu wei shou t'ou
sung.

Riches and honour are entirely the result of diligence and
economy ; poverty is altogether occasioned by a
slack hand.

勤 儉 富 貴 之 本，懶 惰 貧 賤 之 苗

Ch'in chien fu kuei chih pen, lan to p'in chien chih miao.

Diligence and economy are the root of wealth and
honour ; idleness is the off shoot of poverty and
disgrace.

耐 得 貧 守 得 富

Nai tê p'in shou tê fu.

He who can endure in poverty ; will keep his position
when wealthy. ?

玩 得 化 水 無 形

Wan tê hua shui wu hsing.

A gay life melts away a fortune.

家 貧 如 水 洗，家 寬 出 少 年

Chia p'in ju shui liu, chia k'uan ch'u shao nien.

A poor family is like a washed garment (i.e. nothing but
itself) a prosperous family has a youthful appearance.

富 貴 深 山 有 遠 親，貧 窮 骨 肉 是 閒 人

Fu kuei shen shan yu yüan ch'in, p'in ch'iung ku jou shih hsien
jên.

To the wealthy, men away in the mountains are relatives;
to the poor, their nearest of kin are strangers.

有 錢 無 子 非 爲 富：有 子 無 錢 不 算 貧

Yu ch'ien wu tzŭ fei wei fu, yu tzŭ wu ch'ien pu suan p'in.

> He who has riches and no sons is not really rich; he who has sons but not money cannot be considered poor.

富 嫌 千 口 少，貧 恨 一 身 多

Fu hsien ch'ien k'ou shao, p'in hen i shen to.

> The rich man considers a thousand people in his family as too few; the poor man regards one person as too many.

發 財 受 窮 總 由 天

Fa ts'ai shou ch'iung tsung yu t'ien,

> Riches and poverty are ordained by Heaven.

Chapter 3. Rich Men.

洗 臉 打 濕 手，吃 飯 打 濕 口

Hsi lien ta shih shou, ch'ih fan ta shih k'ou.

> He wets his hands when washing his face, and his mouth, when eating. Note. All that a rich man does or needs to do.

有 錢 有 酒 必 有 朋 友

Yu ch'ien yu chiu pi yu p'eng yu.

> He who has wealth and wine will always have friends.

大 船 破 了，還 有 三 担 釘

Ta ch'uan p'o liao, huan yu san tan ting.

> When a big ship comes to pieces, there still remain three piculs of nails.

有 錢 長 人 三 十 歲

Yu ch'ien chang jên san shih sui.

> To have money is to add on thirty years' dignity.

英 雄 行 險 道，富 貴 是 花 枝

Ying hsiung hsing hsien tao, fu kuei shih hua chih.

> Heroes walk a dangerous path; the rich are like flowering branches.

有錢到處是揚州

Yu ch'ien tao ch'ü shih Yang Chou.

> If a man has money, every place is Yang-chou to him.

眞財主不穿衣

Chen ts'ai chu pu ch'uan i.

> A really rich man is careless of his dress.

有錢難買不賣貨

Yu ch'ien nan mai pu mai huo.

> Money cannot buy things that are not for sale.

紗帽底下無窮人

Sha mao ti hsia wu ch'iung jên.

> There are no poor men under gauze hats. Note. The gauze hat was the official hat worn under the Ming Dynasty.

手下無人身不貴

Shou hsia wu jên shen pu kuei.

> To be without servants is to be without honour.

家有萬貫不可輕師慢匠

Chia yu wan kuan pu k'o ch'ing shih man chiang.

> However rich you may be, never slight a scholar nor be rude to an artizan.

樹大招風

Shu ta chao fêng.

> A great tree attracts the wind. Note. A rich man is likely to tempt the cupidity of others.

大樹好遮陰

Ta shu hao chê yin.

> Patronage. *Lit.* A great tree affords a pleasant shade.

Chapter 4. Rich and Poor Men.

富貴壓不倒鄉黨，山高遮不住太陽

Fu kuei ya pu tao hsiang tang, shan kao chê pu chu t'ai yang.

> The wealthy cannot supress the village clans, any more than the mountains can hide the sun.

富 人 思 來 年, 窮 人 思 眼 前

Fu jên ssǔ lai nien.ch'iung jên ssǔ yen ch'ien.

> A rich man thinks of the future, a poor man thinks of
> the present.

貧 不 怨 來 富 不 誇, 那 有 久 富 長 貧 家

P'in pu yüan lai fu pu k'ua, na yu chiu fu ch'ang p'in chia.

> If poor, do not murmur, and if rich do not boast ; for
> neither wealth nor poverty are abiding.

人 敬 有 的 狗 咬 醜 的

Jên ching yu ti kou yao ch'ou ti.

> Men honour the well.to-do ; dogs bite the ill-dressed.

有 錢 一 條 龍, 無 錢 一 條 蟲

Yu ch'ien i t'iao lung, wu ch'ien i t'iao ch'ung.

> Having money you are a dragon ; without it, you are
> merely a worm.

有 銀 着 銀 累, 無 銀 得 覺 睡

Yu yin cho yin lei, wu yin tê chiao shui.

> He who has wealth has many cares ; he who has none
> can sleep soundly.

富 人 讀 書, 窮 漢 餵 豬

Fu jên tu shu, ch'iung han wei chu.

> Rich men read books ; poor men rear pigs.

蒿 草 之 下 或 有 蘭 香, 茅 茨 之 屋 或 有 公 王

Hao ts'ao chih hsia huo yu lan hsiang, mao tzǔ chih wu huo yu
kung wang.

> The jungle may hide the fragrant orchid, and a thatched
> roof may cover a future monarch.

窮 沾 富 恩, 富 沾 天 恩

Ch'iung chan fu ên, fu chan t'ien ên.

> The poor enjoy the favour of the rich ; the rich, the
> favour of heaven.

窮 的 伴 富 的, 伴 的 沒 褲 子

Ch'iung ti pan fu ti, pan ti mu k'u tzǔ.

> If the poor man associates with the rich, the poor man
> will soon have no trousers to wear. i.e. He will
> spend beyond his means.

窮 莫 失 志, 富 莫 顚 狂

Ch'iung mo shih chih fu mo tien k'uang.

> If poor, don't lose your self-reliance ; if rich, don't act the fool.

貧 不 可 欺, 富 不 可 恃

P'in pu k'o ch'i, fu pu k'o shih.

> If poor, don't cheat ; if rich, don't presume.

富 貴 多 士, 貧 賤 寡 交

Fu kuei to shih, p'in chien kua chiao.

> The rich have many well-to-do friends ; the poor have few associates.

飽 人 不 知 餓 人 饑, 富 人 不 知 窮 寒 苦

Pao jên pu chih ô jên chi, fu jên pu chih ch'iung han k'u.

> The well-fed know nothing of the hunger of the starving; the wealthy know nothing of the hardships of the poor.

貧 則 易 諂, 富 而 多 驕

P'in tsê i ch'an, fu êrh to chiao.

> It is easy for the poor to turn flatterers, for the rich to become proud.

貧 居 鬧 市 無 人 問, 富 在 深 山 有 遠 親

P'in chu nao shih wu jên wen, fu tsai shen shan yu yüan ch'in.

> No one calls on the poor man though he dwell in the busy market place, but distant relations visit the rich man in his retired mountain home.

只 有 巴 巴 粘 飯, 沒 有 飯 粘 巴 巴

Chih yu pa pa chan fan, mu yu fan chan pa pa.

> The poor cling to the rich, not the rich to the poor. *Lit.* It is the crust which sticks to the rice, not the rice that sticks to the crust.

有 錢 道 眞 語, 無 錢 語 不 眞
不 信 但 看 筵 中 酒, 杯 杯 先 勸 有 錢 人

Yu ch'ien tao chên yü, wu ch'ien yü pu chên, pu hsin tan k'an yen chung chiu, pei pei hsien ch'üan yu ch'ien jên.

> If you have money your words are taken for truth; if not, they are taken for lies. If you doubt it you have only to see the wine at a feast ; cup after cup is first pressed on the rich.

貧 窮 自 在·富 貴 多 憂
P'in ch'iung tau tsai, fu kuei to yu.

The poor have peace ; the rich many troubles.

富 貴 定 要 依 本 分，貧 窮 不 必 枉 思 量
Fu kuei ting yao i pen fen, p'in ch'iung pu pi wang ssŭ liang.

The rich must adhere to duty; the poor should not
indulge vain thoughts.

富 貴 肉 食，貧 賤 藿 食
Fu kuei jou shih, p'in chien huo shih.

The rich eat flesh; the poor eat herbs.

有 錢 高 三 輩，無 錢 低 三 輩
Yu ch'ien kao san pei, wu ch'ien ti san pei.

A man's wealth exalts him three degrees; a man's
poverty degrades him three degrees.

貧 寒 休 要 怨，富 貴 不 須 驕
P'in han hsiu yao yüan, fu kuei pu hsü chiao.

The poor man must not murmur, and the rich man must
not boast.

飽 煖 思 淫 慾，饑 寒 起 盜 心
Pao nuan ssŭ yin yü, chi han ch'i tao hsin.

Food and warmth induce lustful thoughts; hunger and
cold encourage thoughts of stealing.

有 錢 堪 出 衆，無 衣 懶 出 門
Yu ch'ien k'an ch'u chung, wu i lan ch'u men.

The wealthy feel worthy to appear in public; the
ill-dressed don't care to go out of doors.

天 子 脚 下 有 貧 親
T'ien tzŭ chiao hsia yu p'in ch'in.

Even the Emperor has poor relations.

皇 帝 亦 有 草 鞋 親
Huang ti i yu ts'ao hsieh ch'in.

Even the Emperor has straw-sandalled relations.

貧窮則父母不子,富貴則親戚畏懼

P'in ch'iung tsê fu mu pu tzŭ, fu kuei tsê ch'in ch'i wei chü.

When one is poor, his parents disown him but when rich, relations revere him. Note. One of the sayings of 蘇秦 Su Tsi'n, a statesman who flourished in the second century B.C. Being at first unsuccessful in his ventures, he was ill-received by his family, but eventually having become famous, was enthusiastically welcomed to his home.

窮人的氣大,富人的眼大

Ch'iung jên ti ch'i ta, fu jên ti yen ta.

The poor man's rage, and the rich man's eyes, are both great. Note. The rich man is haughty and supercilious.

有錢難買親生子,無錢可討有錢妻

Yu ch'ien nan mai ch'in sheng tzŭ, wu ch'ien k'o t'ao yu ch'ien ch'i.

Though you have money you cannot buy a son of your own; though you have none you may get a wealthy wife.

富人捨錢,窮人捨力

Fu jên shê ch'ien. ch'iung jên shê li.

The rich man expends money, the poor man strength.

貧莫與富鬪,富莫與官鬪

P'in mo yü fu tou, fu mo yü kuan tou.

The poor must not quarrel with the rich, nor the rich with the magistrates.

小富靠勤,大富靠天

Hsiao fu k'ao ch'in, ta fu k'ao t'ien.

The well-to-do man trusts to his diligence ; the millionaire to Heaven.

寧可清貧,勿可濁富

Ning k'o ch'ing p'in, wu k'o cho fu.

Rather be honestly poor than wickedly rich.

富有萬金,窮無寸鐵

Fu yu wan chin, ch'iung wu ts'un t'ieh.

The rich have thousands of gold, the poor not an inch of iron.

一 更 窮, 二 更 富

I keng ch'iung, êrh keng fu.

> Sudden fortune. *Lit.* The first watch poor, the second watch rich.

Chapter 5. Poverty.

窮 乃 士 人 之 常

Ch'iung nai shih jên chih ch'ang.

> Poverty is the common lot of scholars.

好 吃 懶 做, 衣 食 不 彀

Hao ch'ih lan tso, i shih pu kou.

> He who is fond of eating and not inclined to work, will soon be short of food and clothing.

衣 破 眞 是 苦, 笑 破 不 笑 補

I p'o chên shih k'u, hsiao p'o pu hsiao pu.

> He whose clothes are in rags is certainly poor; you may laugh at ragged clothes but not at patched ones.

熬 苦 受 難, 無 錢 措 辦

Ao k'u shou nan, wu ch'ien ts'o pan.

> In great distress and poverty with no money to use.

小 名 叫 喜, 腰 裏 沒 得 一 個 銅 皮

Hsiao ming chiao hsi, yao li mu tê i ko t'ung p'i.

> My little name is Joy, though I haven't a single copper in my girdle.

一 餐 無 飯, 妻 離 子 散

I ts'an wu fan, ch'i li tzŭ san.

> One mealtime without food is enough to break up a household. *Lit.* The wife leaves and the children scatter.

越 奸 越 狡 越 貧 窮, 奸 狡 原 來 天 不 容

Yüeh chien yüeh chiao yüeh p'in ch'iung, chien chiao yuan lai t'ien pu jung.

> The more dishonest and crafty you become, the poorer you will be ; for Heaven will not countenance dishonesty and craftiness.

人 怕 老 來 窮, 穀 怕 午 時 風

Jên p'a lao tai ch'iung. ku p'a wu shih fêng.

Men fear poverty in their old age; the growing corn dreads the noon tide wind.

渴 無 所 飲, 餓 無 所 食

K'o wu so yin, ô wu so shih.

Thirsty with nothing to drink; hungry with nothing to eat.

買 飯 不 飽, 買 酒 不 醉

Mai fan pu pao, mai chiu pu tsui.

He can't buy enough rice to satisfy his hunger or enough wine to make him drunk.

一 文 錢 逼 倒 英 雄 漢

1 wen ch'ien pi tao yiug hsiung han.

A brave fellow may be harassed by the want of one cash.

明 知 王 法, 饑 餓 難 當

Ming chih wang fa, chi ô naŋ fang.

Poverty forces men to commit crime. *Lit.* One may know the king's law well enough, but starvation is hard to bear.

仁 人 廉 士, 窮 不 改 節

Jên jên lien shih, ch'iung pu kai chieh.

Poverty cannot change the virtues of the benevolent and disinterested.

日 無 雞 抓 之 米, 夜 無 鼠 耗 之 糧

Jih wu chi chua chih mi, yen wu shu hao chih liang.

Abject poverty. *Lit.* Without as much rice as a fowl could scratch in the day, or a rat gnaw at night.

飯 甑 裏 跑 出 老 鼠 來

Fan tseng li p'ao ch'u lao shu lai.

Same as above. *Lit.* Rats run away out of his rice boiler.

可 救 燃 眉

K'o chiu jan mei.

The same. *Lit.* Just able to save the eyebrows from being burnt.

開 口 告 人 難

K'ai k'ou kao jên nan.

It is hard to have to tell one's wants.

百 般 奸 狡 百 般 窮

Pai pan chien chiao pai pan ch'iung.

There is poverty for all kinds of rogues.

打 得 廊 簷 下, 誰 敢 不 低 頭

Ta tê lang yen hsia, shui kan pu ti t'ou.

One must submit to circumstances. *Lit.* Who won't bow his head when he knocks it against the eaves.

馬 行 無 力 皆 因 瘦, 人 不 風 流 只 爲 貧

Ma hsing wu li chieh yin shou, jên pu fêng liu chih wei p'in.

Nothing but leanness makes horses go feebly, only poverty keeps men from being gay.

火 燒 眉 毛, 只 顧 眼 前

Huo shao mei mao, chih ku yen ch'ien.

In great straits. *Lit.* When the fire is so close that it singes the eyebrows, one can pay attention to that alone.

無 法 可 制, 上 天 無 路, 下 地 無 門

Wu fa k'o chih, shang t'ien wu lu, hsia ti wu men.

At one's wits end; upwards, no road, downwards, no door.

赤 手 空 拳

Ch'ih shou k'ung ch'üan.

Penniless. *Lit.* Naked-handed and empty-fisted.

人 貧 志 短, 馬 瘦 毛 長

Jên p'in chih tuan, ma shou mao ch'ang.

When poor a man's resolution fails; when lean, a horse's hair grows shaggy.

吃 不 窮 穿 不 窮, 算 計 不 到 一 時 窮

Ch'ih pu ch'iung ch'uan pu ch'iung, suan chi pu tao i shih ch'iung.

A man is not quickly beggared by eating or dressing, but by the failure of his plans.

無錢且耐煩
Wu ch'ien ch'ieh nai fan.
In poverty be patient.

錢當用不辭貧
Ch'ien tang yung pu tz'ŭ p'in.
Do not plead poverty when you ought to spend.

好漢不怕出身低
Hao han pu p'a ch'u shen ti.
A worthy man is not ashamed of his humble origin.

燈臺無油點不光,世上無錢難爲人
Teng t'ai wu yu tien pu kuang, shih shang wu ch'ien nan wei jên.
An empty lamp gives no light; it is hard to act the man without money.

人窮思古債
Jên ch'iung ssŭ ku chai.
When a man becomes poor he recalls old debts due to him.

絕處逢生
Chüeh ch'ü fêng sheng.
When want is extremest, supplies come.

貧無達士將金贈,病有高人說藥方
P'in wu ta shih chiang chin tseng ping yu kao jên shuo yao fang.
If you are poor there is no clever man who will befriend you ; if ill, a doctor will give you a prescription.

貧窮斷六親
P'in ch'iung tuan liu ch'in.
Poverty destroys the six relationships, i.e., of father, mother, elder brother, younger brother, wife and child.

火燂鑊底就知窮
Huo t'an huo ti chiu chih ch'iung.
When the fire burns out the bottom of the cooking-pot you will know what poverty is

Chapter 6. Poor Men.

頭頂的沒得,脚踏的沒得
T'ou tiug ti mu tê, chiao t'a ti mu tê.
He has nothing over his head or under his feet.

光棍光棍大家帮趁
Kuang kun kuang kun ta chia pang ch'en.
Everybody is obliged to help rascals.

冷竈無烟,人窮無錢
Leng tsao wu yen, jên ch'iung wu ch'ien.
A cold stove has no smoke ; poor folk have no money.

窮得向粗糠火
Ch'iung tê hsiang ts'u k'ang huo.
One so poor that he is glad to get before a chaff fire.

稻草烟多;窮人氣多
Tao ts'ao yen to ch'iung jên ch'i to.
Rice straw gives out much smoke; poor men give out much wrath.

見貧苦親鄰須多温恤
Chien p'in k'u ch'in lin hsü to wen hsi.
Be kind and pitiful when you meet poor relatives and neighbours.

破帽底下有人
P'o mao ti hsia yu jên.
There is many a good man under a shabby hat.

井裏蛙蟇總難翻身
Ching li wa ma tsung nan fan shên.
A frog in a well finds it hard to turn round.

家無積攢爲口奔馳
Chia wu chi tsan wei k'ou pen ch'ih.
He who has no store at home, must run about for a living.

遇貧窮而作驕態者賤莫甚
Yü p'in ch'iung êrh tso chiao t'ai che chien mo shen.
There is nothing more dishonourable than being haughty with the poor.

窮人無病抵半富
Ch'iung jên wu ping ti pan fu.
A healthy poor man is half a rich one.

SECTION 8. AGENCY.

Chapter 1. Cause and Effect.

水 有 源 頭 木 有 根

Shui yu yüan t'ou mu yu ken.

> Every effect has its cause. *Lit.* Rivers have sources, trees have roots.

打 得 雷 大，落 得 雨 小

Ta tê lei ta, lo tê yü hsiao.

> It thunders loudly but rains very little. Comp. Great cry and little wool.

凡 事 必 有 因

Fan shih pi yu yin.

> Every thing must have a cause.

剪 草 除 根，萌 芽 不 發

Chien ts'ao ch'u ken, mêng ya pu fa.

> In cutting grass dig out the foot and it will sprout no more.

風 不 來，樹 不 動

Fêng pu lai shu pu tung.

> Trees don't move without wind.

樹 倒 無 陰

Shu tao wu yin.

> When the tree falls the shade is gone.

輸 了 寡 人 弱 了 國

Shu liao kua jên jo liao kuo,

> Having conquered the king you have weakened the country.

一 粒 老 鼠 屎 打 壞 一 鍋 飯

I li lao shu shih ta huai i kuo fan.

> One speck of rat's dung will spoil a whole pan full of rice.

肉 腐 出 蟲, 魚 枯 出 蠹

Jou fu ch'u ch'ung, yü k'u ch'u tu

> Putrid flesh breeds maggots ; rotten fish generates grubs.

棚 柴 火 焰 高

P'eng ch'ai huo yen kao.

> More fuel more fire.

樹 高 千 丈 葉 落 歸 根

Shu kao ch'ien chang, yeh lo kuei ken.

> Though a tree grow never so high, its falling leaves return to the root.

牆 隙 而 高, 其 崩 必 疾

Ch'iang ch'i êrh kao, ch'i peng pi chi.

> When a wall is cracked and lofty its fall must be speedy.

濁 其 源 而 求 流 之 清

Cho ch'i yüan êrh ch'iu liu chih ch'ing.

> To foul the spring and expect the stream to be pure.

欲 滅 跡 而 足 雪 踪

Yü mieh chi êrh tsu hsüeh tsung.

> He wishes to hide his footprints, but they still remain.
> Note. 雪 equals 顯 明 to manifest.

挖 樹 必 從 挽 子 起

Wa shu pi ts'ung tou tzǔ ch'i.

> In digging up a tree you must begin with the root.

物 各 有 主

Wu ko yu chu.

> Every thing has its owner.

苦 瓠 只 生 苦 瓠 子

K'u kua chih sheng k'u kua tzǔ.

> The bitter gourd only produces other small bitter gourds.

開 好 花 結 好 果

K'ai hao hua chieh hao ko.

> If the flower is good the fruit will be good.

河水滿井水滿

Ho shui man, ching shui man.

> When the river is full the wells are full.

有麝自然香何必當風立

Yu shê tzŭ jan hsiang, ho pi tahg fêng li.

> If there is musk it will give off its perfume ; it is not necessary to stand in the wind.

Chapter 2. Modus Operandi.

若要功夫深，鐵杵磨成繡花針

Jo yao kung fu sheng t'ieh kan mo ch'eng hsiu hua chen.

> If you want remarkable workmanship, grind an iron rod into an embroidery needle.

救人救到頭，殺人殺斷喉

Chiu jên chiu tao t'ou, sha jên sha tuan hou.

> If you save life do it completely; if you kill, kill outright.

拳不離手，曲不離口

Ch'üan pu li shou, ch'ü pu li k'ou.

> Practice makes perfect. *Lit.* Boxing cannot dispense with the hand, nor songs the mouth.

做事做到頭，殺猪殺到喉

Tso shih tso tao t'ou, sha chu sha tao hou.

> Whatever you do, do thoroughly ; if you kill a pig, kill it outright.

要得高人前操

Yao tê kao jên ch'ien ts'ao.

> If you wish to excel, drill before an expert.

萬丈高樓從地起

Wan chang kao lou ts'ung ti ch'i.

> The loftiest towers rise from the ground.

萬事起頭難

Wan shih ch'i t'ou nan.

> Every thing is difficult at first.

知 非 難, 行 之 爲 難

Chih fei nan, hsing chih wei nan.

>It is easier to know how to do a thing than to do it.

見 者 易, 學 者 難

Chien chê i, hsüeh chê nan.

>Easy to look at ; difficult to imitate.

領 其 手 不 能 謝 其 責

Ling ch'i shou pu neng hsieh ch'i tsê.

>Responsibility rests on the originator.

難 者 不 會, 會 者 不 難

Nan chê pu hui, hui chê pu nan.

>It is hard for those who don't know how ; for those who know how, it is easy.

辛 苦 討 得 快 活 吃

Hsin k'u t'ao tê k'uai huo ch'ih.

>Sweet is the bread of labour.

畫 虎 不 成 終 類 犬

Hua hu pu ch'eng chung lei ch'uan.

>Sketch a tiger incompletely and it is only like a dog.

百 般 道 路 百 般 難

Pai pan tao lu pai pan nan.

>Every kind of method has its own difficulties.

看 事 容 易 做 事 難

K'an shih jung i, tso shih nan.

>Looking on is easy ; doing things is difficult.

願 剃 頭 打 濕 腦, 不 剃 頭 乾 的 好

Yüan t'i t'ou ta shih nao, pu t'i t'ou kan ti hao.

>Wet your head if you want to shave it, but if you don't, it is better dry.

篾 籤 子 穿 豆 腐 如 之 何 不 掉

Mieh ch'ien tzu ch'uan tou fu ju chih ho pu tiao.

>If you take up beancurd on a bamboo slip ; how can you hinder it hanging down.

忙 中 有 錯

Mang chung yu ts'o.

> In hurry is error.

從 容 幹 好 事

Ts'ung jung kan hao shih.

> Done leisurely done well.

慢 功 出 細 貨

Man kung ch'u hsi huo.

> Slow work produces fine goods.

若 要 心 腸 堅，鑿 山 通 海 泉

Jo yao hsin ch'ang chien, tso shan t'ung hai ch'üan.

> Would you have a steady aim, bore through the rock to the fountains of the sea.

九 層 之 臺，起 於 累 土

Chiu ts'eng chih t'ai, ch'i yü lei t'u.

> Nine-storied terraces rise by a gradual accumulation of bricks.

渡 人 渡 上 岸

Tu jên tu shang an.

> If you ferry at all, ferry across.

辦 事 太 忙 就 有 參 差 了

Pan shih t'ai mang chiu yu ts'an ch'a liao.

> What is done hastily is not done well.

久 火 練 成 鋼

Chiu huo lien ch'eng kang.

> Iron long fired becomes steel.

費 力 不 討 巧

Fei li pu t'ao ch'iao.

> Anything beyond one's strength is never done well.

箭 在 弦 上，不 得 不 發

Chien tsai hsien shang, pu tê pu fa.

> When the arrow is on the string it must go.

砍 的 沒 得 車 的 圓

K‘an ti mu tê ch‘e ti yüan.

What is chopped has not the roundness of what is turned
by a lathe.

熟 能 生 巧

Shu neng sheng ch‘iao.

Practice makes perfect.

井 修 三 遍 吃 甜 水

Ching hsiu san p‘ien ch‘ih t‘ien shui.

Clean out the well three times and the water will be sweet.

一 畦 蘿 葡 一 畦 菜，各 人 養 的 各 人 愛

I ch‘i lo po i ch‘i ts‘ai, ko jên yang ti ko jên ai.

A patch of turnips and a patch of greens, each one raises
what he likes best.

一 物 服 一 行

I wu fu i hang.

Everything has its special use.

弄 假 成 眞

Lung ch‘ia ch‘eng chên.

Pretence may become reality.

先 到 爲 君，後 到 爲 臣

Hsien tao wei chün, hou tao wei ch‘en.

First come, first served. *Lit.* Who comes first is prince；
the next is minister.

創 業 易，守 業 難

Ch‘uang yeh i, shou yeh nan.

It is easier to build up a fortune than to retain one.

戰 勝 易，守 勝 難

Chan sheng i, shou sheng nan.

It is easier to gain than to secure the advantages of victory.

等 得 黃 河 清，人 壽 幾 何

Teng tê huang ho ch‘ing, jên shou chi ho.

What you have to do, do it without delay. *Lit.* Wait
till the Yellow River becomes clear, and how old will
you be？

挖 樹 尋 根

Wa shu hsin ken.

> To get to the bottom of an affair. *Lit.* To dig up a tree, search for the root.

用 心 計 較 般 般 易, 退 步 思 量 事 事 難

Yung hsin chi chiao pan pan i, t'ui pu ssŭ liang shih shih nan.

> Thoughtful planning makes all things easy ; faint hearted consideration makes all things difficult.

習 慣 成 自 然

Hsi kuan ch'eng tzŭ jan.

> Practice makes perfect.

一 回 生, 二 回 熟

I hui sheng, êrh hui shu.

> The first time, a novice ; the second time, an adept.

七 梢 公 八 水 手, 你 齊 我 不 齊

Ch'i shao kuhg pa shui shou, ni ch'i wo pu ch'i.

> Too many cooks spoil the broth. *Lit.* Seven steersmen and eight sailors; one is uniform the other is not.

七 手 八 脚

Ch'i shou pa chiao.

> The same. *Lit.* Seven hands and eight feet.

罈 子 裏 捉 烏 龜 手 到 擎 拿

T'an tzŭ li cho wu kuei shou tao ch'ing na.

> As easy as to lift a tortoise from a jar.

不 費 吹 灰 之 力

Pu fei ch'ui t'an chih li.

> As easy as blowing off dust.

捉 到 強 盜 連 夜 解

Cho tao ch'iang tao lien yeh chieh.

> Too great haste. *Lit.* To catch a thief and hurry him to the yamen the same night.

燒 香 打 破 罄

Shao hsiang ta p'o ch'ing.

> To do anything too hurriedly. *Lit.* Breaking the *ch'ing* whilst burning incense. Note. The ch'ing is a sonorous stone or gong used in temples.

粥 冷 自 然 稠

Chou leng tzu jan ch'ou.

> Congee naturally thickens as it cools. Note. The design of this proverb is to warn against undue hurry or anxiety in doing anything.

只 有 急 過 的，沒 有 緩 過 的

Chih yu chi kuo ti, mu yu buan kuo ti.

> Mistakes occur through haste, never through doing a thing leisurely.

一 勤 天 下 無 難 事

I ch'in t'ien hsia wu nan shih.

> With diligence nothing is difficult.

忙 行 無 好 步

Mang hsing wu hao pu.

> He who hurries cannot walk with a stately step.

世 上 無 難 事，只 怕 心 不 堅

Shih shang wu nan shih, chih p'a hsin pu chien.

> There is nothing difficult in the world; the only fear is want of perseverance.

千 個 師 傅 千 個 法

Ch'ien ko shih fu ch'ien ko fa.

> A thousand masters, a thousand plans.

說 得 出 來 做 不 出 來

Shuo tê ch'u lai, tso pu ch'u lai.

> Easier said than done.

一 馬 一 鞍

I ma i an.

> One horse, one saddle.

墙 上 畫 魚 一 隻 眼

Ch'iang shang hua yü i chih yen.

> Doing a thing by halves. *Lit.* Painting on the wall a fish with one eye.

放 水 容 易 收 水 難

Fang shui jung i shou shui nan.

> It is easy to pour out water but difficult to gather it up.

一 個 巴 掌 打 不 响

I ko pa chang ta pu hsiang.

> You can't clap with one hand.

十 個 指 頭 不 能 一 般 齊

Shih ko chih t'ou pu neng i pan ch'i.

> One's ten fingers can't be all the same length. i.e., we must take the short with the long.

二 人 同 心 其 利 斷 金

Erh jên t'ung hsin ch'i li tuan chin.

> If two men are of one mind their sharpness will divide metal, i.e., they can accomplish anything.

顛 顛 倒 倒 勿 討 好

Tien tien tao tao wu t'ao hao.

> Careless, slovenly action will never succeed.

長 線 放 遠 遙

Ch'ang hsien fang yüan yao.

> If the string is long the kite will fly high.

半 途 而 廢

Pan t'u êrh fei.

> To go half way and then give up.

造 屋 錯 請 箍 桶 匠

Chao wu ts'o ch'ing ku t'ung chiang.

> Using wrong means. *Lit.* To call the cooper by mistake to build a house.

件 件 通 件 件 鬆

Chien chien t'ung chien chien sung.

> Jack of all trades and master of none.

到 了 河 邊 纔 脫 鞋

Tao liao ho pien ts'ai t'o hsieh.

> When you have reached the river then is the time to take off your shoes.

———

Chapter 3. Necessity of Effort.

不 受 苦 中 苦，難 爲 人 上 人

Pu shou k'u chung k'u, nan wei jên shang jên.

> You will hardly excel others unless you can endure **extreme hardship**.

風 自 天 上 轉，地 下 要 人 喚

Fêng tzǔ t'ien shang chüan, ti hsia yao jên huan.

> The wind descends from heaven, but man on earth must call it down.

勤 儉 勤 儉 茶 飯 隨 便，懶 惰 懶 惰 忍 饑 受 餓

Ch'in chien ch'in chien ch'a fan sui pien, lan to lan to jen chi shou ô.

> Diligence and economy secure plenty to eat and drink; whilst idleness and sloth bring hunger and starvation.

鈍 斧 磨 成 鍼，只 要 工 夫 深

Tun fu mo ch'eng chen, chih yao kung fu shen.

> To grind a blunt axe into a needle only requires hard **labour**.

成 人 不 自 在，自 在 不 成 人

Ch'eng jên pu tzǔ tsai, tzǔ tsai pu ch'eng jên.

> To succeed, you can't take things easy ; if you do, you won't succeed.

不 上 高 山，不 顯 平 地

Pu shang kao shan, pu hsien p'ing ti.

> If you don't ascend the mountain, the plain won't be seen.

不 登 山 不 知 天 之 高，不 臨 溪 不 知 地 之 厚

Pu teng shan pu chih t'ien chih kao, pu lin ch'i pu chih ti chih hou.

> Without climbing mountains you can't know the height of the heavens; unless you go down to the streams you can't know the thickness of the earth.

將 相 本 無 種，男 兒 當 自 強
Chiang hsiang pen wu chung, nan erh tang tzŭ ch'iang.

> Generals and premiers do not spring from seed; men must exert themselves.

擊 石 原 有 火，不 擊 乃 無 烟
Chi shih yüan yu huo, pu chi nai wu yen.

> Strike a flint and you will get fire; if you don't strike it, you won't even get smoke.

路 不 行 不 到，事 不 爲 不 成
Lu pu hsing pu tao, shih pu wei pu ch'eng.

> If you don't make a start you won't arrive ; if you don't begin, you won't accomplish anything.

坐 食 山 崩
Tso shih shan pêng.

> He who does nothing but sit and eat, will wear away a mountain (of wealth).

欲 求 生 快 活，須 下 死 工 夫
Yü ch'iu sheng k'uai huo, hsü hsia ssŭ kung fu.

> If you long for pleasure you must labour hard to get it.
>
> Note. 下 equals 用 to use.

不 入 虎 穴，不 得 虎 子
Pu ju hu hsüeh, pu tê hu tzŭ.

> If you do not enter the tiger's den, you cannot get his cubs.

咬 得 菜 根，百 事 可 做
Yao te ts'ai ken, pai shih k'o tso.

> He is equal to any task who can live on cabbage stalks.

臨 淵 羨 魚 不 如 退 而 結 網
Lin yuan hsien yü pu ju t'ui erh chieh wang.

> Better return and make a net, then go down to the stream and merely wish for fishes.

從 來 好 事 必 竟 多 磨
Ts'ung lai hao shih pi ching to mo.

> Never was a good work done without much trouble.

栽秧割麥兩頭忙

Tsai yang ko mai liang t'ou mang.

> Busily engaged. *Lit.* Planting rice and cutting wheat, busy on all hands.

獨打鼓,獨划船

Tu ta ku, tu hua ch'uan.

> Too busy for pleasure. *Lit.* I have both to beat the drum and row the boat.

不貪辛苦昧,難得世間財

Pu t'an hsin k'u wei, nan te shih chien ts'ai.

> He who is not willing to suffer will find it difficult to obtain the world's wealth.

少年不努力,老來徒傷悲

Shao nien pu nu li, lao lai t'u shang pei.

> If you do not exert yourself in youth, there will be vain regrets in old age.

兵臨告急,必須死敵

Ping lin kao chi, pi hsü ssŭ ti.

> Extreme peril requires extreme effort.

寧可浪風打,勿可壁風吹

Ning k'o lang fêng ta, wu k'o pi fêng ch'ui.

> Better strive against the gale than let a draught blow upon you (from a hole in the wall).

天下無難事,只怕心不專

T'ien hsia wu nan shih, chih p'a hsin pu chuan.

> There is nothing really difficult under Heaven, what is to be feared is lack of application.

有心打石,石自穿

Yu hsin ta shih, shih tzŭ ch'uan.

> Keep striking the stone and it will eventually be perforated.

一不作二不休

I pu tso, erh pu hsiu.

> In the first place don't attempt it, but if you do, keep at it.

不受十分苦,離得一文錢

Pu shou shih fen k'u, nan tê i wen ch'ien.

It is hard to get even a single cash without very hard labour.

Chapter 4. Resolution.

有志者事竟成

Yu chih chê shih ching ch'eng.

Decide to do it, and the thing is done.

有志不在年高,無志空活百歲

Yu chih pu tsai nien kao, wu chih k'ung huo pai sui.

Resolution is independent of great age ; but without it one lives a hundred years in vain.

螺蛳彎彎就自有出頭路

Lo shih wan wan chiu tzŭ yu ch'u t ou lu.

Though the twists and turns of his shell are many, the murex will find a way out.

事怕有心人

Shih p'a yu hsin jên.

Work fears a resolute man.

大丈夫起家容易,眞君子立志何難

Ta chang fu ch'i chia jung i, chen chün tzŭ li chih ho nan.

A worthy man can easily establish a family ; to a determined, truly superior man, what is difficult?.

事業要好只在志氣;事業要大只在勤勞

Shih yeh yao hao chih tsai chih ch'i, shih yeh yao ta chih tsai ch'in lao.

To do a good trade needs nothing but resolution ; to do a large one, nothing but application.

有志吃志,無志吃力

Yu chih ch'ih chih, wu chih ch'ih li.

A resolute man lives by his determination ; an irresolute man has to depend on his physical strength.

平生志氣與天高

P'ing sheng chih ch'i yü t'ien kao.

One with life-long resolution rivals the loftiness of Heaven.

不事王侯，高尙其志

Pu shih wang hou, kao shang ch'i chih.

He who refuses to serve either king or prince is possessed of lofty resolution.

兩眼並不觀河水，一心只望跳龍門

Liang yen ping pu kuan ho shui, i hsin chih wang t'iao lung men.

He cannot see the river at all; his heart is so set on leaping the dragon gate. Note. In this figurative way the resolution with which a scholar attempts to gain his degree is set forth.

士先立志

Shih hsien li chih.

To become a scholar, determination is the chief thing.

舒手就捉天上月，入水能擒海中鰲

Shu shou chiu cho t'ien shang yüeh, ju shui neng ch'in hai chung ao.

To be possessed of resolution. *Lit.* To open the hand in order to grasp the moon in the heavens; to plunge into the sea in order to seize leviathan. Note. The Ao is a fabulous sea-monster supposed to support P'eng Lai Shan, one of the three isles of the genii, which were believed to exist in the China Sea.

錦鱗未變志常存

Chin lin wei pien chih ch'ang ts'un.

Till transformed into a dragon, the glittering scaled fish never lost his resolution. Note. This refers to the belief that the carp of the Yellow River ascend the stream in the third month of each year, and that those which succeed in passing the rapids at Lung Men are change into dragons. This is also figurative of success at public examinations.

自己跌倒自己扒，不要靠著別人家

Tzŭ chi tieh tao, tzŭ chi p'a, pu yao k'ao cho pieh jên chia.

When you fall down get up yourself, and don't rely on others.

餓 死 不 吃 貓 兒 飯, 凍 死 不 穿 老 婆 衣

Ô ssǔ pu ch'i mao erh fan, tung ssǔ pu ch'uan lao p'o i.

Self-reliance. *Lit.* I'd rather pine to death than eat a
cat's rice ; I'd rather freeze to death than wear an
old woman's clothes.

好 蜂 不 探 落 地 花

Hao fêng pu ts'ai lo ti hua.

High aims. *Lit.* The good bee doesn't sip from a fallen
flower.

人 無 志 氣, 刀 無 鋼

Jên wu chih ch'i, tao wu kang.

A man without resolution is like an untempered sword.

虧 本 生 意 無 人 做, 斬 首 生 理 有 人 爲

K'uei pen sheng i wu jen tso, chan shou sheng li yu jen wei.

No one will carry on an unprofitable business, but men
will engage in head-losing occupations.

打 蛇 不 死 轉 背 傷 人

Ta shê pu ssǔ chuan pei shang jên.

Strike a serpent without killing it and it will turn and
bite you.

一 人 拚 命, 萬 夫 莫 當

I jên p'an ming, wan fu mo tang.

When one man disregards his life, ten thousand others
are no match for him.

好 漢 不 吃 眼 前 虧

Hao han pu ch'ih yen ch'ien k'uei.

A valiant man is not openly defeated, i.e., in fair fight.

Chapter 5. Example.

上 梁 不 正 下 梁 歪, 中 梁 不 正 倒 下 來

Shang liang pu cheng hsia liang wai, chung liang pu cheng tao hsia
lai.

When the upper beam is uneven the lower beam is awry ;
than the central beam is uneven all falls to the ground.

跟 好 人 學 好 人，跟 端 公 扛 假 神

Ken hao jên hsüeh hao jên, ken tuan kung k'ang chia shên.

> Follow good men and you will imitate them; follow mediums and you will help to carry false gods. Note These mediums are men who practise sorcery and impersonate spirits.

跟 好 人 學 好 人，跟 討 飯 的 睡 廟 門

Ken hao jên hsüeh hao jên, ken t'ao fan ti shui miao men.

> Follow good men and you will become good a man; follow beggars and you will sleep at the temple gates.

近 飽 者 臭，近 蘭 者 香

Chin pao chê ch'ou, chin lan chê hsiang.

> That which is near putrid fish stinks; that which is near the orchid is fragrant.

上 行 下 效

Shang hsing hsia hsiao.

> What those above do, those below will imitate.

法 司 馬 廣，積 陰 功

Fa Ssu Ma Kuang, chi yin kung.

> Imitate Ssu Ma who laid up much secret merit. Note. This refers to Ssu Ma Kuang 司 馬 光, one of the most prominent authors and statesmen under the Sung Dynasty.

臭 肉 同 味

Ch'ou jou t'ung wei.

> All equally bad. *Lit.* Putrid flesh all smells alike.

一 羊 前 行 衆 羊 後 繼

I yang ch'ien hsing chung yang hou chi.

> When one sheep leads the way all the rest follow.

莫 看 強 盜 吃 肉，只 看 強 盜 受 罪

Mo k'an ch'iang tao ch'ih jou, chih k'an ch'iang tao shou tsui.

> Don't look at the good living of thieves, but look at them suffering punishment.

跟 好 學 好

Ken hao hsüeh hao.

> Following the good you learn to be good.

白 布 掉 在 染 缸 皂 白 難 分

Pai pu tiao tsai jan kang, tsao pai nan fen.

> When white calico has been dipped in the dyeing vat, it is difficult to tell it from black.

爲 老 不 正，敎 壞 子 孫

Wei lao pu cheng, chiao huai tzŭ sun.

> When old men are not upright, they teach their sons and grandsons to be rogues.

照 本 宣 歌

Chao pen hsüan ko.

> Follow example. *Lit.* Sing according to the book.

牽 牛 喝 水，先 打 濕 脚

Ch'ien niu ho shui, hsien ta shih chiao.

> He who leads an ox to drink must first wet his own feet.

照 樣 畫 葫 蘆

Chao yang hua hu lu.

> Follow the example in sketching your calabash.

籮 筐 裝 石 灰，在 處 有 跡 窩

Lo k'uang chuang shih hui, tsai ch'ü yu chi wo.

> Influence of bad men. *Lit.* He who carries lime in a basket, leaves traces wherever he stops.

上 之 所 爲，民 之 歸 也

Shang chih so wei, min chih kuei yeh.

> The people follow the example of their rulers.

大 船 拖 成 漕，小 船 不 用 篙

Ta ch'uan t'o ch'eng ts'ao, hsiao ch'uan pu yung kao.

> When a large vessel has opened a way, it is easy for a small one to follow.

見 善 如 不 及，見 惡 如 探 湯

Chien shan ju pu chi, chien wo ju t'an t'ang.

> Contemplating the good, but thinking it unattainable; contemplating evil, but shrinking from it as from trusting the hand into hot water. Note. See Confucian Analects. Book 16. Chap. II. This was an old saying in Confucius' time. He used it as applicable to some of his disciples.

嫂 嫂 做 鞋 嬬 子 有 樣

Sao sao tso hsieh shen tzŭ yu yang.

> The elder daughter-in-law's shoes are a pattern for the younger.

倒 倒 廟 對 斜 斜 神

Tao tao miao tui hsieh hsieh shen.

> Force of example. *Lit.* The dilapidated temple corresponds to the toppling gods.

挨 金 似 金，挨 玉 似 玉

Ai chin ssŭ chin, ai yü ssŭ yü.

> Like begets like. *Lit.* Near gold it resembles gold; near jade it resembles jade.

跟 三 姑 學 跳 神：跟 好 人 學 好 人

Ken san ku hsüeh t'iao shên, ken hao jen hsüeh hao jen.

> A man is known by the company he keeps. *Lit.* Following the three kinds of women, you learn to exorcise spirits; following good men you learn to be good. See Section on Women.

前 船 受 是 後 船 眼

Ch'ien ch'uan shou shih hou ch'uan yen.

> The front boat is eyes for the boat behind.

一 犬 吠 形，百 犬 吠 聲

I ch'üan fei hsing, pai ch'uan fei sheng.

> One dog barks at something he sees, and a hundred dogs bark in chorus.

看 花 容 易，繡 花 難

K'an hua jung i, hsiu hua nan.

> It is easy to look at (embroidered) flowers; it is difficult to do them.

近 朱 者 赤，近 墨 者 黑

Chin chu chê ch'ih, chin mo chê hei.

> That which touches vermilion becomes red; that which touches ink becomes black.

前 人 開 路，後 人 行

Ch'ien jên k'ai lu, hou jên hsing.

> Those who go first make the road and those who follow walk on it.

Chapter 6. Impossibilities.

不大其棟,不能任重
Pu ta ch'i tung, pu neng jên chung.

Little pillars cannot sustain heavy weights.

針無兩頭利
Chen wu liang t'ou li.

No needle has two sharp points, i e., it is impossible for a man to do two things at once.

按到雞母㲘兒
An tao chi mu pao erh.

To force a hen to hatch chickens.

癩蝦蟆墊床脚硬掙
Lai hsia ma tien ch'uang chiao ying cheng.

A toad propping a bedpost firmly.

螞蟻搬泰山
Ma i pan t'ai shan.

Ants removing the Tai Shan. Note. The Tai Shan is the most famous of the five mountains of China.

一把掌遮不住這日頭
I pa chang chê pu chu che jih t'ou.

You cannot shade off the sun's light, with one hand, i.e., the matter is bound to come out.

隔牆丟瓦,未知撲仰
Ke ch'iang tiu wa, wei chih p'u yang.

Throw a tile over a wall and you cannot tell on which of its sides it has lighted.

後頸窩裏毛,摸得到看不見
Hou ching wo li mao, mo tê tao k'an pu chien.

It is impossible to prophesy the future. *Lit.* One may feel, but not see the hair on the back of one's neck.

巧媳婦難作無米之炊
Ch'iao hsi fu nan tso wu mi chih ch'ui.

A clever daughter-in-law cannot cook without rice.

一 隻 脚 踏 不 得 兩 隻 船

I chih chiao t'a pu tê liang chih ch'uan.

> One foot can't stand on two boats.

牛 不 吃 水，按 不 住 頭

Niu pu ch'ih shui an pu chu t'ou.

> If an ox won't drink you can't make him bend down his head.

單 絲 不 成 線，孤 木 不 成 林

Tan ssŭ pu ch'eng hsien, ku mu pu ch'eng lin.

> A single filament will not make a thread; a single tree cannot make a grove.

巧 媳 婦 只 煮 得 有 米 的 飯

Ch'iao hsi fu chih chu yu mi ti fan.

> A clever daughter-in-law cannot cook without rice. See above.

廟 廊 之 材 非 一 木 之 枝

Miao lang chih ts'ai fei i mu chih chih.

> The temple's halls are not built from one tree.

一 身 不 能 當 二 役

I shen pu neng tang erh i.

> One man cannot do two yamen-runner's work, i.e., you can't do two things at once.

水 裏 按 葫 蘆 你 起 我 落

Shui li an hu lu ni ch'i wo lo.

> One man cannot manage too many affairs. *Lit*. Like pumpkins in water; one bobs up while you press the other down.

事 不 量 力 如 夸 父 追 日

Shih pu liang li ju K'ua Fu chui jih.

> Beyond one's strength as K'ua Fu pursuing the sun. Note. K'ua Fu was a noted worthy who was anxious to see where the sun set, but who died of exhaustion before he accomplished his purpose.

獨 脚 戲 難 唱

Tu chiao hsi nan ch'ang.

> One actor cannot perform a play.

一個蝨子頂不起被窩
I ko shih tzŭ ting pu ch'i pei wo.
> One louse cannot raise a coverlet.

一木焉能支大厦
I mu yen neng chih ta hsia.
> How can one piece of timber build a great house.

這一杯湧酒難得吃
Chě i pei yung chiu nan tê ch'ih.
> This cup of strong wine is hard to swallow.

同邊草鞋各穿一隻
T'ung pien ts'ao hsieh ko ch'uan i chih.
> Sandals for the same foot must be worn by different persons.

誰人保得千年計
Shui jên pao tê ch'ien nien chi.
> Who can guarantee a thing for ever.

象牙不出鼠口
Hsiang ya pu ch'u shu k'ou.
> You can't get ivory out of a rat's mouth.

大海洋洋尋美針
Ta hai yang yang hsin mei chen.
> Seeking for a fine needle in the boundless ocean.

燥籠糠打不出油來
Tsao lung k'ang ta pu ch'u yu lai.
> You can't beat oil out of dry chaff.

海水不可斗量
Hai shui pu k'o tou liang.
> You can't measure the waters of the sea in a peck measure.

畫餅難充飢
Hua ping nan ch'ung chi.
> Drawing cakes won't appease hunger.

千金難買亡人筆
Ch'ien chin nan mai wang jên pi.
> A thousand taels won't buy a dead man's handwriting.

SECTION IX. FORTUNE.

Chapter 1. Fate.

賊 却 火 燒 命 裏 所 招

Tsê chieh huo shao, ming li so chao.

Robbery and fire are decreed by fate.

有 緣 遇 着，無 緣 錯 過

Yu yüan yü cho, wu yüan ts'o kuo.

If so destined, you will meet each other ; if not, you will miss each other.

命 好 不 用 乖，心 好 不 用 齋

Ming hao pu yung kuai, hsin hao pu yung chai.

If your luck is good, you need not practise deceit ; if your heart is good you need not resort to asceticism.

有 福 同 享，有 禍 同 當

Yu fu t'ung hsiang, yu huo t'ung tang.

We will enjoy happiness together, and we will suffer calamity together.

有 鹽 同 鹹，無 鹽 同 淡

Yu yen t'ung hsien, wu yen t'ung tan.

Same as above. *Lit.* Having salt, we will salt our food together ; if there is no salt, together we will put up with its insipidity.

命 裏 帶 六 合，處 處 合 得 着

Ming li tai liu ho, ch'ü ch'ü ho tê cho.

If your luck includes the Six Harmonies, wherever you are you will be all right. Note. The Six Harmonies are the Six Cardinal Points, North, East, South, West, the Zenith and the Nadir.

富 貴 命 裏 排，各 自 等 時 來，

Fu kuei ming li p'ai, ko tzu teng shih lai.

Riches and honour are settled by fate, but each comes at its appointed time.

心好命又好，富貴直到老；心好命不好，天地終須保；命好心不好，中途天折了；心命俱不好，貧賤受煩惱

Hsin hao ming yu hao, fu kuei chih tao lao; hsin hao ming pu hao, t'ien ti chung hsü pao; ming hao hsin pu hao, chung t'u yao chê liao; hsin ming chü pu hao p'in chien shou fan nao.

> When your heart and your luck are both good, riches and honour will be yours till old age ; if your heart is good but your luck not good, the powers of heaven and earth will protect you ; if your luck is good but not your heart, you will be cut off in middle life ; if both your heart and your luck are not good you will suffer distress in poverty and humiliation.

横財不富命窮人

Heng ts'ai pu fu ming ch'iung jên.

> Unjust gains cannot enrich those who are fated to be poor.

醫得病，醫不得命

I tê ping, i pu tê ming.

> Disease may be cured, but not fate.

有緣千里能相會，無緣對面不相逢

Yu yüan ch'ien li neng hsiang hui, wu yüan tui mien pu hsiang fêng.

> Destined for each other, though separated a thousand li, people will meet ; not so destined, though living opposite, will never meet.

福生有基，禍生有胎

Pu sheng yu chi, huo sheng yu t'ai.

> Happiness has its foundation and misery its womb.

命你只有八合米，走盡天下不滿升

Ming ni chih yu pa ko mi, tsou chin t'ien hsia pu man sheng.

> If your fate is to have only eight-tenths of a pint of rice, though you traverse the empire over you won't get a full pint.

世事皆先定，浮生空自忙

Shih shih chieh hsien ting, fou sheng k'ung tzŭ mang.

> The world's affairs are determined beforehand, so it is vain to worry about this transitory life.

萬 般 皆 由 命，半 點 不 由 人

Wan pan chieh yu ming, pan tien pu yu jên.

> Everything is decreed by fate ; not even the slightest thing depends on man.

路 逢 險 處 難 廻 避，事 到 頭 來 不 自 由

Lu fêng hsien ch'ü nan hui pi, shih tao t'ou lai pu tzŭ yu.

> On a road there are unavoidable dangers ; and a time comes in life when affairs are beyond our control.

萬 事 不 由 人 計 較，一 生 都 是 命 安 排

Wan shih pu yu jên chi chiao, i sheng tu shih ming an p'ai.

> Nothing depends on man's own calculations ; his whole life is arranged by fate.

大 家 都 是 命，半 點 不 由 人

Ta chia tu shih ming, pan tien pu yu jên.

> The destiny of every one is fixed without the slightest reference to our own will.

心 高 命 不 高

Hsin kao ming pu kao.

> His heart is loftier than his destiny.

有 意 栽 花 花 不 發，無 心 挿 柳 柳 成 陰

Yu i tsai hua hua pu fa, wu hsin ch'a liu liu ch'eng yin.

> Flowers planted with care never grow ; willows stuck in carelessly may become shady trees

善 惡 隨 人 作，禍 福 自 己 招

Shan wo sui jên tso, huo fu tzŭ chi chao.

> Good and evil are the outcome of men's conduct ; misery or happiness depends on themselves.

人 能，命 不 能

Jên neng, ming pu neng

> The man has ability, but his fate is against him.

城 隍 廟 的 算 盤

Ch'eng huang miao ti suan p'an.

> Fate or Destiny. *Lit.* The abacus in the temple of the city god.

杯 酒 塊 肉 皆 前 定

Pei chiu k'uai jou chieh ch'ien ting.

> Every glass of wine and every slice of meat are
> predestined.

妻 財 子 祿 皆 前 定

Ch'i ts'ai tzŭ lu chieh ch'ien ting.

> Wife, wealth, children, salary, are all predestined.

誰 人 不 愛 子 孫 賢, 誰 人 不 愛 千 鍾 粟, 奈 五 行 不 是 這 般 題 目

Shui jên pu ai tzŭ sun hsien, shui jên pu ai ch'ien chung su, nai
wu hsing pu shih chê pan t'i mu.

> Virtuous children and official emolument who does not
> desire? Alas, these are not the theme of your
> luckless horoscope. Note. One's fate is supposed
> to be closely connected with the Wu Hsing or Five
> Primordial Elements.

莫 道 文 王 卦 不 靈, 只 怕 先 生 斷 不 眞

Mo tao Wen Wang kua pu ling, chih p'a hsien sheng tuan pu chen.

> Don't depend on fortune-tellers. *Lit.* Do not say that
> Wen Wang's Diagrams are powerless; rather fear
> the fortune-teller has explained them wrongly. The
> Eight Diagrams were the basis of a system of
> ancient philosophy, and these were first expounded
> in the 12th Century B.C.

天 之 所 命 人 不 能 違 也

T'ien chih so ming jên pu neng wei yeh.

> What Heaven has decreed man cannot oppose.

一 飲 一 啄 莫 非 前 定

I yin i cho mo fei ch'ien ting,

> Not one sup or bite but is pre-determined.

千 里 姻 緣 一 線 牽

Ch'ien li yin yüan i hsien ch'ien.

> Those destined to be married to each other, though a
> thousand li apart, are drawn together by a single
> thread.

不要觀音面，只要丈夫星現

Pu yao Kuan Yin mien, chih yao chang fu hsing hsien.

> Do not desire the features of Kuan Yin (i.e., great beauty) but that the star of your future husband may appear. Note. This indicates that destiny rather than beauty secures a husband.

財帛兒女命相連

Ts'ai pai erh nü ming hsiang lien.

> Riches and offspring are both matters of destiny.

命中有兒何在早晚

Ming chung yu erh ho tsai tsao wan

> If destined to have sons, what matter whether early or late.

Chapter 2. Luck.

今天攢明天攢，攢來攢去買了一把傘，忽然一陣狂風起，兩手抱住光竹桿

Chin t'ien tsan ming t'ien tsan, tsan lai tsan ch'ü mai liao i pa san, hu jan i chen k'uang fêng ch'i, liang shou pao chu kuang chu kan.

> He who hoards to-day and to-morrow, and by constant hoarding has bought a new umbrella; finds that suddenly a strong wind arises and leaves him nothing but a bare bamboo stick.

命裏有時終須有，命裏無時莫強求

Ming li yu shih chung hsü yu, ming li wu shih mo ch'iang ch'iu.

> If you are destined to good fortune it will come; if not, don't struggle to obtain it.

兵強則滅，木強則折

Ping ch'iang tsê mieh, mu ch'iang tsê chê.

> The strongest army may be destroyed; the sturdiest tree may be broken down.

人在時中，行船遇順風

Jên tsai shih chung, hsing ch'uan yü shun fêng.

> A man in luck is as a boat with a favourable wind.

朝 爲 田 舍 郎，暮 登 天 子 堂

Chao wei t'ien shê lang: mu teng t'ien tzǔ t'ang.

> In the morning only a farmer ; in the evening in the
> emperor's palace.

人 在 時 中 又 胖 又 白，借 錢 五 十 答 應 一 百；
人 不 在 時 又 瘦 又 黑，借 錢 五 十 答 應 沒 得

Jên tsai shih chung yu p'ang yu pai, chieh ch'ien wu shih ta ying i
pai, jên pu tsai shih yu shou yu hei, chieh ch'ien wu shih ta
ying mu tê.

> A lucky man is stout and fair, and if he wishes to borrow
> fifty taels people lend him a hundred ; an unlucky
> man is lean aud swarthy and if he tries to borrow
> fifty taels, they say they haven't any money.

桃 花 二 月 開，菊 花 九 月 開，各 自 等 時 來

T'ao hua erh yüeh k'ai, chü hua chiu yüeh k'ai, ko tzǔ teng shih
lai.

> Peach trees blossom in the second month ; chrysanthemums
> bloom in the ninth month ; each according to its
> own season.

一 發 如 雷，一 敗 如 灰

I fa ju lei, i pai ju hui.

> Some rise as thunder does (suddenly) ; some fall as into
> dust (irretrievably).

戲 不 彀 神 仙 湊

Hsi pu kou, shen hsien ts'ou.

> What is beyond the power of the actors is supplied by
> the gods and fairies. Note. This is said of any in
> straits who happen to meet with opportune help.

上 身 長 坐 官 堂，下 身 長 走 忙 忙

Shang shen ch'ang tso kuan t'ang, hsia shên ch'ang tsou mang mang.

> Long-bodied men become magistrates ; long-legged men
> have to earu their living by running about. Note.
> This is a saying of physioguomical fortune-tellers.

敲 碗 敲 筷，窮 死 萬 代

Ch'iao wan ch'iao k'uai, ch'iung ssǔ wan tai.

> If you rattle your chopsticks against the basin, you and
> your descendants will always be poor. One of the
> superstitious fancies of China.

眼 跳 心 驚，坐 臥 不 寧

Yen t'iao hsin ching, tso wo pu ning.

> With eyes quivering and heart throbbing, no rest either sitting or lying. These symptoms are supposed to be ominous of evil fortune.

人 情 莫 道 春 光 好，只 怕 西 風 有 冷 時

Jên ch'ing mo tao ch'ün kuang hao, chih p'a hsi fêng yu leng shih.

> Don't boast of good fortune. *Lit.* Don't let yourself say too much about the fineness of spring ; but have a fear of westerly winds and cold.

空 手 出 門，抱 財 歸 家

K'ung shou ch'ü men, pao ts'ai kuei chia.

> He goes out empty-handed ; he returns holding great wealth.

一 家 打 牆，兩 家 方 便

I chia ta ch'iang, liang chia fang pien.

> One family builds a wall and two families get the benefit of it.

有 福 傷 財，無 福 傷 己

Yu fu shang ts'ai, wu fu shang chi.

> With good luck he may only suffer in his purse ; if unlucky he will suffer in his person. Note. The case here supposed is that of a man who has broken the law ; if he can pay a fine he may escape corporal punishment.

越 窮 越 見 鬼

Yüeh ch'iung yüeh chien kuei.

> The poorer one is the more devils he meets.

時 來 誰 不 來，時 不 來 誰 來

Shih lai shui pu lai, shih pu lai shui lai.

> When luck comes, who doesn't ; when luck doesn't come, who does ?

稻 場 打 穀 終 有 一 日

Tao ch'ang ta ku, chung yu i jih.

> Good luck certain sometime. *Lit.* A day must come for threshing out the grain.

癩 瘰 跟 月 亮 走，沾 光 沾 光

La li ken yueh liang tsou chan kuang chan kuang.

> A scabbed head in the moonlight gets extra light. Note.
> La li is the common designation of a scalp disease
> that deprives the head of hair and renders it
> unsightly and offensive. Sufferers from this disease
> are commonly made the butts of ridicule, owing to
> the glistening appearance of their heads. This
> proverb expresses the good luck one enjoys following
> another.

矮 子 扒 樓 梯 一 步 高 一 步

Ai tzŭ p'a lou t'i i pu kao i pu.

> When a dwarf ascends a staircase, he gets higher every
> step.

矮 子 打 二 起，純 高 也 總 不 高

Ai tzŭ ta erh ch'i, shun kao yeh tsung pu kao.

> A dwarf sitting with one knee over the other; he looks
> tall but he isn't. Note. 純 高 equals. 頂 高 very
> high.

扯 起 篷 來 走 順 風

Ch'e ch'i p'eng lai tsou shun feng.

> To enjoy good luck. *Lit.* To hoist the sail before a fair
> wind.

那 怕 你 一 筆 抒 破 天

Na p'a ni i pi shu p'o t'ien.

> Who fears that your pen will pierce the sky?

掃 塲 結 大 瓜

Shao ch'ang chieh ta kua.

> A sudden return of luck. *Lit.* The swept area produces
> a large melon.

睡 錯 搖 籮，脫 錯 了 胎

Shui ts'o yao lo, t'o ts'o liao t'ai.

> Born unlucky. *Lit.* You have slept in the wrong
> cradle, and issued from the wrong womb.

運 去 金 成 鐵, 時 來 鐵 似 金

Yün ch'ü chin ch'eng t'ieh shih lai t'ieh ssǔ chin.

> With no luck, gold becomes iron ; in luck, iron resembles gold.

黃 河 尚 有 澄 淸 日, 豈 可 人 無 得 運 時

Huang ho shang yu teng ch'ing jih, ch'i k'o jên wu tê yün shih.

> Even the Yellow River has its clear days ; is there a man who hasn't luck sometimes. ?

貧 無 達 士 持 金 贈, 病 有 高 人 說 藥 方

P'in wu ta shih ch'ih chin tsêng, ping yu kao jên shuo yao fang.

> The poor have no wise friend to succour them ; but the sick have some noble friend to tell them of a remedy.

屋 漏 更 遭 連 夜 雨, 行 船 又 遇 打 頭 風

Wu lou keng tsao lien yeh yü, hsing ch'uan yu yü ta t'ou fêng.

> The leaky house has a succession of rainy nights ; and the boat often beats against unfavourable winds.

各 人 名 下 一 重 天

Ko jên ming hsia i ch'ung t'ien.

> Under each man's name is his own fortune. Note. *Lit.* One storey or division of heaven.

酸 甜 苦 辣 都 嘗 過

Suan t'ien k'u la tu ch'ang kuo.

> Sour, sweet, bitter, pungent, all must be tasted.

天 有 不 測 風 雲, 人 有 旦 夕 禍 福

T'ien yu pu ts'e fêng yün, jên yu tan hsi huo fu.

> The fortunes of men are as uncertain as the winds and clouds of heaven.

善 游 者 溺·善 騎 者 墮

Shan yu chê ni, shan ch'i chê to.

> Good swimmers are sometimes drowned ; good riders are sometimes thrown.

時 來 逢 好 友, 運 去 遇 佳 人

Shih lai fêng hao yu, yün ch'ü yü chia jên.

> In luck, one meets a friend; out of luck, one meets a fair lady.

撥 開 浮 雲 見 青 天

Po k'ai fou yün chien ch'ing t'ien.

When the floating clouds are dispersed we see the clear sky.

兩 干 不 雜

Liang kan pu tsa.

His horoscope is lucky. *Lit.* The two stems don't disagree. Note. 天 干 The " Stems " are the ten characters called T'ien Kan, or Heavenly Stems which with the twelve Ti Chih 地 支 or Earthly Branches are used to form the name of the sixty years of the Chinese cycle.

眼 睛 跳 晦 氣 到

Yen ching t'iao hui ch'i tao.

When the eyes twitch it is a sign of bad luck coming.

馬 有 千 里 之 志, 非 人 不 能 自 往, 人 有 凌 雲 之 志, 非 運 不 能 亨 通

Ma yu ch'ien li chih chih, fei jên pu neng tzǔ wang, jên yu ling yün chih chih fei yün pu neng heng t'ung.

A horse may be able to run a thousand li, but without a rider it can't go ; a man may have a great ambition, but without luck he cannot be successful. Great ambition. *Lit.* A cloud-scaling determination.

狂 風 單 打 下 風 人

K'uang fêng tan ta hsia fêng jên.

A raging wind only strikes those who are in it.

有 朝 一 日 時 運 轉, 富 貴 榮 華 天 降 來

Yu chao i jih shih yün chuan, fu kuei jung hua t'ien chiang lai.

A day will come when luck will change and Heaven will send down wealth and honour.

破 帆 遇 順 風

P'o fan yü shun fêng.

A poor fellow in luck's way. *Lit.* A ragged sail in a fair wind.

甘 羅 十 二 受 秦 恩，太 公 八 十 食 周 祿

Kan Lo shih erh shou Ch'in en, T'ai Kung pa shih Chou lu.

> Kan Lo enjoyed the favour of the state of Ch'in at the age of twelve; T'ai Kung was eighty when he received the emoluments of Chou. Note. Kan Lo was a precocious boy minister who at the age of twelve was entrusted with important diplomatic messages to other princes. Chiang T'ai Kung or Chiang Tzu Ya was a noted statesman under Wen Wang who was called to his position in old age.

一 舉 兩 得
一 舉 兩 便

I chü liang tê or i chü liang pien.

> " To kill two birds with one stone."

一 弓 搭 兩 箭

I kung ta liang chien,

> To shoot two arrows at once.

稻 草 包 珍 珠

Tao ts'ao pao chen chu.

> A pearl wrapped up in straw. Note. Said of able or learned persons whose ill luck it is to live unnoticed and unknown.

選 日 不 如 撞 日

Hsien jih pu ju chuang jih.

> A chance day is better than a chosen one.

瞎 雞 公 撞 米 頭

Hsia chi kung chuang mi t'ou.

> Chance luck. *Lit.* A blind cock chancing on grain

修 橋 補 路 雙 瞎 眼，殺 人 放 火 得 長 命

Hsiu ch'iao pu lu shuang hsia yen, sha jên fang huo tê ch'ang ming.

> He who repairs bridges and mends the public roads becomes blind in both eyes; the assassin and incendiary enjoy long life. Note. This of course is ironical,

看 命 先 生 半 路 死，地 理 先 生 無 處 埋

K'an ming hsien sheng pan lu ssŭ, ti li hsien sheng wu ch'ü mai.

> The fortune-teller dies in the prime of life; the geomancer has no burying place.

Chapter 3. Opportunity.

時 不 至 來 運 不 通，行 船 又 遇 擋 頭 風

Shih pu chih lai yün pu t'ung, hsing chuan yu yü tang t'ou fêng.

> Until the times favour you, you will have no luck ; every time your boat sails it will be against head winds

因 風 吹 火，用 力 不 多

Yin feng ch'ui huo, yung li pu to.

> When the wind blows the fire you need not do it.

近 官 得 貴，近 厨 得 食

Chin kuan tê kuei, chin ch'ü tê shih.

> Those near an official get honour; those near a kitchen, food.

當 取 不 取，過 後 莫 悔

Tang ch'ü pu ch'ü kuo hou mo hui.

> He who neglects a good opportunity, must not complain afterwards.

馬 到 臨 崖 收 韁 晚，禍 至 頭 來 悔 不 及

Ma tao lin yai shou chiang wan, huo chih t'ou lai hui pu chi.

> When the horse is on the brink of the precipice it is too late to pull the reins ; when calamity is upon you, repentance is too late.

籠 內 雞 綱 內 魚 手 到 全 拿

Lung nei chi wang nei yü shou tao ch'ien na.

> Fowls in a hencoop and fishes in a net, can all be caught with the hand.

陽 溝 裡 篾 片 也 有 翻 身 日

Yang kou li mieh p'ien yeh yu fan shen jih.

> Opportunity comes to all. *Lit.* There comes a day when the bits of bamboo in the gutter turn over.

英 雄 無 用 武 之 處

Ying hsiung wu yung wu chih ch'ü.

> A hero without the opportunity of displaying his bravery.

近水樓臺先得月，向陽花木早逢春

Chin shui lou t'ai hsien tê yüeh, hsiang yang hua mu tsao fêng ch'ün.

> Enjoying good opportunities. *Lit.* A water-side tower
> first catches the moon ; trees and flowers in the sun
> earliest meet the spring.

少壯不努力，老大徒傷悲

Shao chuang pu nu li, lao ta t'u shang pei.

> Laziness in youth means sorrow in old age.

一年之計在於春，
一日之計在於寅，
一家之計在於和，
一生之計在於勤

I nien chih chi tsai yü ch'ün, i jih chih chi tsai yü yin,
i chia chih chi tsai yü ho, i shen chih chi tsai yü ch'in.

> A year's opportunities depend on the spring; a day's, on
> the dawn ; a family's, on harmony and a life's, on
> industry.

但有綠楊堪繫馬，處處有路透長安

Tan yu lu yang k'an chi ma, ch'ü ch'ü yu lu t'ou Ch'ang An.

> If you have but a green poplar you can tie your horse
> to it ; all roads lead to the capital. Note. Chang
> An the modern Sian Fu in Shensi was the capital
> during the early years of the Christian era.

條條大路通北京

T'iao t'iao ta lu t'ung Pei Ching.

> Every high road leads to Peking.

船到江心補漏遲

Ch'uan tao chiang hsin pu loü ch'ih

> When the boat has reached the middle of the river it is
> too late to stop the leak.

順風吹火，下水行船

Shun feng ch'ui huo, hsia shui hsing ch'uan.

> A fair wind fans the flame ; the boat glides with the
> stream.

殺人不死反爲仇

Sha jên pu ssŭ fan wei ch'ou.

> If you do not kill a man outright he will always remain
> your enemy.

借 風 過 河
Chieh fêng kuo ho.

To avail oneself of the wind to cross the river.

熱 竈 裏 着 把 火
Jo tsao li cho pa huo

To light a fire in a hot stove.

打 鐵 趁 熱
Ta t'ieh kan jo.

Strike while the iron is hot.

見 幾 而 作
Chien chi êrh tso.

Act, when you see an opportunity.

遇 貴 人 吃 飽 飯·遇 宰 相 穿 朝 衣
Yü kuei jên ch'ih pao fan, yü tsai hsiang ch'uan ch'ao i.

Meet a nobleman and you will get a good meal ; meet a
statesman and you will wear court dress.

瓜 熟 自 落
Kua shu tzŭ lo.

When the melon is ripe it will drop of itself.

快 刀 打 豆 腐 兩 面 光
K'uai tao ta tou fu liang mien kuang.

One whom opportunity serves to please all parties. *Lit.*
A sharp knife cuts bean-curd leaving both sides
smooth.

遇 飲 酒 時 須 飲 酒，得 高 歌 處 且 高 歌
Yü yin chiu shih hsü yin chiu, tê kao ko ch'ü ch'ieh kao ko.

Drink wine at the proper time ; sing aloud when in a
suitable place.

休 別 有 魚 處 莫 戀 淺 灘 頭
Hsiu pieh yu yü ch'ü, mo lien ch'ien t'an t'ou.

Don't leave a spot when there is fish ; and hanker after
a place of shallow rapids.

差一步差一途

Ch'a i pu ch'a i t'u.

> A miss is as good as a mile. *Lit.* Less one step, less
> the ferry.

吃了清水白米飯，江塘邊沿來救人

Ch'ih liao ch'ing shui pai mi fan, chiang t'ang pien yen lai chiu
jên.

> Wasted abilities. *Lit.* You have eaten white rice boiled
> in pure water and all you do is to stroll on the river
> bank with a view to saving life.

時勿際運勿通，手揑黃金變白銅

Shih wu chi yün wu t'ung shou nieh hüang chin pien pai t'ung.

> Losing hold of opportunities is like gold turning to white
> brass in your hand.

苦海無邊，回頭是岸

K'u hai wu pien, hui t'ou shih an.

> A bitter unbounded sea, turn your head and there is the
> shore, i.e. Reform while you have the chance.

白日莫閒過，青春不再來

Pai jih mo hsien kuo, ch'ing ch'ün pu tsai lai,

> Don't pass the days in idleness; youth will not return

SECTION X. THE FIVE RELATIONS.

Chapter. 1. Prince and Minister.

身 在 皇 帝 邊，猶 如 共 虎 眠

Shen tsai huang ti pien, yu ju kung hu mien.

> To attend on the Emperor, is like sleeping with a tiger.

只 有 臣 諫 君，沒 有 君 諫 臣 之 禮

Chih yu ch'en chien chün, mu yu chün chien ch'en chih li.

> The minister admonishes the Prince, not the Prince the minister.

君 不 正 臣 逃 外 國

Chün pu cheng ch'en t'ao wai kuo.

> When the Prince is not upright, ministers fly abroad.

天 上 衆 星 皆 拱 北，世 間 無 水 不 朝 東

T'ien shang chung hsing chieh kung pei, shih chien wu shui pu ch'ao tung.

> All the stars of heaven salute the north; every stream flows towards the east. i.e. The Emperor is the centre of attraction.

一 朝 天 子 一 朝 臣

I ch'ao t'ien tzŭ i ch'ao ch'en.

> The ministers of every dynasty will be like the emperors of that dynasty.

君 要 臣 死 臣 就 死

Chün yao ch'en ssŭ ch'en chiu ssŭ.

> When the prince wants a minister to die, he dies.

朝 廷 無 強 官 之 法

Ch'ao t'ing wu ch'iang kuan chih fa.

> The emperor cannot force men to be magistrates.

衆 星 朗 朗 不 如 孤 月 獨 明

Chung hsing lang lang pu ju ku yueh tu ming.

> The brilliance of all the stars is not equal to that of the moon, i.e. The Emperor excels all others.

國 正 天 心 順，官 清 民 自 安

Kuo cheng t'ien hsin shun, kuan ch'ing min tzŭ an.

> When the kingdom is governed properly, Heaven remains
> complacent; when the officials are upright the people
> are naturally at peace.

聖 天 子 百 靈 相 助

Sheng t'ien tzŭ pai ling hsiang chu.

> All divine influences combine to support an enlightened
> Emperor.

天 子 犯 法 與 民 同 罪

T'ien tzŭ fan fa yü min t'ung tsui.

> If the emperor breaks the law he is an offender like every
> one else.

忠 臣 視 死 無 難 色，節 婦 臨 危 有 笑 容

Chung ch'en shih ssŭ wu nan sê, chieh fu lin wei yu hsiao jung.

> A faithful minister views death unappalled; a virtuous
> woman faces danger with a smile.

忠 臣 不 怕 死，怕 死 不 忠 臣

Chung ch'en pu p'a ssŭ, p'a ssŭ pu chung ch'en:

> A loyal minister is not afraid of death; he who is, is not
> a loyal minister.

伴 君 如 同 羊 伴 虎，一 點 不 到 有 損 傷

Pan chün ju t'ung yang pan hu, i tien pu tao yu sun shang.

> One attends a prince as a sheep a tiger; the slightest
> shortcoming means punishment.

私 臣 不 忠，忠 臣 不 私

Ssŭ ch'en pu chung, chung ch'en pu ssŭ.

> A corrupt minister is not loyal; a loyal minister cannot
> be corrupted.

求 忠 臣 必 入 孝 子 之 門

Ch'iu chung ch'en pi ju hsiao tzŭ chih men.

> You must look for loyal ministers amongst filial sons.

好 馬 不 背 雙 鞍，忠 臣 不 事 二 主

Hao ma pu pei shuang an, chung ch'en pu shih erh chu.

> A good horse cannot wear two saddles, nor a loyal
> minister serve two masters.

君 猶 盃 也, 民 猶 水 也, 盃 方 水 方, 盃 圓 水 圓

Chün yu pei yeh min yu shui yeh, pei fang shui fang pei yüan shui yüan.

> The Prince is the cup, the people are the water; and the water takes the shape of the cup.

王 不 出 頭 誰 作 主

Wang pu ch'u t'ou shui tso wang.

> If the sovereign is not higher than others who would rule? Note. This is a play on the characters 王 and 主, the latter having the dot which gives it the "protruding head" as literally described.

滿 天 星 獨 靠 一 輪 月

Man t'ien hsing tu k'ao i lun yüeh.

> All the stars in the sky depend on the one moon, i.e., The whole Empire depends on its ruler.

天 無 二 日, 民 無 二 王

T'ien wu erh jih, min wu erh wang.

> There are not two suns in the sky nor can there be two rulers of the people.

春 震 帝 王 生, 冬 震 帝 王 崩

Ch'ün chen ti wang sheng, tung chen ti wang pêng.

> An earthquake in spring portends the birth, in winter, the death of a prince.

人 君 如 堂, 羣 臣 如 陞

Jên chün ju t'ai, ch'ün ch'en ju chieh.

> The prince is the audience hall, the ministers the steps to it.

木 從 繩 則 正, 君 從 諫 則 聖

Mu ts'ung shêng tsê cheng, chün ts'ung chien tsê sheng.

> If the mark is followed the wood will the sawed straight; if the prince listens to his counsellors he will be a sage.

大 王 勿 貪 私 人 鬼 勿 怕

Ta wang wu t'an ssŭ jên kuei wu p'a.

> If the ruler is free from covetousness he fears neither men nor devils.

家貧出孝子,國亂見忠臣

Chia p'in ch'u hsiao tzŭ, kuo luan chien chung ch'en.

> Poor families produce filial sons ; a disordered empire discovers faithful ministers.

Chapter. 2. Parents and Children.

龍 生 龍,鳳 生 鳳,老 鼠 生 的 會 打 洞

Lung sheng lung feng sheng feng, lao shu sheng ti hui ta tung.

> Like father, like son. *Lit.* Dragons give birth to dragons ; phoenixes to phoenixes ; the new-born rat is able to gnaw a hole.

人 莫 知 其 子 之 惡,農 莫 知 其 苗 之 碩

Jěn mo chih chih tzŭ chih ô nung mo chih ch'i miao chih shih.

> Parents never know the faults of their children and farmers never know the richness of their crops.

要 得 小 兒 安,須 帶 三 分 饑 餓 寒

Yao tê hsiao êrh an hsü tai san fen chi ô han.

> If you seek the welfare of your children, let them experience a little cold and hunger.

田 要 親 耕,子 要 親 生

T'ien yao ch'in keng, tzŭ yao ch'in sheng.

> Fields are best when ploughed by yourself ; sons are best when they are your own.

他 養 我 小,我 養 他 老

T'a yang wo hsiao, wo yang t'a lao.

> He kept me in youth ; I support him in old age.

兒 大 爺 難 做

Erh ta yeh nan tso.

> When sons are grown up it is hard to control them.

水 總 是 往 下 流 的

Shui tsung shih wang hsia liu ti.

> Love always descends from parent to child. *Lit.* Water always flows downhill.

生 身 父 母 在 一 邊，養 身 父 母 大 如 天

Sheng shen fu mu tsai i pien, yang shen fu mu ta ju t'ien.

> Parents who only give us birth may be neglected; whilst those who rear us must be considered great as heaven.

好 兒 不 種 爺 田 地，好 女 不 穿 嫁 時 衣

Hao erh pu chung yeh t'ien ti, hao nü pu ch'uan chia shih i.

> Good sons do not live on the produce of their parents' fields; good daughters do not always wear their wedding dresses.

長 子 不 離 宗 堂，么 兒 不 離 娘 房

Chang tzǔ pu li tsung t'ang, yao erh pu li niang fang.

> The eldest son does not leave the ancestral home; the youngest does not leave his mother's room.

種 子 隔 年 留，兒 女 前 世 修

Chung tzǔ kê nien liu erh nü ch'ien shih hsiu.

> Seed corn is kept from former years; children are the result of merit in a former existence.

看 兒 歹 好，須 從 幼 小

K'an erh tai hao, hsü t'sung yu hsiao.

> You can tell whether your son will be good or bad from what he is as a child.

國 朝 盛 出 賢 臣，家 道 興 看 子 孫

Kuo ch'ao sheng ch'u hsien ch'en, chia tao hsing k'an tzǔ sun.

> A prosperous dynasty produces virtuous statesmen; in a well-conducted home grandchildren will be seen.

一 樹 之 果 有 酸 有 甜，一 母 之 子 有 愚 有 賢

I shu chih kuo yu suan yu t'ien, i mu chih tzǔ yu yü yu hsien.

> Of the fruit of a tree, some may be sour and some sweet; of the children of one mother some may be stupid and some virtuous.

子 孫 無 福，賴 墳 賴 屋

Tzǔ sun wu fu lai fen lai wu.

> When a man's descendants are not prosperous it is owing to the grave or the house being in an unlucky position.

嬌 兒 不 孝,嬌 狗 上 竈
Chiao erh pu hsiao, chiao kou shang tsao.

> A spoilt child is unfilial; a spoilt dog steals the dinner.

父 不 仁,子 奔 他 鄉
Fu pu jên, tzǔ pen t'a hsiang.

> When the father is unkind the son flies to a distant locality.

父 慈 子 孝,子 孝 媳 賢
Fu tz'ǔ tzǔ hsiao, tzǔ hsiao hsi hsien.

> If the father is kind the son will be filial ; if the son is filial the son's wife will be virtuous.

養 兒 不 知 娘 辛 苦
Yang erh pu chih niang hsin k'u.

> The child knows not what trouble it has given its mother.

養 得 兒 早 享 得 福 早
Yang tê erh tsao hsiang tê fu tsao.

> Youthful parents enjoy happiness early.

兒 多 母 苦
Êrh to mu k'u.

> When children are numerous the mother suffers.

荒 年 不 養 兒,稼 熟 無 兒 用
Huang nien pu yang erh, chia shu wu erh yung.

> If in lean years you cannot rear children ; when there is harvest you will have none to render assistance.

生 個 兒 一 幸,生 個 女 一 悶
Sheng ko erh i hsin, sheng ko nü i men.

> It is a blessing to bear a son; a calamity to bear a daughter.

接 一 個 媳 婦 賣 一 個 兒
Chieh i ko hsi fu mai i ko êrh.

> Receiving a daughter-in-law and selling a son. Note. The case supposed is that of a young man being so enamoured of his wife as to neglect the duties of filial piety.

兒 大 必 發, 女 大 必 塌

Êrh ta pi fa, nü ta pi t'a.

> When the son is grown up he will make money; when the daughter is grown up she will use it. Note. The money will probably be used by the parents in buying fine clothes, etc., for the young lady.

男 跑 一 貴 女 跑 一 賤

Nan p'ao i kuei nü p'ao i chien.

> A runaway son retains respectability; a runaway daughter, loses it.

屋 簷 溝 裏 水 點 點 滴 在 舊 窩 裏

Wu yen kou li shui tien tien ti tsai chiu wo li.

> The same as above. *Lit.* Water always drops from the eaves into the same old holes.

寵 妻 別 母 子 不 孝, 替 兒 嫌 妻 母 不 賢

Ch'ung ch'i pieh mu tzǔ pu hsiao, t'i erh hsien ch'i mu pu hsien.

> The son is unfilial who loves his wife more than his mother; the mother is not good who joins the son in hating his wife.

送 老 歸 山 纔 是 兒, 穿 破 綾 羅 纔 是 衣

Sung lao kuei shan ts'ai shih erh, ch'uan p'o ling lo ts'ai shih i.

> He is really the son who lives long enough to bury his parents; silks and satins that are worn into holes are really clothes.

父 母 老 死 風 流 孝 子

Fu mu lao ssǔ feng liu hsiao tzǔ.

> When parents die in old age, dutiful sons may be merry.

嚴 父 出 孝 子

Yen fu ch'u hsiao tzǔ.

> Strict fathers have filial sons.

父 子 和 而 家 不 退, 兄 弟 和 而 家 不 分

Fu tzǔ ho erh chia pu t'ui, hsiung ti ho erh chia pu fen.

> When father and son agree the family will not fail; when brothers agree the family will not separate.

賭 錢 塲 上 無 父 子

Tu ch'ien ch'ang shang wu fu tzŭ.

> In a gambling house there are no fathers and sons.

後 人 不 好，連 累 上 人

Hou jen pu hao, lien lei shang jen.

> Bad descendants involve ancestors in disgrace. Note.
> A purely Chinese notion according to which the sins
> of descendants are charged upon ancestors; they
> must have committed some awful crime to cause
> their descendants thus to sin.

爹 娘 痛 的 順 心 兒

Tieh niang t'ung ti shun hsin erh.

> The parents' pet is the obedient child.

父 母 難 保 子 孫 賢

Fu mu nan pao tzŭ sun hsien.

> Parents cannot guarantee that their children will be
> virtuous.

父 要 子 亡，子 不 留

Fu yao tzŭ wang, tzŭ pu liu.

> When the father wants his son to die, he dies.

父 在 子 不 敢 自 專

Fu tzai tzŭ pu kan tzŭ chuan.

> Whilst the father lives the son dare not assert himself.

棍 棒 頭 上 出 好 子，嬌 疼 嬌 養 忤 逆 兒

Kun pang t'ou shang ch'u hao tzŭ, chiao t'eng chiao yang wu ni erh.

> Spare the rod, spoil the child. _Lit._ The end of the rod
> produces a good child ; petting and spoiling result in
> a disobedient son.

好 爹 媽 好 親 事，好 兒 女 好 葬 事

Hao tieh ma hao ch'in shih, hao erh nü hao tsang shih.

> Good parents will see that their children marry well ;
> good children will see that their parents have decent
> burial.

虎 生 三 子 必 有 一 豹，人 生 三 子 必 有 一 貴

Hu sheng san tzǔ pi yu i pao, jen sheng san tzǔ pi yu i kuei.

> When a tiger has three cubs at a birth, one of them will
> be a leopard; when a man has three boys at a birth
> one of them will be a distinguished person.

賣 子 莫 摩 頭，摩 頭 眼 淚 流

Mai tzǔ mo mo t'ou, mo t'ou yen lei liu.

> When selling a son do not stroke his head; if you do,
> your tears will flow.

孝 順 還 生 孝 順 子，忤 逆 還 生 忤 逆 兒

Hsiao shun huan sheng hsiao shün tzǔ wu ni huan sheng wu ni erh.

> Dutiful sires beget dutiful sons; undutiful sires beget
> undutiful children.

養 兒 方 知 父 母 恩

Yang erh fang chih fu mu en.

> You must rear children yourself to understand your
> parents' love.

有 兒 靠 兒，無 兒 靠 婿

Yu erh k'ao erh, wu erh k'ao hsü.

> He who has a son must depend on him; he who has not,
> must depend on his son-in-law.

子 孫 勝 似 我，要 錢 做 甚 麼，養 兒 不 如 我，要 錢 做 甚 麼

Tzǔ sun sheng ssu wo, yaŏ ch'ien tso shen mo, yang erh pu ju wo,
yao ch'ien tso shen mo

> If my descendants surpass me, why should I want money
> if they be inferior to me, still why should I do so?

莫 把 眞 心 空 計 較，兒 孫 自 由 兒 孫 福

Mo pa chen hsin k'ung chi chiao, erh sun tzu yu erh sun fu

> Do not spend your honest wit in fruitless scheming; your
> children will get their share of happiness.

但 存 方 寸 地，留 與 子 孫 耕

Tan ts'un fang ts'un ti, liu yü tzu sun keng.

> Reserve the square-inch plot for your descendants to till.
> Note. The "square-inch plot" is the heart, and
> the meaning is that parents must leave a good
> example to be followed by their children.

若 要 愛 子 敎 他 勤 儉

Jo yao ai tzǔ chiao t'a ch'in chien.

> Would you love your child, then teach him industry and temperance.

老 子 趕 兒 不 上 百 步

Lao tzǔ kan erh pu shang pai pu.

> When the father pursues the son with the rod, he must not follow him a hundred paces.

破 窰 出 好 瓦

P'o yao ch'u hao wa.

> The broken kiln may turn out good tiles.

憐 兒 多 與 棒·憎 兒 多 與 食

Lien erh to yü pang, tseng erh to yü shih.

> If you love your child, don't spare the rod; if you hate your child, give him plenty of dainties. Comp. Prov. 13, 24.

杵 頭 出 白 米,棒 頭 出 好 子

Ch'u t'ou ch'u pai mi, pang t'ou ch'u hao tzǔ.

> The pestle produces white rice, and the rod, good children.

父 母 言 語,忍 氣 吞 聲

Fu mu yen yü, jen ch'i t'un sheng.

> When parents chide, children must curb their tempers and hold their tongues.

男 大 避 母,女 大 避 父

Nan ta pi mu, nü ta pi fu.

> Grow up sons must separate from their mothers; grown up daughters from their fathers.

兒 孫 自 有 兒 孫 福,莫 與 兒 孫 作 馬 牛

Erh sun tzǔ yu erh sun fu, mo yü erh sun tso ma niu.

> Sons and grandsons have their destined pleasures; don't for their sakes toil like horses or oxen.

有 理 打 得 爺

Yu li ta tê yeh.

> With right on his side, even a son may correct a father.

在 家 敬 父 母 , 何 必 遠 燒 香

Tsai chia ching fu mu, ho pi yüan shao hsiang.

> Honour your parents at home, why go afar to burn
> incense? i.e. Piety begins at home.

各 人 皮 肉 各 人 疼

Ko jen p'i jou ko jen t'eng.

> Every man loves his own flesh and blood.

打 爺 罵 娘 出 自 本 心

Ta yeh ma niang ch'u tzu pen hsin.

> A man shows his disposition when he strikes his father
> or curses his mother.

浪 子 回 頭 無 價 之 寶

Lang tzu hui t'ou wu chia chih pao.

> A prodigal's repentance is a priceless treasure.

癡 男 勝 過 巧 女

Ch'ih nan sheng kuo ch'iao nü.

> A stupid son is better than a crafty daughter.

長 大 毛 乾 各 自 飛

Chang ta mao kan ko tzŭ fei.

> Full-fledged birds fly away.

好 子 不 要 多

Hao tzŭ pu yao to.

> If sons are filial, you don't want many.

新 娶 媳 婦 初 來 勤

Hsin ch'ü hsi fu ch'u lai ch'in.

> A new daughter-in-law is very diligent on her first arrival.

子 不 嫌 母 醜 , 狗 不 嫌 家 貧

Tzu pu hsien mu ch'ou, kou pu hsien chia p'in.

> A son does not take exception to his mother's ugliness ;
> a dog does not despise a home because of its poverty.

無 志 男 兒 , 把 祖 宗 誇

Wu chih nan erh, pu tsu tsung k'ua.

> Irresolute sons boast of their ancestors.

財帛動人心, 兒女痛人心

Ts'ai pai tʊng jen hsin, erh nü t'ung jen hsin.

Wealth excites men's minds; children awaken their affections.

有兒貧不久, 無子富不長

Yu erh p'in pu chiu, wu tzǔ fu pu ch'ang.

He who has sons cannot long remain poor; he who has none cannot long remain rich.

寧可養頑子, 不可養癡子

Ning k'o yang wan tzu, pʊ k'o yang ch'ih tzu.

Better rear a playful than a stupid child.

三年乳哺長懷抱, 長大成人各自開

San nien ju pu ch'ang huai pao, chang ta ch'eng jen ko tzû k'ai.

Children whom the mother suckled for three years leave her when grown to man's estate.

有兒有女是冤家, 無兒無女是仙家

Yu erh yu nü shih yuan chia, wu erh wu nü shih hsien chia.

It is an unfortunate family where there are sons and daughters; it is a blissful family where there are none. Note. Literally a "fairy" family. This proverb may be quoted in jocular reply to congratulation by the father of a large family.

有錢無子非是貴, 有子無錢非是貧

Yu ch'ien wu tzu fei shih kuei, yu tzǔ wu ch'ien fei shih p'in.

He is not rich who has money but no children; he is not poor who has children but no money.

不患父不慈, 子賢親自樂

Pu huan fu pu tzu, tzu hsien ch'in tzu lê

Don't fear that your father won't love you; for when children are virtuous, parents are naturally glad.

要求順子, 先孝爹娘

Yao ch'iu shun tzǔ, hsien hsiao tieh niang,

If you wish for dutiful children, first shew filial piety to your own parents.

十 個 指 頭 有 長 短

Shih ko chih t'ou yu ch'ang tuan.

> Among the ten fingers there are long and short ones.
> Note. This indicates the various dispositions of
> children.

一 娘 生 九 子 九 子 各 別

I niang sheng chiu tzu chiu tzŭ ko pieh.

> Of the nine sons of one mother, each has his own peculiar
> temperament.

孩 不 離 娘，瓜 不 離 穰

Hai pu li niang, kua pu li jang.

> A child cannot leave its mother any more than a melon
> leave the stalk.

孩 子 往 外 走，帶 着 娘 的 手

Hai tzŭ wang wai tsou, tai cho niang ti shou.

> When a child goes out it carries with it the impression
> of the mother's hand. i.e. It reflects the mother's
> personal care.

閨 女 大 了，似 私 鹽 包

Kuei nü ta liao, ssŭ ssŭ yen pao.

> An unmarried daughter is like a package of smuggled
> salt, i.e., a dangerous possession.

十 分 精 明 使 九 分，留 着 一 分 給 子 孫

Shih fen ching ming shih chiu fen, liu cho i fen chi tzŭ sun.

> Use only nine parts of your shrewdness, reserve one part
> for the benefit of your children

有 錢 不 買 張 口 貨

Yu ch'ien pu mai chang k'ou huo.

> Those who have money don't spend it to buy families.
> *Lit.* Open-mouthed goods, i.e., mouths to feed.

兒 女 乃 是 眼 前 歡

Êrh nü nai shih yen ch'ien huan.

> Children are present joys.

十 八 個 羅 漢 女 趕 不 上 個 點 脚 的 兒

Shih pa ko lo han nü kan pu shang ko tien chiao ti êrh.

Eighteen gifted daughters are not equal to one lame son.
Note. The 十 八 羅 漢 are the eighteen personal
disciples of Buddha, the images of which are to be
seen in Chinese temples. 羅 漢 equals the Sanskrit
Arhan or Arhat means estimable, worthy, etc.

小 兒 的 心 似 佛 心

Hsiao erh ti hsin ssŭ fu hsin.

The heart of a little child is like the heart of Buddha.

養 兒 原 爲 防 備 老

Yang erh yüan wei fang pei lao.

To bring up children is to provide against old age.

世 人 都 曉 神 仙 好，只 有 兒 孫 忘 不 了
癡 心 父 母 古 來 多，孝 順 子 孫 誰 見 了

Shih jên tu hsiao shen hsien hao, chih yu êrh sun wang pu liao
ch'ih hsin fu mu ku lai to, hsiao shun tzŭ sun shui chien liao.

Men all know that the life of gods and genii is ideal, but
they can't forego the desire for children. From
ancient times there have been doting parents, but
who ever has seen dutiful children?

慣 子 如 殺 子

Kuan tzŭ ju sha tzŭ.

To spoil a child is to kill him.

少 一 般 不 成 世 界

Shao i pan pu ch'eng shih kai.

Minus one sort, there can't be a world, i.e. You need
both sons and daughters.

子 孫 賢 要 錢 何 用，子 孫 不 賢 要 錢 何 用

Tzŭ sun hsien yao ch'ien ho yung, tzŭ sun pu hsien yao ch'ien ho
yung.

If your sons and grandsons are virtuous why do you need
money; if they are bad what use will money be?

好 男 勿 吃 分 開 飯，好 女 勿 著 嫁 裝 衣

Hao nan wu ch'ih fen k'ai fan, hao nü wu cho chia chuang i.

A good son will not use his allotted portion, neither will
a good daughter wear her marriage clothes.

祖 宗 積 德 好 兒 孫 戴 紗 帽

Tsu tsung chi tê hao erh sun tai sha mao.

If the ancestors accumulated virtue, the descendants will wear the gauze hat. Note. The gauze hat was worn by officials under the Ming Dynasty.

好 笋 出 在 笆 外

Hao sun ch'u tsai pa wai.

Good bamboo shoots springing up outside the fence. i.e. Good daughters who will be married and leave home.

爹 娘 完 全，兒 女 值 錢

Tieh niang wan ch'üan, erh nü chih ch'ien.

When both parents are living the children are highly esteemed.

好 兒 孫 勿 用 勞 起 屋

Hao erh sun wu yung lao ch'i wu.

Those who have good children need not struggle to build a house for them (they will build it themselves).

有 子 原 是 命，無 子 天 註 定

Yu tzŭ yüan shih ming, wu tzu t'ien chu ting.

To have children is the decree of destiny ; to have no children is also fixed by Heaven.

生 不 奉 養 死 祭 無 益

Sheng pu fêng yang, ssŭ chi wu i.

If a man does not support his parents in their lifetime; after death to sacrifice to them will be useless.

Chapter 3. Husbands and Wives.

兒 討 媳 婦 女 招 郎，人 在 世 間 鬧 一 塲

Erh t'ao hsi fu nü chao lang, jen tsai shih chien nao i ch'ang.

The one thing for which people are striving every day is to secure wives for their sons and husbands for their daughters.

結 親 如 結 義, 兩 家 莫 生 氣
Chieh ch'in ju chieh i, liang chia mo sheng ch'i.

> Arranging marriages is like forming friendships; neither side is averse to it.

門 當 戶 對, 兩 下 成 婚 配
Men tang hu tui, liang hsia ch'eng hun p'ei.

> When families are of equal social rank, marriages may be arranged between them. Note. Literally, when doorways are opposite each other.

女 兒 說 人 家 過 細 訪 查
Nü êrh shuo jên chia kuo hsi fang ch'a.

> In betrothing a daughter it is necessary to make very careful enquiries.

夫 妻 愛 好 同 偕 到 老
Fu ch'i ai hao t'ung chieh tao lao.

> When true love exists between husband and wife, they remain united unto old age.

擡 頭 嫁 女, 低 頭 接 媳 婦
T'ai t'ou chia nü, ti t'ou chieh hsi fu.

> If they raise their heads high in marrying their daughter; bow your head low in receiving her as a daughter-in-law.

好 妻 無 好 漢, 天 下 一 大 半,
好 漢 無 好 妻, 天 下 一 大 堆
Hao ch'i wu hao han, t'ien hsia i ta pan, hao han wu hao ch'i t'ien hsia i ta tui.

> Most of the good wives in the empire have bad husbands; and most of the good husbands in the empire have bad wives.

公 不 離 婆, 稱 不 離 鉈
Kung pu li p'o, ch'eng pu li t'o.

> The husband cannot do without the wife any more than the steelyard can do without the weight.

結 髮 夫 妻 醜 也 好，粗 布 縫 衣 衣 也 牢

Chieh fa fu ch'i ch'ou yeh hao, ts'u pu fêng i i yeh lao.

> An old couple united from childhood may be ugly, but that doesn't matter : coarse cloth often makes good strong clothes. Note. Chieh Fa, indicates the knotting up of the hair in childhood.

嫁 壞 人 葬 壞 墳

Chia huai jên tsang huai fen.

> For a woman to be married to a bad man, is like being buried in a luckless tomb.

過 婚 嫂 連 夜 討

Kuo hun sao lien yeh t'ao.

> Widow marriage must be immediately consummated. Note. If not, the widow may demand a higher price, or accept some one else's higher bid.

死 了 前 夫 嫁 後 夫，一 步 高 一 步

Ssŭ liao ch'ien fu chia hou fu, i pu kao i pu.

> Having lost a first husband and married a second, she has risen each step.

娶 妻 娶 德，娶 妾 娶 色

Ch'ü ch'i ch'ü tê, ch'ü ch'ieh ch'ü sê.

> A man marries a wife for her virtue, a concubine, for her beauty.

公 婆 嫌 還 猶 可，丈 夫 嫌 無 處 躲

Kung p'o hsien huan yu k'o, chang fu hsien wu ch'u to.

> A woman need not fear the dislike of her husband's parents, but there is no escaping the displeasure of her husband.

有 福 之 女 不 落 無 福 之 家

Yu fu chih nü pu lo wu fu chih chia.

> The well-to-do maiden is not married into a poverty stricken family.

男 大 須 婚 女 大 須 嫁

Nan ta hsü hun, nü ta hsü chia.

> Sons and daughters should marry as soon as they are grown up.

會 做 媒 的 罵 兩 頭，不 會 做 媒 的 兩 頭 罵

Hui tso mei ti ma liang t'ou, pu hui tso mei ti liang t'ou ma.

A clever-match-maker can scold both sides; while a
stupid match-maker gets scolded by both.

養 女 不 嫁 讀 書 郎，朝 朝 夜 夜 守 空 房，
有 那 一 日 時 運 到，又 要 討 過 小 婆 娘

Yang nü pu chia tu shu lang, chao chao yeh yeh shou k'ung fang,
yu na i jih shih yün tao, yu yao t'ao kuo hsiao p'o niang.

If you rear a daughter do not marry her to a literary man,
lest day and night she be left alone in the house.
It also may happen that he has a stroke of luck, and
then he will bring home a concubine.

好 漢 不 養 十 八 女

Hao han pu yang shih pa nü.

A wise man does not keep a daughter over eighteen
under his care.

不 怕 姐 兒 生 得 醜，只 怕 媒 人 開 了 口

Pu p'a chieh erh sheng tê ch'ou, chih p'a mei jen k'ai liao k'ou.

Care not that the young lady is ugly, only fear lest the
match-makers should tell the secret.

養 女 望 高 門

Yang nü wang kao men.

Those who rear daughters hope for great suitors.

上 等 之 人 陪 錢 嫁 女，中 等 之 人 養 女 嫁 女，下
等 之 人 賺 錢 嫁 女

Shang teng chih jen p'ei ch'ien chia nü, chung teng chih jen yang
nü chia nü, hsia teng chih jen chuan ch'ien chia nü.

The upper classes endow their daughters on marriage;
the middle classes do nothing but rear and marry
them; and the lower classes make money by
marrying them.

天 上 無 雲 不 下 雨，地 下 無 媒 不 成 親

T'ien shang wu yün pu hsia yü, ti hsia wu mei pu ch'eng ch'in.

Without clouds in the sky it cannot rain; so without
go-betweens a match cannot be made.

一 家 養 女 百 家 求

I chia yang nü pai chia ch'iu.

> When one family rears a daughter a hundred families ask her in marriage.

種 田 不 好 一 時 窮,討 壞 老 婆 一 生 窮

Chung t'ien pu hao i shih ch'iuug, t'ao huai lao p'o i sheng ch'iung.

> Negligent farming may bring temporary poverty, but a mistake in marrying may bring poverty for life.

十 媒 九 誆

Shih mei chiu k'uang.

> Nine out of ten go-betweens are liars.

吃 菜 吃 油 鹽 娶 妾 娶 容 顏

Ch'i ts'ai ch'i yu yen, ch'ü ch'ieh ch'ü jung yen,

> You expect condiments with vegetables; a pretty face with a concubine.

葬 墳 還 可 起,擇 婿 不 可 悔

Tsang fen huan k'o ch'i tsê hsü pu k'o hui.

> You may exhume a coffin, but you may not reject a betrothed son-in-law.

婚 姻 勸 攏,禍 患 勸 開

Hun yin ch'üan lung, huo huan ch'üan k'ai.

> Matrimony, exhort men to complete; strifes, exhort men to put away.

人 倫 有 五 夫 婦 爲 先,大 禮 三 千 婚 姻 最 重

Jen lun yu wu fu fu wei hsien, ta li san ch'ien hun yin tsui chung.

> There are the Five Relationships, and that of husband and wife stands first; there are three thousand Rites, and that of marriage is the most important. Note. The Five Relationships are generally given in the following order, viz., Prince and Minister, Parents and Children, Husband and Wife, Elder and Younger Brothers, and Friends. But in the Yi Ching the relationship of husband and wife stands first hence this saying.

夫 爲 妻 之 綱 夫 正 妻 亦 良

Fu wei ch'i chih kang, fu cheng ch'i i liang.

> The husband is the wife's pattern ; when he is upright, she is good. Note. The word "kang" which originally means the long rope that binds the meshes of a fishing net, signifies that which regulates or reduces to order.

前 世 有 緣 今 世 結

Ch'ien shih yu yüan chin shih chieh.

> Marriage results from ante-natal causes.

夫 以 義 爲 良，婦 以 順 爲 正

Fu i i wei liang, fu i shun wei cheng.

> In the husband, fidelity is the thing that is good ; in the wife, obedience is the thing that is proper.

夫 妻 本 是 同 林 鳥，大 限 到 來 各 自 飛

Fu ch'i pen shih t'ung lin niao, ta hsien tao lai ko tzŭ fei.

> Husband and wife are indeed birds of one grove ; but at the bourn of death each flies away.

癩 痢 討 花 枝

La li t'ao hua chih.

> Ugly men marry pretty wives. *Lit.* Scabbed-heads get flowery boughs.

生 成 一 對，紐 成 一 雙

Sheng ch'eng i tui, niu ch'eng i shuang.

> If they match by nature, couple them by marrying.

夫 妻 相 好 合，琴 瑟 與 笙 簧

Fu ch'i hsiang hao, ch'in sê yu sheng huang.

> Husband and wife in perfect concord, are like the music of the harp and lute.

夫 唱 婦 隨

Fu ch'ang fu sui.

> Conjugal felicity. Lit. The husband sings and the wife accompanies

馬 無 再 配, 人 有 重 婚

Ma wu tsai p'ei, jên wu ch'ung hun.

> Horses will not re-mate but men and women will re-marry.

翻 船 折 桅 一 時 窮, 討 壞 老 婆 一 生 窮

Fan ch'uan chê wei i shih ch'iung, t'ao huai lao p'o i sheng ch'iung.

> When a man's vessel is overturned and its masts broken, it means temporary poverty ; but if he marries a bad wife he may be poor for life.

癡 漢 怕 老 婆, 賢 女 敬 丈 夫

Ch'ih han p'a lao p'o, hsien nü ching chang fu.

> The fool fears his old woman, but a virtuous wife reverences her husband.

清 秀 才 郎 倒 配 不 良 之 婦, 乖 巧 女 子 反 招 愚 拙 之 夫

Ch'ing hsiu ts'ai lang tao p'ei pu liang chih fu, kuai ch'iao nü tzŭ fan chao yü chüeh chih fu.

> A talented bridegroom is sometimes matched with a worthless bride ; and a clever woman is sometimes betrothed to a dolt.

伴 人 合 不 可 伴 人 開

Pan jen ho pu k'o pan jen k'ai.

> When the two have been united they may not be separated.

夫 婦 恩 厚, 兒 女 情 長

Fu fu ên hou, erh nü ch'ing ch'ang.

> Loving husbands and wives enjoy the enduring affection of their sons and daughters.

只 許 男 大 一 層, 不 可 女 長 一 歲

Chih hsu nan ta i ts'eng, pu k'o nü ch'ang i sui.

> A man may be ten years older than his wife ; she must not be one year older than he.

男 無 妻 家 無 主, 女 無 夫 身 無 主

Nan wu ch'i chia wu chu, nü wu fu shen wu chu.

> A man without his wife has a home without a mistress ; a woman without a husband is without a protector.

夫 婦 不 和 奴 婢 欺

Fu fu pu ho nu pei ch'i.

> When husband and wife disagree they become the dupes of their slaves.

夫 乃 婦 之 天, 妻 乃 夫 之 奴

Fu nai fu chih t'ien, ch'i nai fu chih nu.

> Husbands are as Heaven to their wives; wives are the slaves of their husbands.

夫 妻 無 隔 夜 之 仇

Fu ch'i wu kê yeh chih ch'ou.

> Husband and wife have no enmities that can survive a night.

我 不 淫 人 婦, 人 不 淫 我 妻

Wo pu yin jên fu, jên pu yin wo ch'i.

> If I keep to my wife, others will keep to theirs.

好 漢 不 打 妻, 好 狗 不 咬 雞

Hao han pu ta ch'i hao kou pu yao chi.

> A good man will not beat his wife; a good dog will not worry a fowl.

莫 罵 酉 時 妻, 一 夜 受 孤 悽

Mo ma yu shih ch'i i yeh shou ku ch'i.

> Do not curse your wife in the evening, or you will have to sleep alone.

吃 醋 不 討 小

Ch'ih ts'u pu t'ao hsiao.

> If your wife is jealous do not get a concubine. Note. Literally " to drink vinegar ". This is a synonym for domestic unpleasantness caused through jealousy. It originated with the wife of Fang Hsuen Ling, 房 玄 齡 a noted minister of the Tang dynasty, who rather than receive a concubine into the house, took a bowl of vinegar, thinking it to be poison.

輕 家 雞 愛 野 雞

Ch'ing chia chi ai yeh chi.

> He detests his own wife and loves other women. *Lit.* He lightly esteems the domestic fowl, but loves the wild pheasant. "Yeh chi" is a common term for loose women.

華屋量人斗，嬌妻渡客船

Hua wu liang jen tou, chiao ch'i tu k'o ch'uan.

> Fine houses are skeps by which men are measured; pretty wives are ferry boats. Note. The moral of this proverb is neither covet fine houses nor pretty wives, for, out of the one you will be turned by death and after your death, the other will marry again.

枕邊之言莫聽

Chen pien chih yen mo t'ing.

> Take no notice of what you hear said on the pillow.

家花沒得野花香，野花沒得家花長

Chia hua mu te yeh hua hsiang, yeh hua mu tê chia hua ch'ang.

> Domestic flowers are not as fragrant as wild flowers, but wild flowers do not last so long.

賢婦令夫貴，惡婦令夫賤

Hsien fu ling fu kuei, ô fu ling fu chien.

> A virtuous wife brings honour to her husband; a bad one brings shame. Comp. Prov. 12. 4.

醜婦拙奴，無價之寶

Ch'ou fu chüeh nu, wu chia chih pao.

> Ugly wives and stupid maids are priceless treasures.

妻妾切忌艷妝

Ch'i ch'ieh ch'ieh chi yen chuang.

> Avoid gorgeously dressed wives or concubines.

家有賢妻，男人不遭橫事

Chia yu hsien ch'i, nan jen pu tsao heng shih.

> A virtuous wife saves her husband from evil ways.

強嘴婆娘只怕打

Ch'iang tsui p'o niang chih p'a ta.

> A wilful wife only fears a beating.

一家女兒吃不得兩家飯

I chia nä erh ch'ih pu tê liang chia fan.

> She who is wife to one man cannot eat the rice of two.

寡 婦 門 前 是 非 多

Kua fu men ch'ien shih fei to.

Slanders cluster round a widow's door.

穿 衣 見 父 母，脫 衣 見 丈 夫

Ch'uan i chien fu mu, t'o i chien chang fu.

In the presence of your parents be properly dressed ; in the presence of your husband undress will do.

起 早 了 得 罪 丈 夫，起 晏 了 得 罪 公 婆

Ch'i tsao liao tê tsui chang fu, ch'i yen liao tê tsui kung p'o.

If she rises early, she offends her husband ; if late, his father and mother.

有 福 死 夫 前，無 福 死 夫 後

Yu fu ssǔ fu ch'ien wu fu ssǔ fu hou.

Happy the wife who dies before her husband ; unhappy she who dies after him.

下 氣 小 心 纔 是 婦 女

Hsia ch'i hsiao hsin ts'ai shih fu nü.

Good tempered and careful,—she is a good wife indeed.

好 馬 不 吃 回 頭 草，好 妻 不 嫁 二 丈 夫

Hao ma pu ch'ih hui t'ou ts'ao, hao ch'i pu chia erh chang fu.

A good horse will not turn back to eat grass; a good wife will not marry a second husband.

忠 臣 不 事 二 君，貞 女 不 嫁 二 夫

Chung ch'en pu shih erh chün, chen nü pu chia erh fu.

A loyal minister will serve but one prince; a virtuous woman but one husband.

寡 婦 好 比 無 舵 之 舟

Wu to chih chou.

A widow is like a rudderless boat.

先 來 新 婦 晚 來 婆，要 粥 要 飯 自 來 提

Hsien lai hsin fu wan lai p'o, yao chou yao fan tzǔ lai t'i.

The daughter-in-law came first, the step-mother-in-law after ; so if the mother wants gruel or rice she must get it for herself.

好 人 家 婦 女 不 喫 兩 家 茶

Hao jên chia fu nü pu ch'ih liang chia ch'a.

Respectable women do not drink the tea of two families.

i.e. They do not marry second husbands.

一 日 夫 妻 百 日 恩

I jih fu ch'i pai jih ên.

One day husband and wife implies a hundred days' kindness.

Chapter 4. Elder and Younger Brothers.

小 時 是 兄 弟,長 大 各 鄉 里

Hsiao shih shih hsiung ti, chang ta ko hsiang li.

Those who are brothers in childhood, when grown up are scattered over the country side.

兄 弟 如 手 足

Hsiung ti ju shou tsu.

Brothers resemble hands and feet.

左 拳 打 右 手,雖 勝 不 如 無

Tso ch'uan ta yu shou, sui sheng pu ju wu.

Though the left hand conquer the right, no advantage is gained.

衣 裳 破 尚 可 補,手 足 斷 難 得 連

I shang p'o shang k'o pu, shou tsu tuan nan tê lien.

Torn clothes may be mended, but a hand or foot cannot be joined on again.

兄 弟 不 和,旁 人 欺

Hsiung ti pu ho, p'ang jen ch'i.

When brothers disagree they are imposed upon by others.

難 得 者 兄 弟,易 得 者 田 地

Nan tê chê hsiung ti. i tê chê t'ien ti.

Brothers are harder to get than fields.

兄 弟 雖 親,財 利 各 別

Hsiung ti sui ch'in, ts'ai li ko pieh.

Though brothers are so closely akin each keep his own money.

兄 弟 殺 人·各 分 手 足

Ti hsiung sha jên, ko fen shou tsu.

> Though a brother commit a murder, it does not involve his brethren.

齒 牙 也 有 相 撞 的 日 子

Ch'ih ya yeh yu hsiang chuang ti jih tzŭ.

> Brothers sometimes disagree. *Lit.* Top and bottom teeth sometimes clash together.

碟 碗 也 有 相 撞 的 日 子

Tieh wan yeh yu hsiang chuang ti jih tzŭ.

> Same as above. *Lit.* Dishes and basins will sometimes get smashed together.

天 下 最 難 得 者 兄 弟

T'ien hsia tsui nan tê chê hsiung ti.

> The most difficult thing on earth to get is a brother.

兄 弟 相 害·不 如 友 生

Hsiung ti hsiang hai pu ju yu sheng.

> Kind friends are better than unkind brothers.

好 煞 了 是 他 人·壞 煞 了 是 自 己

Hao sha liao shih t'a jen, huai sha liao shih tzŭ chi.

> However good he may be he is still a stranger; however bad he may be, he is part of oneself. Note. This has reference to the value of a friend as opposed to a brother.

勿 以 思 毫 利·便 傷 骨 肉 情

Wu i ssŭ hao li, pien shang ku jou ch'ing.

> Never allow the slightest consideration of profit to injure the affection between kith and kin.

妯 娌 和 氣 家 不 散

哥 兒 們 和 氣 順 氣 丸

Chou li ho ch'i chia pu san.

Ko êrh men ho ch'i shun ch'i wan.

> If sister-in-law live in harmony, the family will not be divided; if brothers live in harmony everything will go well. *Lit.* A harmony pill.

Chapter 5. Friends.

說 得 脫 得 八 合
Shuo tê t'o tê pa ko.

> You can get rid of him by giving him a trifle. Note. Pa ko, means eight tenths of a sheng, Chinese pint measure. A small amount. This proverb may be applied with regard to a destitute chum or importunate creditor.

交 義 不 交 財, 交 財 兩 不 來
Chiao i pu chiao ts'ai chiao ts'ai liang pu lai.

> Friendship must rest on goodness rather than gain; if on gain it will not be permanent.

交 官 窮 交 客 富. 交 和 尙 得 緣 薄
Chiao kuan ch'iung chiao k'o fu, chiao ho shang tê yüan pu.

> If you have intercourse with officials you will be beggared, if with merchants you will get rich; if you mix with Buddhist priests you will be asked for a subscription.

三 朋 四 友, 碗 酒 筷 肉
San p'eng ssu yu, wan chiu k'uai jou.

> "A jolly good fellow" *Lit.* A cup of wine and a taste of meat with every friend.

衣 冠 不 正, 朋 友 之 過
I kuan pu cheng, p'eng yu chih kuo.

> Friends are at fault when a man is allowed to wear his dress awry.

得 相 交 且 相 交, 不 相 交 且 開 交
Tê hsiang chiao ch'ieh hsiang chiao, pu hsiang chiao ch'ieh k'ai chiao.

> If you can be friendly, be so; if not, separate.

朝 兄 弟 暮 仇 敵
Chao hsiung ti mu ch'ou ti.

> Brothers in the morning and foes at night.

人 到 無 情 切 莫 相 交
Jen tao wu ch'ing ch'ieh mo hsiang chiao.

> Never make friends of ungenial men.

人 熟 是 寶

Jen shu shih pao.

> A well-known friend is a treasure.

五 湖 四 海 都 是 朋 友

Wu hu ssu hai tu shih p'eng yu.

> Men are friends all over the empire.

藕 斷 絲 不 斷

Ou tuan ssu pu tuan.

> Lingering friendship. *Lit.* The lotus root may be broken, but its silken fibres remain united.

得 意 忘 言 無 所 不 談

Tê i wang yen wu so pu t'an

> When friendship is real men can talk without reserve.

鴉 片 烟 籤 子，遇 着 瓷 瓦 刮

Ya p'ien yen ch'ien tzu. yü cho tzǔ wa kua.

> A miserable friendship. *Lit.* An opium smoker's probe scraped by a bit of pot.

氷 炭 之 交

Ping t'an chih chiao.

> Impossible alliance. *Lit.* Friendship between ice and coal.

固 結 不 可 解

Ku chieh pu k'o chieh.

> You can't separate firm friends.

酒 逢 知 己 飲，詩 向 會 人 吟

Chiu fêng chih chi yin, shih hsiang hui jen yin.

> Drink only with familiar friends; recite poetry only with a poet.

相 識 滿 天 下，知 心 能 幾 人

Hsiang shih man t'ien hsia, chih hsin neng chi jen.

> One's acquaintances may fill the empire, but one's familiar friends must be few.

相 逢 好 似 初 相 識，到 老 終 無 怨 恨 心

Hsiang fêng hao ssu ch'u hsiang shih, tao lao chung wn yuan hen hsin.

> If the politeness of first acquaintance characterise all succeeding intercourse; nothing disagreeable will ever arise.

相 逢 不 飲 空 歸 去，洞 口 桃 花 也 笑 人

Hsiang fêng pu yin k'ung kuei ch'ü, tung k'ou t'ao hua yeh hsiao jên.

> If friends meet and part without a friendly glass, the peach blossom round the grotto will deride them. Note. A literary reference to the famous allegory of T'ao Ch'ien 陶 潛 one of China's famous poets.

有 錢 有 酒 多 兄 弟，急 難 何 曾 見 一 人

Yu ch'ien yu chiu to hsiung ti, chi nan ho ts'eng chien i jen.

> With money and wine you have plenty of friends; but who will you see when in trouble?

結 交 須 勝 己 似 我 不 如 無，但 看 三 五 日 相 見 不 如 初

Chieh chiao hsü sheng chi ssu wo pu ju wu, tan k'an san wu jih hsiang chien pu ju ch'u.

> Unless your friend be your superior, you had better have none; and for a few days observe whether his subsequent greetings equal his first.

樂 莫 樂 兮 新 相 知，悲 莫 悲 兮 生 別 離

Lo mo lo hsi hsin hsiang chih, pei mo pei hsi sheng pieh li.

> No joy equals that of making a new friend; no sorrow that of being separated from friends.

虎 鹿 不 同 遊

Hu lu pu t'ung yu.

> Tigers and deer do not stroll together.

四 海 交 遊 都 成 蘭 味

Ssu hai chiao yu tu ch'eng lan wei.

> He who has friends in every place, finds every place agreeable.

烏 鴉 不 與 鳳 凰 棲

Wu ya pu yü fêng huang ch'i.

> The crow does not roost with the phoenix.

對 面 與 語, 心 隔 千 山

Tui mien yü yü, hsin kê ch'ien shan.

> Though conversing face to face, their hearts are divided as by a thousand hills.

人 要 好 水 也 甜

Jen yao hao shoi yeh t'ien.

> When men are friendly even water is sweet.

一 年 難 相 與 一 個 人, 一 時 便 得 罪 一 個 人

I nieu nan hsiang yü i ko jen, i shih pien tê tsui i ko jen.

> It is difficult to make a friend even in a year, but it is easy to offend one in an hour.

伴 生 不 如 伴 熟

Pan sheng pu ju pan shu.

> Better associate with one well-known than with a stranger.

有 酒 有 肉 多 兄 弟, 患 難 之 時 一 個 無

Yu chiu yu jou to hsiung ti, huan nan chih shih i ko wu.

> With wine and good feeding you will have plenty of friends; but in trouble you will not have one.

意 合 則 吳 越 相 親, 意 不 合 則 骨 肉 爲 仇 敵

I ho tsê Wu yueh hsiang ch'in, i pu ho tsê ku jou wei ch'ou ti.

> When purposes agree, the most hostile grow friendly; when they disagree, near relatives become enemies. Note. Wu and Yueh were two ancient states, often at enmity with each other.

女 無 明 鏡 不 知 面 上 精 粗, 士 無 良 友 不 知 面 上 虧 踰

Nü wu ming ching pu chih mien shang ching ts'u, shih wu liang yu pu chih mien shang k'uei yü.

> Without a good mirror no lady can know her true appearance; without a true friend no gentleman can know his own errors of conduct.

一 人 計 短, 二 人 計 長

I jen chi tuan, erh jen chi ch'ang.

> Two are better than one. *Lit.* One man's plan is short; the plan of two is long.

世 事 靜 方 見，人 情 淡 始 長

Shih shih ching fang chien, jen ch'ing tan shih ch'ang.

> When the worlds' affairs are calm we can judge of them ;
> when affection is moderate it will endure.   Note. 始
> here equals. 纔, then, in that case.

久 旱 逢 甘 雨，他 鄉 遇 故 知

Chiu han fêng kan yü, t'a hsiang yü ku chih.

> Meeting an old friend in a distant country is like
> refreshing rain after a long drought.

朋 友 相 交，所 杖 者 信

P'eng yü hsiang chiao, so chang chê hsin.

> Mutual confidence is the prop of friendship.

膠 漆 自 謂 堅，不 如 雷 與 陳

Chiao ch'i tzŭ wei chien, pu ju Lei yü Ch'en.

> Glue and varnish bind fast but are not equal to the
> love of Lei and Ch'en.   Note. 雷 and 陳 two
> scholars of the Han Dynasty, the Damon and
> Pythias or David and Jonathan of Chinese history.

人 之 相 知，貴 相 知 心

Jên chih hsiang chih, kuei hsiang chih hsin

> The best kind of acquaintance is the acquaintance with
> each other's hearts.

猩 猩 惜 猩 猩，好 漢 愛 好 漢

Hsing hsing hsi hsing hsing,, hao han ai hao han.

> The wild man sympathises with the wild man, and one
> brave man loves another.

站 乾 岸 兒

Chan kan an erh.

> A faithless friend. *Lit.* To stand on the dry shore,
> i.e., without any attempt to save life.

人 是 舊 的 好，衣 裳 是 新 的 好

Jen shih chiu ti hao, i shang shih hsin ti hao.

> Old friends are best friends; best clothes are new clothes.

好 朋 友 勤 算 帳

Hao p'eng yu ch'in suan chang.

> Good friends settle their accounts at once.

你 有 我 有 就 是 朋 友

Ni yu wo yu chiu shih p'eng yu.

> When you and I have (money) then we are friends.

眞 朋 友 淡 淡 如 水, 假 朋 友 蜜 蜜 調 油

Chen p'eng yu tan tan ju shui, chia p'eng yu mi mi t'iao yu.

> True friendship is flavourless like water; (i.e. reserved)
> false friendship is like honey mixed with oil, (i.e.
> fulsome.)

朋 友 高 搭 牆

P'eng yu kao ta ch'iang.

> Friends should have a high wall between them, i.e., too
> much familiarity breeds contempt.

厨 房 有 人 好 吃 飯, 朝 裏 有 人 好 作 官

Ch'ü fang yu jen hao ch'ih fan, ch'ao li yu jen hao tso kuan

> With a friend in the cook-house you can get something
> to eat ; with a friend at court you can obtain office.

———

Chapter 6.　Various.

酒 肉 朋 友 柴 米 夫 妻

Chiu jou p'eng yu, ch'ai mi fu ch'i.

> Friends while good dinners last ; husband and wife while
> fuel and food remain

打 虎 還 是 親 兄 弟, 上 陣 定 要 父 子 兵

Ta hu huan shih ch'in hsiung ti, shang chen ting yao fu tzŭ ping.

> It is best to hunt a tiger or go into battle with one's
> own relatives.

子 登 父 業, 妻 受 夫 分

Tzŭ teng fu yeh, ch'i shou fu fen.

> Sons receive their fathers' fortune ; wives share their
> husbands' lot.

父 母 恩 深 終 有 別, 夫 妻 義 重 也 分 離

Fu mu ên shen chuug yu pieh, fu ch'i i chung yeh fen li.

> Parents though very loving must be parted from their
> children ; husband and wife though most faithful,
> must also separate.

天 上 雷 公，地 下 母 舅

T'ien shang lei kung, ti hsia mu chiu.

> In heaven above—the god of thunder ; on earth below—
> the maternal uncle. Note. Of all relations on the
> mother's side her brothers have the greatest influence.

是 親 不 是 親，非 親 却 是 親

Shih ch'in pu shih ch'in, fei ch'in ch'ioh shih ch'in.

> One though related, is no relation ; another, though not
> related, is a relation.

竈 裏 不 熄 火，路 上 不 斷 人

Tsao li pu hsi huo, lu shang pu tuan jen.

> Whilst fire remains in your cooking stove, guests will
> never cease to arrive.

妻 賢 夫 禍 少，子 孝 父 心 寬

Ch'i hsien fu huo shao, tzŭ hsiao fu hsin k'uan

> His griefs are few whose wife is virtuous; his heart is
> enlarged, whose sons are dutiful.

知 臣 莫 若 君，知 子 莫 若 父，知 弟 莫 若 兄，知 弟 莫 若 師

Chih ch'en mo jo chun, chih tzŭ mo jo fu, chih ti mo jo hsiung,
chih ti mo jo shih.

> Princes know their Ministers, fathers their children,
> elder-brothers their younger-brothers, and teachers
> their scholars, better than anyone else.

欲 知 其 君 先 視 其 臣，欲 知 其 人 先 視 其 友，欲 知 其 父 先 視 其 子

Yü chih ch'i chün hsien shih ch'i ch'en, yü chih ch'i jên hsien shih
ch'i yu, yü chih ch'i fu hsien shih ch'i tzŭ.

> Would you know the character of a prince, then first
> observe his ministers; would you become acquainted
> with a man, first look at his friends; would you
> know a father, first consider his son.

不 是 冤 家 不 成 兒 女，不 是 對 頭 不 成 夫 妻

Pu shih yüan chia pu ch'eng erh nü, pu shih tui tou pu ch'eng
fu ch'i.

> If we were not an injured family, we should have neither
> sons nor daughters ; if we were not at enmity we
> should never have been husband and wife. Note.
> This is used in reply to congratulation, in a jocular
> and self depreciatory sense.

家貧見孝子, 國亂顯忠臣

Chia p'in chien hsiao tzu kuo luan hsien chung ch'en.

> Poverty in a family brings out the dutiful sons; and confusion in the state reveals the loyal minister.

視朝廷重則爵祿輕, 視父母重則妻子輕, 視兄弟重則財產輕

Shih ch'ao t'ing chung tsê chio lu ch'ing, shih fu mu chung tsê ch'i tzǔ, ch'ing shih hsiong ti chung tsê ts'ai ch'an ch'ing.

> He who honours his prince will think lightly of rank and emolument; he who honours his parents will honour his wife and child less; he who honours his brothers will think lightly of money and heritage.

五倫之要在敬, 十義之全惟誠

Wu lun chih yao tsai ching, shih i chih ch'üan wei ch'eng.

> The most important thing in the Five Relationships is Respectfulness; the perfect embodiment of the Ten Virtues is Sincerity. Note. The ten virtues are those which belong to the ten members of the five relationships.

妻賢子孝一身閒, 雨順風調萬事足

Ch'i hsien tzu hsiao i shen hsien, yü shun feng t'iao wan shih tsu.

> He has perfect tranquillity whose wife is virtuous and sons obedient; and all things are satisfactory when rains are seasonable and winds moderate.

夫妻面前莫說眞, 朋友面前莫說假

Fu ch'i mien ch'ien mo shuo chen, p'eng yu mien ch'ien mo shuo chia.

> The honest truth must not be told between husband and wife; lies must not be told between friend and friend. Note. This proverb supposes that the truth between husband and wife cannot be told, because both are immoral.

天下無不是的父母, 世間最難得者兄弟

T'ien hsia wu pu shih ti fu mu, shih chien tsui nan tê chê hsiung ti.

> One's father and mother never do wrong; brothers are very difficult to find.

無 錢 休 入 衆，遭 難 莫 尋 親

Wu ch'ien hsiu ju chung, tsao nan mo hsin ch'in.

> Without money do not enter a crowd ; in adversity do
> not seek your relatives.

兄 弟 如 手 足，夫 妻 如 衣 服

Hsiung ti ju shou tsu, fu ch'i ju i fu.

> Brothers are as hands and feet ; husband and wife as
> clothes.

新 親 熱 極 極，老 親 丟 過 壁

Hsin ch'in jo chi chi, lao ch'in tiu kuo pi.

> New-come relatives eagerly welcomed; old ones thrown
> into the corner.

SECTION XI. MORALS.

Chapter. 1. Conscience.

爲 人 不 做 虧 心 事，半 夜 敲 門 心 不 驚

Wei jen pu tso k'uei hsin shih, pan yeh ch'iao men hsin pu ching.

Men who never violate their consciences, are not afraid of a knock at their door at midnight.

講 良 心 沒 飯 吃

Chiang liang hsin mu fan ch'ih.

Be particular about conscience and you will have nothing to eat.

莫 虧 良 心

Mo k'uei liang hsin.

Do not violate your conscience

再 三 須 重 事，第 一 莫 欺 心

Tsai san hsü chung shih ti i mo ch'i hsin.

In paying special attention to important affairs, the chief thing is not to cheat your conscience.

莫 把 良 心 放 在 背 上

Mo pa liang hsin fang tsai pei shang.

Keep a good conscience. *Lit.* Do not put your conscience on your back.

大 沒 良 心 大 發 財，小 沒 良 心 小 發 財

Ta mu liang hsin ta fa ts'ai, hsiao mu liang hsin hsiao fa ts'ai.

The less of conscience the more of wealth; the more of conscience the less of wealth.

豈 能 盡 如 人 意，但 求 無 愧 我 心

Ch'i neng chin ju jên i, tan chiu wu k'uei wo hsin.

How can we please others in everything; let us only seek not to shame our own conscience.

莫 作 心 上 過 不 去 之 事，莫 起 事 上 行 不 去 之 心

Mo tso hsin shang kuo pu ch'ü chih shih, mo ch'i shih shang hsing pu ch'ü chih hsin.

Never do what your conscience will not allow; never desire what is improper to be done.

養 性 須 修 善 欺 心 莫 吃 齋

Yang hsing hsü hsiu shan, ch'i hsin mo ch'ih chai.

> To nourish your disposition you must cultivate virtue ; if you cheat your conscience don't assume to be an ascetic.

欺 心 折 盡 平 生 福, 行 短 天 敎 一 世 貧

Ch'i hsin chê chin p'ing sheng fu, hsing tuan t'ien chiao i shih p'in.

> Cheat your conscience and a whole life's happiness is destroyed ; let your conduct be faulty and Heaven will cause you to have a life of poverty.

吃 了 匾 担 橫 了 腸 子

Ch'ih liao pien tan heng liao ch'ang tzŭ.

> To violate conscience. *Lit.* To distend the bowels by swallowing a carrying pole.

吃 了 煤 炭 黑 了 良 心

Ch'ih liao mei t'an hei liao liang hsin.

> Same as above. *Lit.* To blacken the heart by eating coal.

是 非 之 心 人 皆 有 之

Shih fei chih hsin jên chieh yu chih.

> Every man can discriminate between right and wrong.

陰 田 不 如 心 田, 陰 宅 不 如 陰 德

Yin t'ien pu ju hsin t'ien, yin tsê pu ju yin tê.

> A grave-yard plot is not so good as a heart-plot ; a grave is not so good as unassuming virtue. Note. 陰 田 is a common term for the heart, the field or plot for the cultivation of virtue.

Chapter 2. Good Works.

好 事 難 成 惡 事 多

Hao shih nan ch'eng ô shih to.

> It is difficult to do good deeds, there are so many evil ones.

點 塔 七 層 不 如 暗 處 一 燈

Tien t'a ch'i t'seng pu ju au ch'ü i teng

> A single lamp in a dark place is better than illuminating a seven storied pagoda.

爲 善 則 流 芳 百 世

Wei shan tsê liu fang pai shih.

> The fragrance of virtuous conduct will last for a hundred
> generations.

行 滿 天 下 無 怨 惡

Hsing man t'ien hsia wu yüan wu.

> Good deeds may fill the empire without provoking any
> one's dislike.

但 行 好 事, 莫 問 前 程

Tah hsing hao shih mo wen ch'ien ch'eng.

> Do good regardless of consequences.

善 事 可 作: 惡 事 莫 爲

Shan shih k'o tso, ô shih mo wei.

> Good deeds may be done but not evil ones.

勿 以 惡 小 而 爲 之, 勿 以 善 小 而 不 爲

Wu i ô hsiao erh wei chih, wu i shan hsiao erh pu wei.

> Do not consider any vice trivial, and so practise it ; do
> not consider any virtue trivial, and so neglect it.

爲 善 鬼 神 欽, 作 惡 被 天 鑑

Wei shan kuei shen ch'in, tso ô pei t'ien chien.

> Do good, and the spirits will honour you; do evil, and
> you will suffer the chastisement of Heaven.

一 善 改 千 惡

I shan kai ch'ien ô.

> One good deed will correct a thousand bad ones.

善 門 難 開

Shan men nan k'ai.

> It is difficult to begin doing good deeds. *Lit.* The door
> of goodness is hard to open. Note.—Good deeds
> once commenced may require more money and time
> than can be expended without injury to the doer.

勸 世 文 勸 世 人, 勸 動 人 心 不 害 人

Ch'üan shih wen ch'üan shih jên, ch'üan tung jên hsin pu hai jên.

> Religious books and preachers, influence, but do not
> injure men.

修 道 雖 無 人 見，存 心 自 有 天 知

Hsiu tao sui wu jeu chien, ts'un hsin tzu yu t'ien chih.

> The cultivation of virtue, although unseen by men, if persevered in, will be known of Heaven.

一 毫 之 惡 勸 人 莫 作，一 毫 之 善 與 人 方 便

Ĭ hao chih ô ch'üan jen mo tso, i hao chih shan yü jeu fang pien.

> Exhort men not to commit the slightest sin ; the smallest virtue is advantageous to men.

公 修 公 德，婆 修 婆 德，各 修 各 德

Kung hsiu kung tê, p'o hsiu p'o tê, ko hsiu ko tê.

> Man and wife each cultivate their own virtue.

說 好 不 爲 好，做 好 方 爲 好

Shuo hao pu wei hao, tso hao fang wei hao.

> Talking good isn't being good ; doing good is.

黑 處 作 揖，各 人 憑 心

Hei ch'ü tso i, ko jen p'ing hsin.

> Do good as you think best. *Lit.* Bowing in the dark is according to every man's own fancy.

勿 登 山 而 綱 禽 鳥，勿 臨 水 而 毒 魚 蝦

Wu teng shan erh wang ch'in niao, wu lin shui erh tu yü hsia.

> Do not go out on the hills to net birds ; nor down to the waters to poison fishes and shrimps. i.e. Don't take life.

勿 宰 耕 牛 勿 棄 字 紙

Wu tsai keng niu, wu ch'i tzŭ chih.

> Never kill the draught ox, nor throw away written paper.

在 家 出 家，在 世 出 世

Tsai chia ch'ü chia, tsai shih ch'u shih.

> In the family separate from the family ; in the world separate from the world. Comp. John 17.15.

無 事 不 可 對 人 言

Wu shih pu k'o tui jen yen.

> He does nothing that cannot be told to others. Note.—Ssu Ma Kuang, 司 馬 光 a noted statesman of the Sung Dynasty said of himself that "all his life long he had done nothing that he could not tell to others." Comp. Acts 23:1.

下 坡 容 易·上 坡 難

Hsia p'o jung i, shang p'o nan.

　　It is easier to run down hill than to run up.

十 世 修 來 同 船 渡, 百 世 修 來 共 枕 眠

Shih shih hsiu lai t'ung ch'uan tu, pai shih hsiu lai kung chen mien.

　　Surely those who have in ten lives cultivated virtue, may
　　　cross in the same boat ; as those who have in a
　　　hundred may sleep in the same bed. Note.—Pre-
　　　natal cultivation of virtue implies cultivation of
　　　friendly relations.

人 不 勸 不 善, 鐘 不 打 不 鳴

Jen pu ch'üan pu shan, chung pu ta pu ming.

　　Men will no more be virtuous without exhortation, than
　　　a bell will sound without being struck.

言 善 非 難·行 善 爲 難

Yeu shan fei nan, hsing shan wei nan.

　　To talk about good deeds is easy, to do them is difficult.

救 人 一 命 勝 造 七 級 浮 屠

Chiu jên i ming sheng chao ch'i chi fou t'u.

　　To save one man's life is better than to build a seven-
　　　storied pagoda. Note.—Fou T'u, the last two
　　　characters are used to represent the sound of Buddha.
　　　In this case they represent the old name of an Indian
　　　pagoda.

人 到 無 求 品 自 高

Jen tao wu ch'iu p'in tzŭ kao.

　　His conduct is naturally exalted who will not condescend
　　　to beg.

見 死 不 救 一 行 大 罪

Chien ssŭ pu chiu, i hang ta tsui.

　　To neglect to save life is one of the greatest crimes.

欲 修 仙 道 先 修 人 道, 人 道 不 修 仙 道 遠 矣

Yü hsiu hsien tao hsien hsiu jen tao, jen tao pu hsiu hsien tao yuan i.

　　If a man wishes to attain the excellence of the Immortals
　　　he must first cultivate human virtues ; if the human
　　　virtues are not cultivated, he will not reach to the
　　　excellence of the Immortals.

若 是 一 行 善 勝 起 九 層 塔

Ju shih i hsing shan sheng ch'i chiu ts'eng t'a.

If you do one good deed it is better than building a
nine-storied pagoda.

———

Chapter. 3. Reproof and Good Counsel.

要 得 好 問 三 老

Yao tê hao wen san lao.

If you wish to be right ask three aged men.

沒 有 吃 肉 也 看 見 猪 走

Mu yu ch'ih jou yeh k'an chien chu tsou.

You may not have tasted their flesh but you have seen
pigs walking about. Note.—Used by a superior to
an inferior, this conveys rebuke; otherwise, it means
that, though lacking actual experience, one has a
certain amount of knowledge of the subject referred
to.

打 草 驚 蛇 殺 雞 嚇 猴

Ta ts'ao ching she sha chi ho hou.

To reprove one for another's warning. *Lit.* To beat the
grass to frighten the snake ; to kill the fowl to
frighten the monkey.

指 張 良 罵 韓 信 爲 着 誰 來

Chih Chang Liang ma Han Hsin wei cho shui lai.

The same as above. *Lit.* He points at Chang Liang
and curses Han Hsin. Note.—Chang Liang and
Han Hsin, were two ministers of Kao Tsu, first of
the Han emperors, whose reign dates from 206 B.C.

指 東 瓜 罵 葫 蘆

Chih tung kua ma hu lu.

The same. *Lit.* He points at the great melon and
curses the gourd.

指 桑 罵 槐

Chih sang ma huai.

The same. *Lit.* He points at the mulberry and curses
the ash.

賢不責愚

Hsien pu tsê yü.

> A wise man will not reprove a fool.

彎木頭自必有直木匠

Wan. mu t'ou tzu pi yu chih mu chiang.

> Faults must be corrected by competent persons. *Lit.*
> Crooked trees must come under the straightening
> hand of the carpenter.

買把扇子遮臉

Mai pa shan tzǔ chê lien

> Buy a fan to cover your face. Note.—Said to another
> this conveys reproof; said of one's self, apology.

君有臣諫，父有子諫

Chün yu ch'en chien, fu yu tzǔ chien.

> Princes have censors, fathers have sons, that reprove
> them.

說話時短，記話時長

Shuo hua shih tuan, chi hua shih ch'ang.

> It takes little time to reprove a man; but it takes a long
> time to forget reproof.

甘言疾也，苦言藥也

Kan yen chi yeh, k'u yen yao yeh.

> Flattery is sickness; reproof is medicine.

苦口是良藥

K'u k'ou shih liang yao.

> A bitter mouth is good medicine.

守口莫談人過短，自短何曾說與人

Shou k'ou mo t'an jen kuo tuan, tzǔ tuan ho ts'eng shuo yü jen.

> Shut your mouth and do not talk about the faults of
> others; and why should you mention your own.

莫說他人先輸了自己

Mo shuo t'a jen hsien shu liao tzu chi.

> Before you blame others, confess yourself in fault.

自 恨 無 枝 葉, 莫 怨 太 陽 偏

Tzu hen wu chih yeh, mo yüan t'ai yang p'ien.

> Be vexed with yourself that you have neither branch nor leaf; do not accuse the sun of partiality.

責 人 之 心 責 己, 恕 己 之 心 恕 人

Tsê jen chih hsin tsê chi, shu chi chih hsin shu jên,

> Blame yourself as you would blame others; excuse others as you would excuse yourself.

生 平 只 會 量 人 短, 何 不 回 頭 把 自 量

Sheng p'ing chih hui liang jen tuan, ho pu hui t'ou pa tzǔ liang.

> Why do not those who are continually judging of other men's faults, turn about and judge themselves. Comp. Matthew 7:3.

先 正 自 己, 後 正 他 人

Hsien cheng tzǔ chi, hou cheng t'a jen.

> First put yourself right, then others.

道 吾 好 者 是 吾 賊, 道 吾 惡 者 是 吾 師

Tao wu hao chê shih wu tsei, tao wu ô chê shih wu shih.

> He who flatters me is my enemy; he who reproves me is my teacher.

洗 臉 碍 住 鼻 子

Hsi lien ai chu pi tzu.

> To butt against the nose in washing the face. Note. The meaning here is of encountering unpleasantness or danger in the performance of duty.

不 應 我 的 舵

Pu ying wo ti to.

> He won't listen to my advice. *Lit.* He won't obey my helm.

不 能 正 己, 焉 能 正 人

Pu neng chen g chi, yen neng cheng jên.

> If you can't correct yourself, how can you correct others?

責己者於無過中求有過·責友者於有過中求無過

Tsê chi chê yü wu kuo chung ch'iu yu kuo, tsê yu chê yü yu kuo
chung ch'iu wu kuo.

> Reprove yourself as though seeking for something to
> blame; reprove your friends as though seeking to
> excuse their faults.

烟舘酒店不可走,花街柳巷莫亂行

Yen kuan chiu tien pu k'o tsou, hua chieh liu hsiang mo luan hsing.

> Shun opium dens and wine shops; avoid houses and
> places of ill-fame.

打破碗說碗,打破碟說碟

Ta p'o wan shuo wan, ta p'o tieh shuo tieh.

> If you have broken a bowl, say it is a bowl, if you have
> broken a dish say it is a dish.

善人聽說心中刺,惡人聽說耳邊風

Shan jen t'ing shuo hsin chung tz'ü, ô jen t'ing shuo erh pien fêng.

> Reproof stings the heart of a good man, but to an evil
> man is merely a breath of wind.

一朝失足,百身莫贖

I chao shih tsu, pai shen mo shu.

> Make a false step one day, and a hundred lifetimes will
> not redeem it.

Chapter 4. Virtue and Vice.

正直爲人,正直爲神

Cheng chih wei jen, cheng chih wei shen.

> To be an upright man is to become an upright spirit.

恃德者昌恃惡者亡

Shih tê chê ch'ang shih ô chê wang.

> Those who trust to virtue prosper; those who trust to
> vice are destroyed.

從善如登,從惡如崩

Ts'ung shan ju teng, ts'ung ô ju pêng.

> To follow virtue is to ascend; to follow evil is to fall in
> ruin.

餓 死 的 事 小，失 節 的 事 大

Ô ssŭ ti shih hsiao, shih chieh ti shih ta.

> It is a little thing to starve to death; it is a serious matter to lose one's virtue.

重 仁 義，輕 死 亡

Chung jen i. ch'ing ssŭ wang.

> Consider benevolence and righteousness important, and death of no consequence.

寧 死 不 可 背 理

Ning ssŭ pu k'o pei li.

> Better die than turn your back on what is right.

仁 義 禮 智 信 理 所 當 遵

Jên i li chih hsin li so tang tsun.

> Benevolence, Righteousness, Propriety, Wisdom and Fidelity are the principles which ought to be followed.

衣 食 足 而 後 禮 義 興

I shih tsu erh hou li i hsing.

> Let there be plenty of food and clothing, and propriety and righteousness will flourish.

守 分 安 命 順 時 聽 天

Shou fen an ming shun shih t'ing t'ien.

> Accept your destiny, do your duty; be satisfied with your position; and obey the voice of heaven.

不 怕 說 壞 了，就 怕 做 壞 了

Pu p'a shuo huai liao, chiu p'a tso huai liao.

> Fear not when men speak evil of you; fear lest you should do evil.

做 惡 爲 易：做 善 爲 難

Tso ô wei i, tso shan wei nan.

> It is easy to do evil, it is hard to do good.

義 爲 心 之 制，又 爲 事 之 宜

I wei hsin chih chih, keng wei shih chih i.

> When righteousness controls the heart, the actions cannot but be right.

作 事 須 循 天 理，出 言 要 順 人 情

Tso shih hsü hsün t'ien li, ch'u yen yao shun jen hsin.

> In our actions we should accord with the will of heaven ;
> in our words we should consider the feelings of men.

眞 的 假 不 得；假 的 眞 不 得

Chen ti chia pu tê, chia ti chen pu tê.

> Truth must always be true and falsehood false.

善 欲 人 見 不 是 眞 善；惡 恐 人 知 便 是 大 惡

Shan yü jen chien pü shih chen shan, ô k'ung jên chih pien shih ta ô.

> Virtue practised to be seen is not real virtue ; vice which
> fears to be seen is real vice.

善 不 可 失，惡 不 可 長

Shan pu k'o shih, ô pu k'o chang.

> Never lose virtue nor promote vice.

諸 惡 莫 作，衆 善 奉 行

Chu ô mo tso, chung shan fêng hsing.

> All vice avoid, all virtue follow.

善 乃 福 之 基；惡 乃 禍 之 兆

Shan nai fu chih chi, ô nai huo chih chao.

> Virtue is the foundation of happiness ; vice the presage
> of misery.

富 潤 屋，德 潤 身

Fu yün wu, tê yün shen.

> Riches adorn the house ; virtue adorns the person.

善 不 積 不 足 以 成 名，惡 不 積 不 足 以 滅 身

Shan pu chi pu tsu i ch'eng ming, ô pu chi pu tsu i mieh shen.

> When virtue is not accumulated fame cannot be attained ;
> if wickedness be not accumulated it will not destroy
> the body.

善 惡 施 也，禍 福 報 也，天 報 屬 陰 地 報 屬 陽

Shan ô shih yeh, huo fu pao yeh, t'ien pao shu yin, ti pao shu yang.

> Good and Evil are the outward acts ; Misery and Happi-
> ness are the recompense, the recompense of Heaven
> is concealed, the recompense of Earth is manifest.

寧 在 直 中 取，不 向 曲 中 求

Ning tsai chih chung ch'ü, pu hsiang ch'ü chung ch'iu.

Take what you can get in a straightforward way rather than seek to acquire by crooked means.

十 年 行 善 不 足，一 日 作 惡 有 餘

Shih nien hsing shan pü tsu, i jih tsu ô yu yü.

To do good for ten years is not sufficient ; to do evil for a single day is too much.

善 惡 雖 小，須 要 分 別 黑 白

Shan ô sui hsiao, hsü yao fen pieh hei pai.

It may not be very good or very evil but it is necessary to discriminate as between white and black.

善 惡 隨 人 作，禍 福 自 己 招

Shan ô sui jên tso, huo fu tzǔ chi chao.

Men are free to do good or evil; misery or happiness are of their own making.

智 欲 圓 而 行 欲 方，膽 欲 大 而 心 欲 小

Chih yü yüan erh hsing yü fang, tan yü ta erh hsin yü hsiao.

Let your wisdom be round (all inclusive) and your actions square; shew great courage and keep a small (humble) heart.

善 人 流 芳 百 世，惡 人 遺 臭 萬 年

Shan jen liu fang pai shih, ô jêu, i ch'ou wan nien.

A virtuous man hands down a good name for a hundred generations ; an evil man leaves a reproach for a myriad years.

爲 善 善 日 增，改 過 過 日 減，莫 問 能 不 能 但 問 肯 不 肯

Wei shan shan jih tseng, kai kuo kuo jih chien, mo wen neng pᵞ neng tan wen k'en pu k'en

Be good and good days will be added unto you; reform, and evil days will diminish. Do not ask am I able, but am I willing.

Chapter 5. Virtues.

1. CONCESSION AND FORBEARANCE.

忍字高忍字高，忍字頭上一把刀，
爲人能效張公忍，自然快活無煩惱

Jên tzŭ kao jên tzŭ kao, jên tzŭ t'ou shang i pa tao,
Wei jên neng hsiao Chang Kung jên, tzŭ jan k'uai huo wu fan nao.

> Forbearance is a noble word;
> Above its head behold a sword;
> Whoe'er in this is like Chang Kung,
> Must happy be and never bored.

Note.—Chang Kung was a certain superior man noted
for writing out one hundred instances of the application of the word "Forbearance", as well as for his
own exemplification of its meaning.

任他雪山高萬丈，太陽一出自然消

Jên t'a hsüeh shan kao wan chang, t'ai yang i ch'u tzu jan hsiao.

> Let him alone! A snow mountain, ten thousand feet
> high, will melt as soon as the sun shines upon it.

效張公多書忍字

Hsiao Chang kung to shu jên tzŭ.

> Imitate Chang Kung who wrote so much on Forbearance.

彎彎扁擔不得斷

Wan wan pien tan pu tê tuan.

> Carrying poles which bend easily do not break.

忍得一時之氣，免得百日之憂

Jên tê i shih chih ch'i, mien tê pai jih chih yu.

> To repress a moment's anger may save you a hundred
> days of sorrow.

少間弗忍，終身之羞

Shao chien fu jen, chung shen chih hsiu.

> A moment's want of forbearance may mean the shame
> of a lifetime.

忍一句息一怒，饒一着退一步

Jên i ch'ü hsi i nu, jao i cho t'ui i pu.

> Endure provocation; repress wrath; forgive an offence;
> and yield a point.

得忍且忍，得耐且耐

Tê jên ch'ieh jên, tê nai ch'ieh nai.

When it is proper to forbear, forbear.

不忍不耐，小事成大

Pu jên pu nai, hsiao shih ch'eng ta.

Want of forbearance causes small offences to become great ones.

忍字家中寶

Jên tzŭ chia chung pao.

The word " Forbearance " is a household treasure.

不忍一時有禍·三思百歲無妨

Pu jên i shih yu huo, san ssŭ pai sui wu fang.

Without forbearance you will be in trouble at once; think it over and you will have nought to fear for a hundred years.

吃虧是不佔便宜

Ch'ih k'uei shih pu chan pien i.

Whoever is willing to suffer, covets not another's advantage.

饒人算人之本，輸人算人之機

Jao jen suan jen chih pen, shu jên suan jên chih chi.

To forgive is considered man's duty; to win is considered man's ingenuity.

終身讓路不枉百步，終身讓畔不失一段

Chung shen jang lu pu wang pai pu, chung shen jang pan pu shih i tuan.

In life-long concession of road and dyke, one neither loses a hundred paces nor a single plot.

行不讓路，坐不讓席

Hsing pu jang lu, tso pu jang hsi.

He will neither concede on a road nor at a feast.

將 相 頂 頭 堪 走 馬，公 侯 肚 裏 好 撐 船

Chiang hsiang ting t'ou k'an tsou ma, kung hou tu li hao ch'eng
ch'uan.

> You may walk your horse over a general's or premier's
> head; and pole your boat in the body of a duke or
> marquis. Note.—This strange proverb is intended
> to express the boundless generosity and forbearance
> of the gentlemen mentioned.

放 糢 糊 些 不 可 頂 眞

Fang mo hu hsieh, pu k'o ting chen.

> Affect a little indistinctness, rather than insist upon
> absolute correctness.

處 世 讓 一 步 爲 高，待 人 寬 一 分 是 福

Ch'ü shih jang i pu wei kao, tai jên k'uan i fen shih fu.

> In life it is noble to yield even one step; and it is
> happiness to treat men with even a little generosity.

讓 人 非 我 弱，守 己 任 他 強

Jang jen fei wo jo, shou chi jên t'a ch'iang.

> One may give way to another not from weakness but
> because of self-control.

饒 人 非 我 弱，癡 漢 入 牢 門

Jao jen fei wo jo, ch'ih han ju lao men.

> One may give way to another, not from weakness, but
> because one is not fool enough to risk imprisonment.

心 直 口 快 招 人 致 怪

Hsin chih k'ou k'uai chao jên chih kuai.

> To be severe and outspoken is to provoke the censure of
> men.

君 子 不 念 舊 惡

Chün tzŭ pu nien chiu ô.

> The superior man forgets past injuries.

小 不 忍 亂 大 謀

Hsiao pu jên luan ta mou.

> A little impatience will spoil a great scheme.

2. CONTENTMENT.

飽 餐 三 飯 常 知 足，得 一 帆 風 便 可 收

Pao ts'an san fan ch'ang chih tsu, tê i fan fêng pien k'o shou.

With three good meals a day be content ; take in your sail after a good run before the wind. i.e. Be satisfied.

知 足 常 足，終 身 不 辱

Chih tsu ch'ang tsu, chung shen pu ju.

To be always contented means a lifetime without disgrace.

得 意 不 可 再 往

Tê i pu k'o tsai wang.

Having obtained your wish be content.

人 生 得 過 隨 時 過

Jên sheng tê kuo sui shih kuo.

Be content with what is sufficient to pass over the present time.

比 上 不 足，比 下 有 餘

Pi shang pu tsu, pi hsia yu yü.

Compared with superiors, I have less ; compared with inferiors, I have more.

得 過 且 過

Tê kuo ch'ieh kuo.

Be content with whatever you have.

人 要 知 足，天 為 賜 福

Jên yao chih tsu, t'ien wei tz'ŭ fu.

Heaven will prosper the contented man.

養 心 莫 善 於 寡 欲

Yang hsin mo shan yü kua yü.

To nourish virtue there is nothing better than to make the desires few.

知 足 者 貧 賤 亦 樂，不 知 足 者 富 貴 亦 憂

Chih tsu chê p'in chien i lê, pu chih tsu chê fu kuei i yu.

He who is content, though poor, is happy ; he who is not content, though rich, is sad.

3. FILIAL PIETY.

世 間 好 事 忠 和 孝, 天 下 良 謀 讀 與 耕

Shih chien hao shih chung ho hsiao, t'ien hsia liang mou tu yü keng.

No virtues equal loyalty and filial piety; no employments equal those of learning and agriculture.

但 存 忠 孝 還 天 地

Tau ts'un chung hsiao huan t'ien ti.

Only preserve loyalty and filial piety, and you will recompense heaven and earth.

千 經 萬 典, 孝 義 爲 先

Ch'ien ching wan tien, hsiao i wei hsien.

In all the classics filial piety and righteousness are considered of first importance.

萬 善 孝 爲 先

Wan shan hsiao wei hsien.

Of a myriad virtues filial piety is the first.

萬 惡 淫 爲 首, 百 行 孝 爲 先

Wan ô yin wei shou, pai hsing hsiao wei hsien.

Of a myriad vices, fornication is the chief ; of a hundred virtues, filial piety is the first.

孝 心 感 動 天 和 地

Hsiao hsin kan tung t'ien ho ti.

Filial piety moves heaven and earth.

子 孝 父 心 寬

Tzŭ hsiao fu hsin k'uan.

A filial son is the joy of his father.

一 子 不 孝, 有 子 皆 滅

I tzŭ pu hsiao, yu tzŭ chieh mieh.

One unfilial son involves others in ruin.

兒 不 賢 媳 不 孝

Erh pu hsien, hsi pu hsiao.

When the son lacks virtue, the daughter-in-law lacks filial piety.

父 母 不 寬 難 顯，兒 女 的 孝 道 來

Fu mu pu k'uan nan hsien, erh nü ti hsiao tao lai.

If parents are not lenient, children are not likely to be filial.

君 不 正 臣 必 不 忠，父 不 慈 子 定 不 孝

Chün pu cheng ch'en pi pu chung, fu pu tz'ŭ tzŭ ting pu hsiao.

If the prince is not upright the minister is certain not to be loyal; if the father is not kind the son is sure to be unfilial.

不 孝 有 三 無 後 爲 大

Pu hsiao yu san wu hou wei ta.

There are three things which are unfilial, and to have no posterity is the greatest of them.

孝 親 十 六 兩，後 輩 兒 孫 還 一 斤

Hsiao ch'in shih liu liang, hou pei êrh sun huan i chin.

He who is filial to the extent of sixteen ounces, will be repaid a full catty by his descendants.

百 行 孝 爲 先，論 心 不 論 事 論 事 世 間 無 孝 子

Pai hsing hsiao wei hsien, lun hsin pu lun shih lun shih shih chien wu hsiao tzŭ.

Of the hundred virtues filial piety is the chief, but it must be judged by the intentions not by the acts; if judged by the acts there are no filial sons in the world.

事 君 要 忠，事 親 要 孝

Shih chün yao chung, shih ch'in yao hsiao.

Serve the sovereign with fidelity and your parents with filial piety.

上 查 吃 荣，斷 種 絕 代

Shang ch'a ch'ih ts'ai tuan chung chüeh tai.

If you become a vegetarian you separate from your ancestors and cut off posterity.

孝 順 新 婦 值 孝 堂

Hsiao shun hsin fu chih hsiao t'ang.

A dutiful daughter-in-law will attend upon her dead mother-in-law, i.e., will not leave the place of mourning.

有命之父母不知孝子

Yu ming chih fu-mü pu chih hsiao tzŭ.

Lucky parents do not know what it is to have filial sons.

久病牀前無孝子

Chiu ping ch'uang ch'ien wu hsiao tzŭ.

There are no filial sons at the bedside of those who are long ill.

4. GENEROSITY AND KINDNESS.

常捨常有，富貴長久

Ch'ang shê ch'ang yu, fu kuei ch'ang chiu.

He who is constantly giving always has; riches and honour abide with him.

萬事留一線之路

Wan shih liu i hsien chih lu.

Always leave some way of escape (i.e. to the erring).

喚起風來大家涼

Huan ch'i fêng lai ta chia liang,

To call up a breeze that all may be cooled.

見人一善，忘其百非

Chien jen i shan wang ch'i pai fei.

To see a man do a good deed is to forget all his other faults.

牽瞎子過橋

Ch'ien hsia tzŭ kuo ch'iao.

·To conduct a blind man over a bridge.

刻苦自己，厚待別人

K'o k'u tzŭ chi, hou tai pieh jen.

To stint oneself and treat others generously.

打燈籠照別人

Ta teng lung chao pieh jên.

To use one's own lantern to lighten another's path.

不看金面看佛面

Pu k'an chin mien k'an fu mien.

> Do not consider the gilt face of the idol but the face of
> Buddha behind it. Note.—The "gilt face" rep-
> resents the offender, "the face of Buddha" the
> intercessor ; and the request is that for the inter-
> cessor's sake the offender may be forgiven.

濟人之急,救人之危

Chi jên chih chi, chiu jen chih wei.

> Help men in their necessities and rescue them from
> danger.

只有千里人情,沒有千里威風

Chih yu ch'ien li jên ch'ing, mu yu ch'ien li wei fêng.

> It is only kindness and not severity, that can impress at
> the distance of a thousand li.

施恩莫望報,望報莫施恩

Shih êu mo wang pao, wang pao mo shih ên.

> Better not do kindnesses at all, than do them in the hope
> of reward.

行時時之方便,作種種之陰功

Hsing shih shih chih fang pien, tso chung chung chih yin kung.

> Continually do acts of kindness ; perform every sort of
> secret virtue.

順水推舟做人情

Shun shui t'ui chou tso jên ch'ing.

> To row with the stream in doing a favour. Note.—For
> instance,—to give books to one fond of study, or
> wine to one who likes it.

人情大過王法

Jên ch'ing ta kuo wang fa.

> Kindness is greater than law.

待人須當量大

Tai jen hsü tang liang ta.

> Men must be treated with great generosity.

單 竹 不 成 排

Tan chu pu ch'eng p'ai.

> Mutual Help. *Lit.* A single bamboo doesn't form a row.

明 中 去，暗 中 來

Ming chung ch'ü. an chung lai.

> What you give openly you will receive in secret.

嚴 霜 單 打 獨 根 草

Yen shuang tan ta tu ken ts'ao.

> The frost only destroys the solitary blades of grass, i.e.
> Mutual help will avert evil.

佛 以 慈 悲 爲 本，方 便 爲 門

Fu i tz'ǔ pei wei pen, fang pien wei men.

> Buddha makes compassion the root, and good works the
> door (to salvation). Note. 方便 indicates in
> Buddhism the practice of charitable deeds.

5. GRATITUDE.

吃 王 水 土，報 王 恩

Ch'ih wang shui t'u, pao wang ên.

> Fed on the king's land, recompense the king's favour.

食 王 爵 祿，報 王 恩

Shih wang chio lu pao wang ên.

> Enjoying the king's dignities and emoluments, recom-
> pense the king's favour.

心 不 負 人，面 無 慚 色

Hsin pu fu jên, mien wu ts'an sê.

> He who is grateful has nothing to blush for.

得 人 點 水 之 恩，須 當 湧 泉 之 報

Tê jên tien shui chih ên, hsü tang yung ch'ien chih pao.

> For the favour of a drop of water, pay back a gushing
> fountain.

得 人 錢 財，與 人 消 災

Tê jên ch'ien ts'ai, yü jen hsiao tsai.

> If you share a man's wealth, try to lessen his misfortunes.

寧 可 負 我, 切 莫 負 人

Ning k'o fu wo, ch'ieh mo fu jen.

> Better that others be ungrateful to me than that I should be so to others.

羊 有 跪 乳 之 恩, 鴉 有 反 哺 之 義

Yang yu kuei ju chih en, ya yu fan fu chih i.

> Lambs have the grace to suck kneeling; and young crows have the goodness to return part of their food to their parents. Note.—This latter phrase is explained both in a literal and metaphorical sense. Literally the crow is said to disgorge its food for its parents to eat. Metaphorically it returns the food received in use by nourishing its parents when they are old.

隨 分 耕 耡 收 地 利, 他 時 飽 煖 謝 蒼 天

Sui fen keng ch'u shou ti li, t'a shih pao nuan hsieh ts'ang t'ien.

> Contentedly till the ground and receive its increase; when you are warmed and fed, thank Heaven.

施 惠 勿 念, 受 恩 莫 忘

Shih hui wu nien, shou ên mo wang.

> Be forgetful of favours given; be mindful of blessings received.

知 恩 不 報, 非 爲 人 也

Chih ên pu pao, fei wei jen yeh.

> It is unmanly to be ungrateful for favours received.

忘 恩 背 義, 禽 獸 之 徒

Wang ên pei i, ch'in shou chih t'u.

> He is but a brute who forgets favours received and turns his back upon righteousness.

吃 人 的 口 軟, 得 人 的 手 軟

Ch'ih jên ti k'ou juan, tê jen ti shou juan.

> He who eats another's food and receives another's favour, is tender in speaking of, and dealing with him.

恩 將 仇 報

Ên chiang ch'ou pao.

> To return evil for good.

一 粥 一 飯 當 思 來 處 不 易

I chou i fan tang ssŭ lai ch'ü pu i.

> Over a bowl of congee or rice, one should remember the trouble it has cost to supply it.

受 恩 不 報 非 君 子

Shou en pu pao fei chün tzŭ.

> He who is ungrateful for favours received is not a princely man.

身 披 一 縷 常 思 織 女 之 勞，日 食 三 餐 每 念 農 夫 之 苦

Shen p'i i lü ch'ang ssu chih nü chih lao, jih shih san ts'an mei nien nung fu chih k'u.

> When you put on your clothes, remember the weaver's labour; when you take your daily food, remember the husbandman's hard work.

受 人 恩 而 不 忍 負 者，爲 子 必 孝 爲 臣 必 忠

Shou jên ên erh pu jen fu che, wei tzŭ pi hsiao wei ch'en pi chung.

> He who is grateful for favours received, will be filial as a son and loyal as a minister.

飲 水 思 源

Yin shui ssŭ yüan.

> When you drink from the stream, remember the spring.

食 笋 須 記 栽 竹 人

Shih sun hsü chi tsai chu jen.

> When you eat bamboo-sprouts, remember the planter of the bamboos.

Chapter 6. Vices.

1. FLATTERY.

論 巴 結 不 過 是 千 百 把 總

Lun pa chieh pu kuo shih ch'ien pai pa tsung,

> As to flattery, it is only petty officers who can practise it. i.e. Only inferiors flatter superiors. "Petty officers": *Lit.* Lieutenant 千 總, Sub-Lieutenants 百 總, etc.

大 老 爺 出 門 放 四 炮 奉 承 不 到 家

Ta lao yeh ch'u men fang ssu p'ao feng ch'eng pu tao chia.

On the departure of a high official to fire a salute of four guns is insufficient flattery.

只 在 熱 竈 裏 着 把 火

Chih tsai jo tsao li cho pa huo.

Flattering only the rich, *Lit.* Only to add fuel to a hot stove.

呵 哄 不 彀 添 鹽 酌 醋

Ho hung pu kou t'ien yen cho ts'u.

Importunate flattery. *Lit.* His humbug fails, so he adds more salt and pours on more vinegar.

奉 承 富 貴 人 畢 竟 有 何 益, 欺 負 貧 窮 人 與 汝 結 仇 隙

Fêng ch'eng fu kuei jen pi ching yu ho i, ch'i fu p'in ch'iung jen. yü ju chieh ch'ou ch'i.

What ultimate benefit is there in flattering the high and wealthy? Insult the poor and needy and you give occasion for enmity.

2. HYPOCRISY AND DECEIT.

無 中 生 有, 畫 蛇 添 足

Wu chung sheng yu, hua shê t'ien tsu.

He makes something out of nothing. He draws snakes and adds feet. i.e. Exaggerates.

欺 老 莫 欺 幼 欺 人 心 不 明

Ch'i lao mo ch'i yu, ch'i jên hsin pu ming.

If you deceive the aged, do not deceive the young; he who deceives has a darkened conscience.

打 破 腦 殼 騙 人

Ta p'o nao k'o p'ien jên.

To break one's head in order to deceive. Note.—This is done by beggars sometimes in order to extort money.

畫 水 無 魚 空 作 浪, 繡 花 雖 好 不 聞 香

Hua shui wu yü k'ung tso lang, hsiu hua sui hao pu wen hsiang.

A painted picture of water without fishes, only represents imitation waves; embroidered flowers, though beautiful, have no fragrance.

指 鹿 爲 馬
Chih lu wei ma.

> Wilful misrepresentation. *Lit.* To point a stag out as
> a horse. Note.—This was done by Chao Kao 趙 高
> a powerful but traitorous minister of the Chin 秦
> Dynasty, to his master the emperor Erh Shih 二 世.

孫 悟 空 的 跟 兜，打 不 過 佛 爺 巴 掌 心
Sun Wu K'ung ti ken tou, ta pu kuo fu yeh pa chang hsin.

> Not to be deceived. *Lit.* Sun Wu Kung's somersaults
> never carried him beyond the extent of Buddha's
> palm. Note.—Sun Wu Kung is the leading
> character in the Hsi Yu Chi 西 遊 記, a popular
> Chinese novel, who began life as a monkey. He
> tried to turn a somersault that would carry him to
> the confines of the universe, but found after all that
> he had only reach the fingers of Buddha's hand.

不 可 面 是 背 非
Pu k'o mien shih pei fei.

> Do not say "yes" before a man's face, and "no" behind
> his back.

不 可 口 是 心 非
Pu k'o k'ou shih hsin fei.

> Do not say one thing and mean another.

眞 菩 薩 面 前 莫 燒 假 香
Chen p'u sa mien ch'ien mo shao chia hsiang.

> Do not burn false incense before a true god.

欺 善 怕 惡
Ch'i shan p'a ô.

> To deceive the good and fear the bad.

瞞 上 不 瞞 下
Man shang pu man hsia.

> If you deceive your superiors, don't deceive your inferiors.

色 不 迷 人 人 自 迷
Se pu mi jen jen tzu mi.

> It is not beauty that beguiles men ; men beguile
> themselves.

富 貴 若 從 奸 巧 得，世 間 呆 子 嗑 西 風
Fu kuei jo ts'ung chien ch'iao tê, shih chien tai tzŭ ho hsi fêng.

> If villainy and cunning obtain all that is valuable, the world's simple people must live on the west wind. Note. 嗑 equals 喝.

一 隻 手 揑 香，一 隻 手 揑 鎗
I chih shou nieh hsiang, i chih shou nieh ch'iang.

> Incense in one hand, a spear in the other. Comp. Psalm. 55. 21.

老 虎 掛 素 珠 假 慈 悲
Lao hu kua so chu chia tz'ŭ pei.

> For a tiger to wear a string of praying beads is hypocritical tenderness.

賴 佛 偸 食 鞋
Lai fu t'ou shih hsieh.

> Trusting to Buddha's help to steal food and shoes, i.e., making a cloak of religion.

3. INGRATITUDE.

一 腔 熱 血 化 爲 冰 炭
I ch'iang jo hsieh hua wei ping t'an.

> He freezes my heart's warm blood into icy cold coal. Note.—This refers to unappreciated service or kindness.

不 因 漁 父 引，怎 得 見 波 濤
Pu yin yü fu yin, tsen tê chien po t'ao.

> If he had not had a fisherman to direct him, how could he ever have seen the waves. Note.—These are said to be the words of Tung Kao Kung 東 皇 公 who thus complains of the ingratitude of Wu Tzu Ssu 伍 子 胥, a high official in the State of Ts'u 楚, to whom he had rendered signal service, but by whom his service had been forgotten.

吃 飯 不 知 牛 辛 苦，穿 衣 不 知 紡 織 人
Ch'ih fan pu chih niu hsin k'u, ch'üan i pu chih fang chih jên.

> To feed and clothe oneself without ever recognising the trouble our food has cost the ox, or our clothes the weaver.

不 以 我 爲 德，反 以 我 爲 仇
Pu i wo wei tê, fan i wo wei ch'ou.

> He does not look upon me as a friend but as an enemy.

關 門 養 虎，虎 大 傷 人
Kuan men yang hu, hu ta shang jen.

> If you rear a tiger indoors, when it is full-grown it will injure somebody.

念 完 經，打 和 尙
Nien wan ching ta ho shang.

> To beat the priest after he has recited the prayers.

4. MEANNESS.

又 要 驢 子 走 得 好，又 要 驢 子 不 吃 草
Yu yao lü tzŭ tsou tê hao, yu yao lü tzŭ pu ch'ih ts'ao.

> He wants his donkey to run well and yet not eat any food.

無 奈 東 瓜 何，捉 得 瓠 子 磨
Wu nai tung kua ho, cho tê hu tzŭ mo.

> You can't endure the pumpkin and so you would grind down the melon.

說 大 話，用 小 錢
Shuo ta hua yung hsiao ch'ien.

> To promise much and give little. *Lit.* To speak great words and use small cash. Note.—Formerly, when the government was in straits, small cash was issued, and many of these coins continue in circulation.

指 甲 殼 太 深 了
Chih chia k'o t'ai shen liao.

> A grasping nature. *Lit.* His finger nails are too long.

抓 別 人 帽 子 去 打 彩
Chua pien jen mao tzŭ tiu ta ts'ai.

> Making presents with other's property. *Lit.* To seize another's hat and throw it on the stage.

用 別 人 的 大 方，用 自 己 的 手 緊

Yung pien jên ti ta fang, yung tzŭ chi ti shou chin.

> To be generous with other people's things, and grasping with what is one's own.

熱 臉 挨 冷 臉

Jo lien ai leng lien.

> Toadyism. *Lit*. To place one's warm cheek alongside another's cold one.

猴 子 檢 到 一 塊 薑，吃 了 怕 辣 丟 了 又 捨 不 得

Hou tzŭ chien tao i k'uan chiang, ch'ih liao p'a la tiu liao yu shê pu tê.

> The monkey seizes a piece of ginger, fears to eat it because it is hot; and is not willing to throw it away. Comp. The dog in the manger.

丟 在 冷 水 盆 裏 去 了

Tiu tsai leng shui p'en li ch'ü liao.

> To slight. *Lit*. To throw into a tub of cold water.

老 鷹 飛 過 拔 蓬 毛

Lao ying fei kuo pa p'eng mao.

> A grasping character. *Lit*. Pulling a bunch of feathers out of the kite flying by.

偷 割 稻，佈 施 粥

T'ou ko tao, pu shih chou.

> Stealthily cutting a neighbour's rice in order to make gruel to be given in charity.

挖 東 墻 補 西 墻

Wa tung ch'iang pu hsi ch'iang.

> Robbing Peter to pay Paul. *Lit*. Taking from the eastern wall to repair the western one.

到 處 不 用 錢，到 處 惹 人 嫌

Tao ch'ü pu yung ch'ien, tao ch'ü jo jen hsien.

> If wherever you go you spend no money, you will be an object of dislike.

鐵 驢 子 似 的 沒 毛 可 拔

T'ieh lü tzŭ ssu ti mu mao k'o pa.

A stingy man. *Lit.* Like an iron donkey, you can't get a hair out of him.

5. QUARRELLING AND VIOLENCE.

借 秦 伐 楚 悶 氣 出 透

Chieh ch'in fa ch'u men ch'i ch'u t'ou.

Cat's-paw. *Lit.* Using Ch'in to punish Ch'u, he gives vent to his ill-temper. Note — 秦, 楚, two of the ancient Feudal States.

猴 急 豹 跳 強 打 惡 要

Hou chi pao t'iao ch'iang ta ô yao.

With the quickness of a monkey or like a leopard leaping, he demands and extracts with force.

在 生 是 一 根 草．死 了 是 一 個 寶

Tsai sheng shih i ken ts'ao, ssu liao shih i ko pao.

Alive, he is but a blade of grass; dead, he is a treasure. Note.—The meaning is that though a man may be worthless as a blade of grass whilst living, if murdered, his family would demand satisfaction and probably make money out of the affair.

與 人 發 怒，切 莫 爭 鬥

Yü jen fa nu ch'ieh mo cheng tou.

If you are angry with anybody, on no account come to blows.

人 情 留 一 線，久 後 好 相 見

Jên ch'ing liu i hsien, chiu hou hao hsiang chien.

Retain a thread of kindly feeling, it will make it easier when you meet again.

半 斤 八 兩

Pan chin pa liang.

Six of one and half a dozen of the other. *Lit.* Half a catty, eight ounces.

唆 狗 咬 猪

So kou yao chu.

To excite a quarrel. *Lit.* To incite a dog to worry a pig.

相 打 無 好 拳，相 罵 無 好 言

Hsiang ta wu hao ch'üan, hsiang ma wu hao yen.

> They are not good fists which fight, nor good words which curse.

雞 子 與 石 子 鬥

Chi tzǔ yü shih tzu tou.

> A hopeless quarrel. *Lit.* A hen's egg fighting a rock.

霸 王 強 喪 烏 江，韓 信 強 喪 渭 陽

Pa Wang ch'iang sang Wu Chiang, Han Hsin ch'iang sang Wei Yang.

> Pa Wang was violent but he died at Wu Chiang: Han Hsin was violent but he died at Wei Yang. Note.—Pa Wang or Hsiang Chi 項 籍, ruler of Ch'u 楚 was noted for his brutality. Han Hsin, also a ruler of Ch'u, was famous for his prowess in arms.

鷸 蚌 相 持，漁 人 得 利

Yü pang hsiang ch'ih yü jen te li.

> When the heron and mussel quarrelled, the fisherman got the benefit. Note.—The reference in this proverb is to a fable ascribed in the Narrative of the Contending States to Su Tai 蘇 代, a prominent statesman who lived in the third century B.C. The mussel nipped the heron's beak as the heron was endeavouring to extract the mussel, and as neither would give way they were caught by the fisherman.

道 路 不 平，旁 人 鏟 修

Tao lu pu p'ing p'ang jen ch'an hsiu.

> When the road is uneven, those who live on each side level it. Note.—This is said when bystanders take up an ill-used man's quarrel, and punish for him his oppressor.

男 不 可 與 女 鬥，刀 不 可 與 斧 鬥

Nan pu k'o yü nü tou, tao pu k'o yü fu tou.

> A man must not quarrel with a woman; the axe must not quarrel with the knife. i.e. The woman will get the worst of it.

知 事 少 時 煩 惱 少，識 人 多 處 是 非 多

Chih shih shao shih fan nao shao, shih jen to ch'ü shih fei to.

> He who meddles little with other peoples' affairs will
> have few troubles; he who mixes with many people
> will often get wrong.

家 中 不 和 鄰 里 欺，鄰 里 不 和 說 是 非

Chia chung pu ho lin li ch'i, lin li pu ho shuo shih fei.

> A quarrelsome family neighbours despise: quarrelsome
> neighbours slander each other.

大 事 化 小，小 事 化 無

Ta shih hua hsiao, hsiao shih hua wu.

> Convert great quarrels into small ones, and small ones
> into nothing.

扯 胡 琴 的 事

Ch'ê hu ch'in ti shih.

> Quarrelling over a trifling affair. Note.—This seems to
> be identical with a common English expression "a
> fiddling business". *Lit.* Wrangling about a fiddle.

寃 仇 可 解 不 可 結

Wan ch'ou k'o chieh pu k'o chieh.

> One may reconcile enmities but not produce them.

罵 一 聲 江 西 老 表 大 家 有 分

Ma i sheng Chiang Hsi lao piao ta chia yu fen.

> Whoever calls a man a cousin from Kiangsi, insults the
> public generally. Note.—This is essentially a Hupeh
> proverb. About the beginning of the Ta Ching
> Dynasty rebels devasted Hupeh to such an extent
> that it had to be repopulated with Kiangsi men. To
> call a man "a Kiangsi cousin" is really to curse
> him, and for a Hupeh man to do so is to curse his
> own relation, and in thus doing to offend the public.

灣 到 船 嗜 罵

Wan tao ch'uan shê ma.

> To anchor in order to quarrel.

劈 破 竹 總 夾 烟

P'i p'o chu tsung chia yen.

> Each half of the riven bamboo smokes. Note.—Said of men, who when a quarrel is over, retain some remains of caloric.

開 弓 莫 放 箭, 打 人 不 如 嚇 人 強

K'ai kung mo fang chien, ta jen pu ju ho jen ch'iang.

> Draw your bow but do not discharge the arrow; it is better to frighten a man than to strike him.

是 非 難 逃 衆 口

Shih fei nan t'ao chung k'ou.

> Quarrels cannot escape the verdict of public opinion.

打 莫 打 人 痛 處, 罵 莫 罵 人 羞 處

Ta mo ta jen t'ung ch'ü, ma mo ma jen hsiu ch'ü.

> Neither beat a man on a wound, nor curse him about a disgrace.

公 說 公 有 理, 婆 說 理 更 長

Kung shuo kung yu li, p'o shuo li keng ch'ang.

> The old man claims to be right and the old woman to be more so.

蚊 蟲 遭 扇 打 嘴 傷 人 心

Wen ch'ung tsao san ta tsui shang jen hsin.

> The mouth wounds the heart, as when a mosquito provokes a rap from a fan.

一 竹 篙 子 打 一 船 人

I chu kao tzŭ ta i ch'uan jen.

> Indiscriminate cursing. *Lit.* One bamboo pole beats a whole boat-load of people.

怪 人 須 要 俾 人 知

Kuai jên hsü yao pei jên chih.

> If you are offended with a person, you must tell him the reason.

兩 個 學 生 打 架 爲 筆

Liang ko hsüeh sheng ta chia wei pi.

> Two students fighting for a pencil. Note.—A specimen of the innuendo. The last two characters, identical in sound with expressing doubt, are used to convey that meaning. 未 必.

事 怕 當 面

Shih p'a tang mien.

> When men come face to face their differences vanish.

江 中 雖 大, 船 亦 有 相 撞

Chiang chung sui ta, ch'uan i yu hsiang chuang.

> Although the river is broad there are times when boats collide.

他 仇, 我 不 仇, 寃 家 卽 了 休

T'a ch'ou, wo pu ch'ou, yüan chia chi liao hsiu.

> Although he hates me, if I do not hate him, enmity will soon be at an end.

淘 得 河 水 混 有 魚 拿

T'ao tê ho shui hun yu yü na.

> When you stir up the mud in the river water you can catch fish.

結 寃 與 人 謂 之 種 禍

Chieh yüan yä jên wei chih chung huo.

> Forming resentments with men may be called planting misery.

來 猫 去 狗, 不 爭 自 有

Lai mao ch'ü kou, pu cheng tzŭ yu.

> If the dog goes when the cat comes there will be no quarrelling.

大 水 冲 了 龍 王 廟, 一 家 不 認 的 一 家 人

Ta shui ch'ung liao Lung Wang Miao, i chia pu jen ti i chia jên.

> When the flood carries away the Dragon King's Temple it is a case of one family not recognising another. Note.—The Dragon is supposed to control the waters.

大 事 不 如 小，小 事 不 如 了

Ta shih pu ju hsiao, hsiao pu ju liao.

A trivial quarrel is better than a grievous one : but a settlement is better than a trivial quarrel.

6. SELFISHNESS.

各 人 吃 飯 各 人 飽 各 人 生 死 各 人 了

Ko jên ch'ih fan ko jên pao, ko jên sheng ssŭ ko jên liao.

Each man eats to satisfy his own hunger ; each man lives and dies only for himself.

貪 他 一 斗 米 失 却 半 年 糧，爭 他 一 脚 豚 反 失 一 羣 羊

T'an t'a i tou mi shih ch'io pan nien liang, cheng t'a i chiao t'un fan shih i ch'ün yang.

Coveting another man's one measure of rice, he loses half a year's food ; wrangling over a quarter of a pig, he loses a flock of sheep.

於 今 的 人 眼 皮 子 薄

Yü chin ti jên yen p'i tzŭ po.

Nowadays men's eyelids are thin, i.e., they can see everything and want everything they see.

各 是 各，你 顧 你，我 顧 我

Ko shih ko, ni ku ni wo ku wo.

Each for himself ; you look after yourself and I will look after myself.

田 也 空 地 也 空，換 了 多 少 主 人 翁，
金 也 空 銀 也 空，死 後 何 曾 在 手 中，
妻 也 空 子 也 空，黄 泉 路 上 不 相 逢

T'ien yeh k'ung ti yeh k'ung, huan liao to shao chu jen wêng,
Chin yeh k'ung yin yeh k'ung, ssŭ hou ho ts'eng tsai shou chung,
Ch'i yeh k'ung tzŭ yeh k'ung, Huang Ch'üan lu shang pu hsiang fêng.

" Vanity of vanities, all is vanity ". *Lit.* Fields and lands are all vanity, they are constantly changing hands ; gold and silver are all vanity, after death they cannot be retained ; wives and children are al vanity, you never meet them in Hades.

你 走 你 的 陽 關 大 路, 我 過 我 的 獨 木 橋

Ni tsou ni ti yang kuau ta lu, wo kuo wo ti tu mu ch'iao.

> Go you along your great highway, and I'll get across my
> one-pole bridge.

勿 舍 己 而 芸 人 之 田

Wu shê chi erh yün jên chih t'ien.

> Do not neglect your own in order to weed another's
> field.

搬 罾 的 守 埠 頭

Pan tseng ti shou fou t'ou.

> Each fisherman sticks to his own fishing ground.   Note.—
> The "tseng" is the large square net often seen on
> the river banks.

脚 彎 手 彎 往 懷 裏 彎

Chiao wan shou wan wang huai li wan.

> To act selfishly.   *Lit.* Both feet and hands bend towards
> the bosom.

逐 鹿 者 不 顧 兎

Chu lu chê pu ku t'u.

> The stag-hunter will not look at the hare.

剮 眼 睛 不 怕 瞎

Kua yen ching pu p'a hsia.

> To grasp at gain regardless of suffering inflicted on
> others.   *Lit.* To gouge out another's eyes fearless
> of blinding him.

幹 大 事 惜 身 而 避, 見 小 利 亡 命 而 來

Kan ta shih hsi shen erh pi, chien hsiao li wang ming erh lai.

> When there is important business to be transacted, he
> spares himself the trouble ; but let him hear of a
> little profit, and he will risk his life to get it.

貪 圖 小 利, 大 事 難 成

T'an t'u hsiao li, ta shih nan ch'eng.

> He who covets small gain, will not be able to accomplish
> great transactions.

打 進 財 卦

Ta chin ts'ai kua.

> To cast the die that brings in the wealth.

人 無 百 歲 壽，枉 作 千 年 計

Jên wu pai sui shou, wang tso ch'ien nien chi.

> Since men live not a hundred years, it is vain to scheme for a thousand.

赤 身 而 來，赤 身 而 去

Ch'ih shen erh lai ch'in shen erh ch'ü.

> Naked we come, and naked we go. Note.—This sentiment is the same as that expressed in Job. 1.21, and 1 Tim. 6.7. It is intended to act as a check on covetousness.

世 界 做 完 空 手 去

Shih chieh tso wan k'ung shou ch'ü.

> Man goes empty-handed when his work on earth is done.

盈 箱 滿 籠 替 人 藏，何 曾 件 件 穿 到 老

Ying hsiang man lung t'i jên ts'ang, ho ts'eng chien chien ch'uan tao lao.

> He who fills his boxes and trunks with clothes, only lays them up for others ; for how can he live to wear each one of them out.

從 來 多 少 好 樓 臺，半 成 瓦 礫 生 青 草

Ts'ung lai to shao hao lou t'ai, pan ch'eng wa li sheng ch'ing ts'ao.

> Of all the noble edifices of the past, one half of them are in ruins overgrown with grass.

世 上 錢 多 賺 不 盡，朝 裏 官 多 做 不 了

Shih shang ch'ien to chuan pu chin, ch'ao li kuan to tso pu liao.

> There is more money on earth than you can gain ; and more offices in the palace than you can fill.

公 眾 堂 屋 無 人 掃

Kung chung t'ang wu wu jen shao.

> There is no one to sweep a common hall.

先 有 自 己, 後 有 他 人

Hsien yu tzǔ chi hou yu t'a jên.

> Yourself first, others afterwards, i.e., "Charity begins at home".

莫 道 君 行 早, 更 有 早 行 人

Mo tao chün hsing tsao, keng yu tsao hsing jên.

> Don't boast of being first, for others indeed are before you.

坐 錢 眼 子 摸 錢 邊

Tso chien yen tzǔ mo ch'ien pien.

> Avarice. *Lit.* Sitting in the hole of a copper cash and feeling the edge of the coin.

螳 螂 捕 蟬 不 知 黃 雀 在 後

T'ang lang pu ch'an pu chih huang ch'iao tsai hou.

> The mantis seizes the cicada not knowing that the oriole is just behind.

7. SLANDER.

是 非 只 爲 多 開 口 煩 惱 皆 因 強 出 頭

Shih fei chih wei to k'ai k'ou, fan nao chieh yin ch'iang ch'u t'ou.

> Slander arises from nothing but too much talk ; offences all come because someone will intrude himself.

任 他 風 浪 起, 穩 坐 釣 魚 臺

Jên t'a fêng lang ch'i wen tso tiao yü t'ai.

> Let his wind and waves arise, I shall sit secure on my fishing terrace. Note.—Said by one conscious of innocence amidst slander.

人 好 說 不 壞, 水 退 石 還 在

Jen hao shuo pu huai, shui t'ui shih huan tsai.

> Slander cannot make a good man bad ; as when the water has receded the rock still remains.

坐 在 屋 裏 犯 夜

Tso tsai wu li fan yeh.

> How can I be guilty of crime, since I never stirred out of my house. Note.—Said in contradiction of slander.

七 處 放 火，八 處 燒 烟

Ch'i ch'u fang huo, pa ch'ü shao yen.

Slander spreads like fire. *Lit.* Light a fire in seven places, and in eight places there will be fire and smoke.

無 風 三 尺 浪，平 地 一 聲 雷

Wu fêng san ch'ih lang, p'ing ti i sheng lei.

Baseless slander. *Lit.* To have waves three feet high without wind, and thunder on a level plain.

事 怕 一 句 言

Shih p'a i chü yen.

A single (slanderous) sentence will injure any cause.

誰 人 背 後 無 人 說，那 個 人 前 不 說 人

Shui jên pei hou wu jên shuo, na ko jên ch'ien pu shuo jên.

What man, behind his back, is not spoken against; and who, before others, does not speak against men?

是 非 終 日 有，不 聽 自 然 無

Shih fei chung jih yu, pu t'ing tzŭ jan wu.

Slander is of daily occurrence, but if nobody would listen to it, it would soon cease.

莫 待 是 非 來 入 耳，從 前 恩 愛 反 成 仇

Mo tai shih fei lai ju erh, ts'ung ch'ien en ai fan ch'eng ch'ou.

Don't wait for slander to enter into your ears, lest it turn former love into hatred.

跳 得 黃 河 洗 不 清

T'iao tê Huang Ho hsi pu ch'ing.

One may leap into the Yellow River, and yet not be washed clean. Note.—The meaning is that one cannot clear oneself of slander.

楚 人 多 謠

Ch'u jên to yao.

The men of Ch'u like to spread rumours.

當 面 說 話 不 成 是 非

Tang mien shuo hua pu ch'eng shih fei.

What is said to a man's face is not slander.

平 白 地 造 謠 言

P'ing pai ti chao yao yen.

> Slander may spring up without a cause.

謠 言 不 動 智 者

Yao yen pu tung chih chê.

> Idle slanders do not affect wise men.

第 一 傷 天 害 理，好 講 閨 門 是 非

Ti i shang t'ien hai li, hao chiang kuei men shih fei.

> The thing which most wounds Heaven and injures Right, is the spreading of slander about women.

黃 犬 背 後 吠

Huang ch'uan pei hou fei.

> The yellow cur barks behind one's back.

耳 不 聽 肚 不 煩

Erh pu t'ing tu pu fan.

> When the ear will not listen, the heart escapes sorrow.

根 深 不 怕 風 搖 動，樹 正 何 愁 月 影 斜

Ken shen pu p'a feng yao tung, shu cheng ho ch'ou yüeh ying hsieh.

> Slander unheeded. *Lit.* When the root is deep, there is no need to fear the wind; when the tree is straight, why trouble if the moon gives slanting shadows.

扯 張 拉 李

Ch'e Chang la Li.

> To throw the blame on others. To drag Chang and pull Li.

自 己 有 錯，休 怪 別 人

Tzu chi yu ts'o, hsiu kuai pieh jen.

> Don't blame others for your own faults.

舌 頭 底 下 壓 死 人

Shê t'ou ti hsia ya ssŭ jen.

> Under the tongue men are crushed to death.

人 多 處 是 非 多

Jên to ch'ü shih fei to.

> Many men, many tongues. *Lit.* Where many people dwell there will be many faults (spoken about).

平 生 只 會 說 人 短, 何 不 回 頭 把 自 量

P'ing sheng chih hui shuo jên tuan, ho pu hui t'ou pa tzǔ liang.

> Why do not those who are only able to slander others turn round and examine themselves.

一 人 傳 虛, 百 人 傳 實

I jen ch'uan hsü, pai jên ch'uan shih.

> One man circulates a false story and a hundred men tell it as true.

明 鎗 容 易 躲, 暗 箭 也 難 防

Ming ch'iang jung i to, an chien yeh nan fang.

> It is easy to avoid a spear in the daylight but it is difficult to guard against an arrow in the dark.

經 目 之 事 猶 恐 未 眞, 背 後 之 言 豈 能 全 信

Ching mu chih shih yu k'ung wei chen, pei hou chih yen ch'i neng ch'üan hsin.

> If what we see is doubtful, why believe all that is spoken behind one's back.

8. STEALING.

銅 牆 鐵 壁, 只 要 費 點 力

T'ung ch'iang t'ieh pi, chih yao fei tien li.

> To dig through brass and iron walls only requires a little extra exertion.

風 吹 鴨 蛋 殼, 財 去 人 安 樂

Fêng ch'ui ya tan k'o, ts'ai ch'ü jên an lê.

> If you lose your wealth you can still be happy, for after all it is only a few duck-egg shells scattered by the wind.

遠 賊 必 要 近 脚

Yuan tsei pi yao chin chiao.

> A thief who is a stranger, needs an accomplice, who is not one.

強 盜 沿 街 走・無 贓 不 定 罪

Ch'iang tao yen chieh tsou, wu tsang pü ting tsui.

Though thieves infest the streets, if they have no stolen goods, they can't be convicted.

賭 者 盜 之 源

Tu chê tao chih' yüan.

Gambling is the source of robbery.

拏 賊 要 拏 贓，拏 姦 要 拏 雙

Na tsei yao na tsang, na chien yao na shuang.

In arresting a thief you must also obtain the stolen property; in arresting a prostitute you must also secure her paramour.

偷 雨 不 偷 雪，偷 風 不 偷 月

T'ou yü pu t'ou hsüeh, t'ou fêng pu t'ou yüeh.

Thieves steal in the rain, but not when it is snowing; they steal when the wind blows but not when the moon shines.

失 物 難 疑 人

Shih wu nan i jên.

Having lost anything do not suspect men of stealing it.

黑 毛 猪 兒 家 家 有

Hei mao chu erh chia chia yu.

Everybody has a black pig.　Note.—This is used to repel a charge of theft.

箱 子 裏 衣 裳 有 件 數

Hsiang tzŭ li i shang yu chien shu.

All the clothes in the box are counted.　Note.—This is a caution to would-be thieves.

偷 雞 摸 狗 總 不 改 性

T'ou chi mo kou tsung pu kai hsing.

He who steals fowls and entices dogs, will never change his disposition.

偷 得 利 而 後 有 害

T'ou tê li erh hou yu hai.

Nothing in the end is got by thieving.

強 盜 遇 着 賊 打 刦

Ch'iang tao yü cho tsei ta chieh.

Robbers get plundered by thieves.

小 時 偷 針 大 時 偷 金

Hsiao shih t'ou chen ta shih t'ou chin.

He who steals a needle when young when grown up will
steal gold.

偷 吃 不 肥，做 賊 不 富

T'ou ch'i pu fei, tso tsei pu fu.

You won't get fat by stealing food, nor rich by becoming
a thief.

走 魚 是 大 的

Tsou yü shih ta ti.

The fish that gets away is always a large one, i.e., things
that have been stolen are always the best.

9. VARIOUS VICES.

把 臉 一 皮，百 事 大 吉

Pa lien i p'i pai shih ta chi.

Don't consider your reputation and you may do anything
you like.

嫖 賭 家 財 盡，囊 空 自 然 休

P'iao tu chia ts'ai chin, nang k'ung tzŭ jan hsiu.

He who wastes his fortune in profligacy, when his purse
is empty must come to a stop.

逸 則 思 淫

I tsê ssu yin.

Leisure breeds lasciviousness.

水 一 傾 則 不 可 覆，性 一 縱 則 不 可 反

Shui i ch'ing tsê pu k'o fu, hsing i tsung tsê pu k'o fan.

Water once spilt cannot be gathered up again; passions
once indulged cannot be restrained.

醜 媳 婦 難 免 不 見 公 婆 的 面

Ch'ou hsi fu nan mien pu chien kung p'o ti mien.

Vice cannot be concealed. *Lit.* An ugly daughter-in-law
cannot help but be seen by her mother-in-law.

但 將 冷 眼 觀 螃 蟹,看 你 橫 行 到 幾 時

Tan chiang leng yen kuan p'ang hsieh, k'an ni heng hsing tao chi shih.

> I look at you with an unprejudiced eye, as at a crab, to see to what extent you will carry on your perverse practices. Note.—The point of the saying is in the fact that the crab is supposed to walk sideways, and the term 橫 行 indicates this as well as "perverse practices".

歪 嘴 吹 喇 叭 斜 氣

Wai tsui ch'ui la pa hsieh ch'i.

> Depraved conduct. *Lit.* A wry-mouthed man blows a trumpet with deflected breath.

偶 然 犯 事 呌 做 過,立 心 犯 法 呌 做 惡

Ou jan fan shih chiao tso kuo, li hsin fan fa chiao tso ô.

> Accidental transgression is called error ; wilful transgression, sin.

不 知 者 不 爲 罪

Pu chih chê pu wei tsui.

> What is done in ignorance is not sin.

人 不 可 一 日 無 業

Jên pu k'o i jih wu yeh.

> Men ought not to be one day without employment.

停 手 就 停 口

T'ing shou chiu t'ing k'ou.

> He who will not work shall not eat. Comp. II. Thess 3.10.

你 是 二 十 四 孝,大 賢 人

Ni shih erh shih ssŭ hsiao, ta hsien jen.

> You are the Twenty-four Examples of Filial Piety,—an exceedingly good man. Note.—This is said sarcastically with a play on the words 賢 人 equalling 閒 人 a lazy lout. Every Chinese schoolboy knows the Twenty-four virtuous examples who lived in the good old days.

SECTION XII. ON RELIGION.

Chapter 1. Heaven or God.

萬 事 由 天 莫 強 求, 何 必 苦 苦 用 機 謀

Wan shih yu t'ien mo ch'iang ch'iu, ho pi k'u k'u yung chi mou.

> Since all things are ordained by Heaven do not struggle to obtain them ; why should you expend your strength in scheming.

皇 天 不 負 苦 心 人

Huang t'ien pu fu k'o hsin jen.

> Imperial Heaven never turns from those who sorrow.

人 便 如 此 如 此, 天 理 未 然 未 然

Jen pien ju tz'ŭ ju tz'ŭ, t'ien li wei jan wei jan.

> Man would have things so and so, but Heaven negatives his plans.

謀 事 在 人, 成 事 在 天

Mou shih tsai jen, ch'eng shih tsai t'ien.

> It is man's part to scheme ; it is Heaven's to accomplish.

天 之 應 人 敏 如 影 響

T'ien chih ying jen min ju ying hsiang.

> Heaven responds to man as quickly as shadow to form or echo to voice.

天 生 一 人 · 必 有 衣 祿

T'ien sheng i jên, pi yu i lu.

> Heaven never sends a man without providing him clothes and income.

人 眼 不 見 天 眼 見 · 人 不 知 道 天 知 道

Jen yen pu chien t'ien yen chien, jen pu chih tao t'ien chih tao.

> What man sees not and knows not, Heaven sees and knows.

紐 得 過 人 來 紐 不 過 天

Niu tê kuo jen lai niu pu kuo t'ien.

> Man can be bound but Heaven cannot.

天 生 一 人 地 生 一 穴

T'ien sheng i jen ti sheng i hsüeh.

> For each man whom Heaven sends, earth provides a grave.

吃 飯 不 瞞 天

Ch'ih fan pu man t'ien.

> Heaven knows how each man gets his living.

人 善 人 欺 天 不 欺；人 惡 人 怕 天 不 怕

Jen shan jen ch'i t'ien pu ch'i, jen ô jen p'a t'ien pu p'a.

> Men deceive good men, and fear bad men, but Heaven does not.

天 眼 昭 昭，報 應 甚 速

T'ien yen chao chao, pao ying shen su.

> Heaven sees clearly and rewards quickly.

人 間 私 語 天 聞 若 雷，暗 室 虧 心 神 目 如 電

Jen chien ssu yü t'ien wen jo lei, an shih k'uei hsin shen mu ju tien.

> Our whispers thunder into the ear of Heaven; our secret evil deeds flash into the eyes of the gods.

吉 人 天 相

Chi jen t'ien hsiang.

> Heaven stands by the good man.

人 有 千 算 不 如 天 一 算

Jen yu ch'ien suan pu ju t'ien i suan.

> A thousand human schemes may be thwarted by one scheme of Heaven.

雷 打 天 補

Lei ta t'ien pu.

> Thunder strikes and Heaven repairs.

人 見 目 前，天 見 久 遠

Jen chien mu ch'ien, t'ien chien chiu yüan.

> Man only sees the present, Heaven sees into the future.

人 靠 天 工，船 靠 舵 公

Jen k'ao t'ien kung, ch'uan k'ao to kung.

> Man depends on Heaven as a ship on her pilot.

不 怨 天 不 尤 人

Pu yüan t'ien pu yu jen.

> Neither repine against Heaven, nor blame men.

托 天 之 福

T'o t'ien chih fu.

> To enjoy the favour of Heaven.

命 在 於 天, 數 在 於 人

Ming tsai yü t'ien, shu tsai yü jen.

> It is Heaven's to destine (life), it is man's to shorten or prolong his days.

民 心 卽 天 心

Min hsin chi t'ien hsin.

> The heart of the people is the heart of Heaven.

盡 其 在 我, 聽 其 在 天

Chin ch'i tsai wo, t'ing ch'i tsai t'ien.

> It is for me to put forth the utmost effort ; it rests with Heaven to give me success.

盡 人 事 而 聽 天 命

Chin jen shih erh t'ing t'ien ming.

> When you have fully done your duty, abide by the will of Heaven.

願 天 常 生 好 人, 願 人 常 行 好 事

Yüan t'ien ch'ang sheng hao jen, yüan jen ch'ang hsing hao shih.

> Would that Heaven would always produce good men, and that men would always do good.

天 道 無 私

T'ien tao wu ssŭ.

> The ways of Heaven are impartial.

人 不 知 天 知

Jen pu chih t'ien chih.

> Man may not know, but Heaven knows.

天 養 人 胖 腯 腯, 人 養 人 皮 包 骨

T'ien yang jen p'ang t'un t'un, jen yang jen p'i pao ku.

> When Heaven rears a man he grows very fat ; when men rear one, he is nought but skin and bone.

瞞 得 過 人 來，瞞 不 過 天

Man tê kuo jên lai, man pu kuo t'ien.

> You may deceive men ; you can't deceive Heaven.

天 地 爲 大，父 母 爲 尊

T'ien ti wei ta, fu mu wei tsun.

> Heaven and Earth are the greatest ; father and mother are the most to be honoured.

天 知 地 知 你 知 我 知

T'ien chih, ti chih, ni chih, wo chih.

> Heaven knows, Earth knows, you know, and I know.
> Note.—This was the saying of a virtuous official of the Han Dynasty, Yang Tsen, 楊 震 when a bribe was offered to him.

死 生 有 命，富 貴 在 天

Ssu sheng yu ming, fu kuei tsai t'ien.

> Death and life are pre-determined ; riches and honours depend upon Heaven.

人 善 天 從 願，家 和 福 自 生

Jen shan t'ien ts'ung yuan, chia ho fu tzŭ sheng.

> Heaven complies with the wishes of good men ; happiness springs naturally in harmonious homes.

稍 善 雖 無 人 見 存 心 自 有 天 知

Shao shan sui wu jen chien ts'un hsin tzŭ yu t'ien chih.

> The smallest desire to do good is, though unseen by man, certainly known to Heaven.

人 害 人 不 死，天 害 人 纔 害 死 了

Jên hai jên pu ssŭ, t'ien hai jên ts'ai hai ssŭ liao.

> Injuries from men may not be fatal; but Heaven utterly destroys.

天 高 皇 帝 遠

T'ien kao huang ti yüan.

> Heaven is high and the emperor far away, i.e., I can do as I like.

天 上 有 路 無 人 走，地 獄 無 門 鑽 進 去

T'ien shang yu lu wu jen tsou, ti yü wu men tsuan chin ch'ü.

> There is a road to Heaven but men will not walk in it;
> hell has no gate but men will bore through to get
> there.

人 有 善 願 天 必 從 之

Jen yu shan yüan t'ien pi ts'ung chih.

> Heaven acts in accordance with the man of good desires.

天 綱 恢 恢 疏 而 不 漏

T'ien wang hui hui su erh pu lou.

> The net of Heaven is large and wide but it lets nothing
> through.

天 不 愛 道，地 不 愛 寶

T'ien pu ai tao ti pu ai pao.

> Heaven does not spare truth; the earth does not spare
> its treasures. Note. 愛 here equals 愛惜 to
> grudge, to spare.

老 天 爺 餓 不 死 瞎 家 雀 兒

Lao t'ien yeh ô pu ssǔ hsia chia ch'iao erh.

> Old Father Heaven doesn't starve even a blind sparrow.
> Comp. Matt. 6:26.

天 爲 大 人，人 爲 小 天

T'ien wei ta jên, jen wei hsiao t'ien.

> Heaven (God) is man on a large scale; man is Heaven
> (God) on a small scale.

萬 事 只 有 天 作 主，算 來 半 點 不 由 人

Wan shih chih yu t'ien tso chu, suan lai pan tien pu yu jên.

> Everything is controlled by Heaven; the smallest affairs
> are beyond the power of man to calculate.

Chapter 2. Rewards and Punishments.

哀 樂 失 時 殃 咎 必 至

Ai lê shih shih yang chiu pi chih.

> He who mourns or rejoices at the wrong time, will
> eventually meet misfortune.

只 圖 眼 前 快 活 不 管 死 後 罪 惡

Chih t'u yen ch'ien k'uai huo, pu kuan ssŭ hou tsui ô.

He only thinks of present happiness and does not trouble about the future punishment of sin.

善 積 者 昌，惡 積 者 喪

Shan chi chê ch'ang, ô chi chê sang.

Those who lay up goodness prosper; those who lay up evil are destroyed

懲 治 兇 惡 枷 責 發 落

Ch'eng chih hsiung ô chia tsê fa lo.

In order to punish wickedness the cangue and the bamboo are used.

一 生 懶 惰，忍 饑 受 餓

I sheng lan to, jên chi shou ô.

Whoever lives in idleness must suffer hunger.

修 橋 補 路 活 該 死，殺 人 作 賊 吃 飽 飯

Hsiu ch'iao pu lu huo kai ssŭ, sha jên tso tsei ch'ih pao fan.

Charitable repairers of bridges and roads are doomed to die; murderers and thieves have food enough and to spare. Comp. Eccles. 8:14.

自 作 必 要 自 受

Tzŭ tso pi yao tzŭ shou

Each must take the consequences of his own actions. Comp. Prov. 12:14.

爲 惡 不 滅 祖 有 餘 德，爲 善 不 昌 祖 有 餘 殃

Wei ô pu mieh tsu yü yü tê, wei shan pu ch'ang tsu yu yü yang.

If evil doers are not destroyed it is owing to the superfluous merit of their ancestors; if good people do not prosper it is because of retribution not meted out to their ancestors.

遠 報 則 在 兒 孫，近 報 就 在 自 己

Yüan pao tsê tsai erh sun, chin pao chiu tsai tzu chi.

Distant punishment falls on a man's descendants; immediate punishment on the man himself.

莫 說 眼 前 無 報 應，或 是 來 早 與 來 遲

Mo shuo yen ch'ien wu pao ying, huo shih lai tsao yü lai ch'ih.

> Don't say there is no retribution; it will come sooner or later.

今 生 作 福，來 生 消 受

Chin sheng tso fu, lai sheng hsiao shou.

> Do good now and be rewarded hereafter.

吃 得 苦 中 苦，做 得 人 上 人

Ch'i tê k'u chung k'u, tso tê jên shaug jen.

> He who endures hardship will become a man above other men.

只 見 活 人 受 罪，那 見 死 鬼 帶 枷

Chih chien huo jên shou tsui, na chien ssǔ kuei tai chia.

> We only see the living punished; whoever saw a departed spirit wearing the cangue.

閻 王 面 前 一 塊 牌 總 不 由 人 算

Yen wang mien ch'ien i k'uai p'ai tsung pu yu jên suan.

> The tablet before Yen Wang contains the words " Not according to man's reckoning". Note.—Yen Wang is the ruler of Hades and punishments are supposed to be administered according to his knowledge of each man's deeds.

雷 打 眼 前 報

Lei ta yen ch'ien pao.

> To be struck by lightning is to receive present punishment.

善 惡 到 頭 終 有 報，只 爭 來 早 與 來 遲

Shan ô tao t'ou chung yu pao, chih cheng lai tsao yü lai ch'ih.

> In the end, good and evil will have its reward, the question is will it come sooner or later.

種 蔴 得 蔴，種 豆 得 豆

Chung ma tê ma, chung tou tê tou.

> He who sows hemp will reap hemp, he who sows beans will reap beans. Comp. Gal. 6:7.

各人修各人得

Ko jên hsiu ko jên tê.

Every man gets what he cultivates.

善有善報惡有惡報，若還不報日子未到

Shan yu shan pao ô yu ô pao, jo huan pu pao jih tzŭ wei tao.

Good has its own reward, evil its own punishment; if
there is no apparent punishment it is because the
time has not arrived. Comp. Prov. 11:21.

爲善最樂，爲惡難逃

Wei shan tsui lê wei ô nan t'ao.

Those who do good are very happy; those who do evil
cannot escape.

殺人可恕，情理難容

Sha jên k'o shu, ch'ing li nan jung.

A murderer may be excused, but one can't put up with
specious excuses. Note. 情理 is the whole aspect
of a case, and sometimes arguments are brought
forward that are so puerile as to be an offence
against common sense; The proverb is of course an
exaggeration.

善必壽老，惡必早亡

Shan pi shou lao, ô pi tsao wang.

The good live long, the evil die early.

大難不死，必有厚祿

Ta nan pu ssŭ pi yu hou lu.

He is certain of a rich reward who escapes in a hazardous
enterprise.

賞以勸善，罰以懲惡

Shang i ch'uan shan, fa i ch'eng ô.

Rewards are used to stimulate goodness; punishment to
repress evil.

雪裡埋人，久後自明

Hsüeh li mai jên, chiu hou tzŭ ming.

Good or evil deeds are sure to be discovered. *Lit.* A
body buried in the snow will eventually be revealed.

大 屈 必 有 大 伸
Ta ch'ü pi yu ta shen.

> Grievous wrong necessitates signal redress. *Lit.* A
> great bend must have a great straightening.

總 有 一 天 穿 疱 的 日 子
Tsung yu i t'ien ch'uan pao ti jih tzǔ.

> There must come a day when the tumour will be
> punctured.

見 色 而 起 淫，心 報 在 妻 女
Chien sê erh ch'i yin, hsin pao tsai ch'i nü.

> If you look on beauty with lustful eyes, you will suffer
> for it in your wife and daughters.

心 正 不 怕 雷 打
Hsin cheng pu p'a lei ta

> The upright in heart fear no thunderbolts.

功 德 隨 時 積，衣 飯 逐 日 生
Kung tê sui shih chi, i fan chu jih sheng.

> Embrace every chance of laying up merit; and your daily
> wants will be regularly supplied.

積 福 有 福 在，行 善 有 陰 功
Chi fu yu fu tsai, hsing shan yu ying kung.

> There is happiness in doing good, and secret merit in
> virtuous deeds.

要 知 前 世 因，今 生 受 者 是，要 知 來 世 因，今 生 作 者 是
Yao chih ch'ien shih yin, chin sheng shou chê shih, yao chih lai
shih yin, chin sheng tso chê shih.

> If you want to know what you were in a previous state
> of existence, you can tell from your fate in this ; if
> you want to know what you will be in a future state,
> you can tell from what you do now.

今 世 便 修 來 世 福
Chin shih pien hsiu lai shih fu.

> You prepare in this world your happiness in the next.

難 得 討 人 身 的

Nan tê t'ao jên shen ti.

A human body is hard to beg. Note.—This is said in
warning to wicked men. The idea is that it will be
impossible for a bad man to obtain a human body in
the future life ; he will have to assume the form of
a beast, a bird, or a reptile.

人 有 三 分 怕 鬼, 鬼 有 七 分 怕 人

Jên yu san fen p'a kuei, kuei yu ch'i fen p'a jên.

Ghosts fear men much more than men fear them.

匿 怨 而 用 暗 箭 禍 延 子 孫

Ni yüan erh yung an chien huo yen tzŭ sun.

He who from secret malice shoots an arrow at another in
the dark, brings calamity on his descendants.

黃 犬 食 肉 白 犬 當 罪

Huang ch'üan shih jou pai ch'üan tang tsui.

The yellow dog eats the pork but the white dog suffers
for it.

惡 人 自 有 惡 人 磨, 蝎 蟆 自 有 蛤 蚆 拖

Ô jên tzŭ yu ô jen mo, i ko tzŭ yu ko pa t'o.

One evil man troubles another evil man; just as the toad
catches the small lizard.

善 惡 之 報 如 影 隨 形

Shan ô chih pao ju ying sui hsing.

The recompence of good and evil is as the shadow
following the substance.

畏 刑 自 可 免 刑

Wei hsing tzŭ k'o mien hsing.

To fear punishment is the best way of avoiding it.

積 善 之 家 必 有 餘 慶, 積 不 善 之 家 必 有 餘 殃

Chi shan chih chia pi yu yü ch'ing, chi pu shan chih chia pi yu yu
yang.

The family that accumulates virtue will have a superabundance of felicity; the family that increases in
evil deeds will have a superabundance of misery.

有 心 爲 善 雖 善 不 賞，無 心 爲 惡 雖 惡 不 罰

Yu hsin wei shan sui shan pu shang, wu hsin wei ô sui ô pu fa.

Those who are intentionally good, though good, will not
be rewarded ; those who are unintentionally evil,
though evil, will not be punished.

Chapter 3   Temples and Worship.

患 病 不 好 求 神 上 表

Huan ping pu hao ch'iu shen shang piao.

When sick, pray to the gods.

瞞 得 過 人 來 瞞 不 過 神

Man tê kuo jen lai man pu kuo shen.

You may deceive men but you cannot deceive the gods.

鐃 鈸 一 響 紋 銀 三 兩

Nao pa i hsiang wen yin san liang.

Every time the cymbals clash there go three taels of
silver.   Note.—This illustrates the expensiveness of
idol worship.

人 無 神 不 行，神 無 人 不 靈

Jen wu shen pu hsing, shen wu jen pu ling.

Men cannot do anything without the gods ; gods cannot
show their efficacy without men.

人 有 誠 心，神 有 感 應

Jen yu ch'eng hsin, shen yu kan ying.

When men are sincere, the gods are moved and they
answer

遇 好 菩 薩 打 一 個 好 卦，遇 歹 菩 薩 打 一 個 歹 卦

Yü hao p'u sa ta i ko hao kua, yu tai p'u sa ta i ko tai kua.

Find a good or bad idol and you will cast a good or bad
fortune.

每 日 清 晨 一 炷 香, 謝 天 謝 地 謝 三 光
所 求 處 處 田 禾 熟, 惟 願 人 人 壽 命 長

Mei jih ch'ing shen i chu hsiang hsieh t'ien hsieh ti hsieh san kuang,
So ch'iu ch'ü ch'ü t'ien ho shu, wei yuan jên jên shou ming ch'ang.

> Light your stick of incense at the break of every day;
> To Heaven, Earth, Sun, Moon, and Stars, devout thanks-
>   giving pay ;
> Pray that in every place crops may ripen in the sun ;
> Wish for every man a long career of life to run.

假 銀 子 肚 裏 空, 銅 錢 買 哄 詛 宗

Chia yin tzǔ tu li k'ung, t'ung ch'ien mai hung tsu tsung

> You use good copper cash to buy sham silver with which
>   to cheat your ancestors.

人 無 神 靈 寸 步 難 行

Jên wu shen ling ts'un pu nan hsing.

> It is hard for man to move an inch without divine
>   assistance.

萬 事 勸 人 休 瞞 昧, 舉 頭 三 尺 有 神 明

Wan shih ch'uan jen hsiu man mei, chü t'ou san ch'ih yu shen ming.

> In everything exhort men to avoid deceit, for only three
>   feet above our heads are the gods watching.

橫 心 進 得 衙 門, 橫 心 進 不 得 廟 門

Heng hsin chin tê ya men, heng hsin chin pu tê miao men.

> You may carry deception into the yamên, but you
>   cannot into the temple.

一 跪 三 叩 首'早 晚 一 鑪 香

I kuei san k'ou shou, tsao wan i lu hsiang.

> Kneel once, bow your head thrice, and offer incense
>   morning and evening.

祈 因 報 本, 朝 山 進 香

Ch'i ên pao pen, ch'an shan chin hsiang.

> Praying for blessings to reward one's parents, we go up
>   the hill to burn incense.

搬 菩 薩 洗 澡 枉 勞 神

Pan p'u sa hsi tsao wang lao shen.

> He who removes an idol to bathe it, puts the god to
>   needless inconvenience.

三斧頭砍定楊泗菩薩的像

San fu t'ou k'an ting Yang Ssǔ p'u sa ti hsiang.

> Three strokes of an axe are enough to complete an image
> of the idol Yang Ssu. Note.—Yang Ssu is the god
> of the sailors, a beardless divinity with a somewhat
> rudely carved triangular head.

楊泗老爺鬍子安不上

Yang Ssu lao yeh hu tzǔ, an pu shang.

> A beard should not be put on the God of Sailors.
> Note.—The force of the proverb is in the last three
> words, and is used to condemn any impropriety.

求佛求一尊

Ch'iu fu ch'iu i tsun.

> If you pray to a Buddha, pray to one only.

窮人害病,求符扛神

Ch'iung jên hai ping, ch'iu fu kang shen.

> When the poor are sick they use charms and carry about
> idols.

公公十分公道,婆婆一片婆心

Kung Kung shih fen Kung tao, P'o P'o i p'ien p'o hsin.

> Grandfather is perfectly just, and grandmother altogether
> motherly. Note.—Kung Kung and P'o P'o are the
> common colloquial designations of the T'u Ti P'u
> Sa or Gods of Agriculture.

三天不吃飯,像個鐵羅漢

San t'ien pu ch'ih fan, hsiang ko t'ieh Lo Han.

> Who fasts three days resembles an Iron Lohan. Note.—
> The "Iron Lohans" are the cast iron images of the
> disciples of Buddha. common in Buddhist temples.
> In popular belief, the spirits of the dead are allowed
> to roam about at times and visit their earthly abodes
> and it is their presence which causes sickness and
> death. If any escape their influence, they are
> afterwards as sturdy as "Iron Lohans".

閒時不燒香,急時抱佛脚

Hsien shih pu shao hsiang, chi shih pao fu chiao.

> When all is well you do not offer incense, but when in
> pressing need you embrace Buddha's feet.

勿 敬 神 明, 但 聞 雷 聲

Wu ching shen ming, tan wen lei sheng.

> If you don't fear the gods listen to the sound of thunder.

土 菩 薩 過 江 自 身 難 保

T'u p'u sa kuo chiang tzŭ shen nan pao.

> When an earthen god crosses the river it can't take care of itself.

人 望 神 力, 草 望 春 生

Jen wang shen li, ts'ao wang ch'un sheng.

> Men look to the gods for strength as the grass waits for the spring.

暗 室 鬼 神 知

An shih kuei shen chih.

> The gods know what is done in secret.

當 鄉 土 地 當 鄉 靈

Tang hsiang T'u Ti tang hsiang ling.

> The village T'u Ti is only efficacious at home. Note.— T'u Ti Shen is the God of the Soil. See above.

東 頭 的 土 地, 西 頭 不 靈

Tung t'ou ti T'u Ti, hsi t'ou pu ling.

> The T'u Ti of the east end is powerless at the west end.

昔 爲 唐 朝 進 士 第, 今 作 當 莊 土 地 神

Hsi wei T'ang Ch'ao chin shih ti, chin tso tang chuang T'u Ti shen.

> Once a famous scholar of the T'ang Dynasty, but now only a local god in a village. Note.—The original of the T'u Ti is popularly supposed to have been Han Yu 韓 愈 otherwise known as Han Wen Kung 韓 文 公 a noted statesman of the T'ang 唐 Dynasty. (See Smith's Proverbs).

有 事 抱 佛 腿, 無 事 把 佛 推

Yu shih pao Fu t'ui, wu shih pa Fu t'ui.

> When anything is the matter to cling to Buddha's foot; when there is nothing to push him aside.

琢坭匠不拜佛，老底兒在他心裏

To ni chiang pu pai Fu, lao ti erh tsai t'a hsin li.

> The image maker does not worship Buddha, he knows what he is made of. Note 老底兒 the bottom or base, indicates the fundamental facts of the case.

坭佛勸土佛

Ni Fu ch'uan t'u Fu.

> The mud Buddha reproving the clay Buddha, i.e., the kettle calling the pan black.

不食不殺，便是菩薩

Pu shih pu sha pien shih p'u sa.

> He who abstains from eating (flesh) and killing is a P'u-sa. Note.—This common term for idol is a contraction of 菩提薩埵 Bodhisatva, i.e, one who is enlightened to such an extent as to almost equal Buddha himself.

十兩通神，百兩通天

Shih liang t'ung shen, pai liang t'ung t'ien.

> Ten taels will move the gods, one hundred will move Heaven itself.

能上大廟去作鬼，不上小廟去爲神

Neng shang ta miao ch'ü tso kuei, pu shang hsiao miao ch'ü wei shen.

> Better be a demon in a large temple than a god in a small one.

Chapter 4. Priests and Nuns.

和尚娶親說過光陰

Ho shang ch'ü ch'in, shuo kuo kuang yin.

> Unfulfilled promises. *Lit.* A Buddhist priest talks of getting married, but time passes without him doing so.

檢到一本經，念也念不清

Chien tao i pen ching, nien yeh nien pu ch'ing.

> He takes up a prayer-book and reads, but can't read properly.

禿子做和尚

T'u tzu tso ho shang.

Bald-headed men are ready made Buddhist priests.

無結梢做和尚

Wu chieh shao tso ho shang.

Only those become Bonzes who have absolutely nothing
to lose.

鄉爲鄉鄰爲鄰，和尚只爲出家人

Hsiang wei hsiang lin wei lin, ho shang chih wei ch'u chia jên.

In villages and hamlets men live together; the Bonze
alone foresakes his family.

黃泥饅頭好供佛

Huang ni man t'ou hao kung Fu.

Mud loaves are good enough to offer to Buddha, i.e., if
you make it alright with the priest.

燒紙風颳了，念經和尚飽

Shao chih fêng kua liao, nien ching ho shang pao.

The burnt cash-paper is blown away by the wind; it is
the recital of the prayers that feeds the priests.

若要佛法興，還是僧讚僧

Jo yao Fu fa hsing, huan shih seng tsan seng.

If Buddhism is to flourish then let Bonze praise Bonze.

和尚剃辮子無法

Ho shang t'i pien tzŭ wu fa.

A Bonze shaving off his queue; it can't be done.
Note —Used in the sense of "to make the best of
a bad job".

SECTION XIII. ON JOYS AND SORROWS.

Chapter 1. Happiness.

善 人 得 福 爲 之 賞, 惡 人 得 福 爲 之 殃

Shan jen tê fu wei chih shang, ô jen tê fu wei chih yang.

> The happiness of good men is their reward ; the happiness of evil men is their calamity.

牛 耕 田 馬 吃 穀, 別 人 養 兒 他 享 福

Niu keng t'ien ma ch'ih ku, pieh jen yang erh t'a hsiang fu.

> "The ox ploughs the field while the horse eats the grain ;
> One rears a son and another gets the gain"

添 人 進 口 越 吃 越 有

T'ien jen chin k'ou, yüeh ch'ih yüeh yu.

> The more members of the family, the more there will be to eat.

有 福 不 會 享, 扯 起 篷 來 盪 槳

Yu fu pu hui hsiang, ch'e ch'i p'eng lai t'ang chiang.

> He who has prosperity and is not able to enjoy it, is like a boatman who hoists the sail and still has to use his oars.

一 人 有 福, 拖 帶 滿 屋

I jên yu fu, t'o tai man wu.

> If one man is blest the whole house shares in his happiness.

一 天 一 咒, 添 福 添 壽

I t'ien i chou, t'ien fu t'ien shou.

> To curse a man every day only adds to his happiness and long life.

心 閒 蓄 頭 髮, 身 閒 蓄 指 甲

Hsin hsien hsiu t'ou fa, shen hsien hsiu chih chia.

> When a man's mind is at rest his hair grows long ; when he has nothing to do his finger nails grow long.

鬧 裏 有 錢, 靜 處 安 身

Nao li yu ch'ien, ching ch'ü an shen.

> In the hum of the market there is money, but in seclusion there is rest.

比神仙還舒服

Pi shen hsien huan shu fu.

> More comfortable than the gods.

高不得低不得就好

Kao pu tê ti pu te chiu hao.

> It is good to be neither too high nor too low.

福自天來

Fu tzǔ t'ien lai.

> Happiness comes from Heaven.

有福不可享盡

Yu fu pu k'o hsiang chin.

> Do not exhaust your happiness.

沒有梧桐樹，叫不着鳳凰來

Mu yu wu t'ung shu, chiao pu cho fêng huang lai.

> Without a Wu T'ung tree, you cannot get the phoenix
> to visit you. Note.—The meaning of this proverb is,
> that without some inducement, certain benefits can-
> not be obtained. The Wu t'ung tree is supposed
> to be a favourite resting place of the phoenix.

家和人和萬事和

Chia ho jen ho wan shih ho.

> Having harmony in the family and being in harmony
> with all men, all your affairs will be harmonious.

平安兩字值千金

Ping an liang tzǔ chih ch'ien chin.

> The two words Peace and Rest, are worth a thousand
> pieces of gold.

百事從順，大吉大利

Pai shih ts'ung shun ta chi ta li

> When all our affairs are in order, great is our felicity
> and profit.

福至心靈

Fu chih hsin ling.

> When happiness comes the mind grows more intelligent.

爽 口 食 多 偏 作 病, 快 心 事 過 恐 生 殃

Shuang k'ou shih to p'ien tso ping, k'uai hsin shih kuo k'ung sheng yang.

> An immoderate use of dainties generally ends in disease; and pleasure when past is converted into pain.

門 前 無 債 主, 家 中 無 病 人

Men ch'ien wu chai chu chia chung wu ping jen.

> Happy circumstances. *Lit.* No creditor at the door, and no one sick in the house.

快 活 不 知 時 日 過

K'uai huo pu chih shih jih kuo.

> The happy know not how time flies.

清 閒 兩 字 錢 難 買

Ch'ing hsien liang tzǔ ch'ien nan mai.

> What is indicated by the two words tranquility and leisure, no money can buy.

多 惜 福 少 惹 災

To hsi fu shao jê tsai.

> Be very careful of happiness and provoke not calamity.

人 生 無 似 清 閒 好, 得 到 清 閒 豈 偶 然

Jen shen wu ssu ch'ing hsien hao, tê tao ch'ing hsien ch'i ou jan.

> Since life has nothing in it to equal tranquility; is it a thing to be obtained by chance.

隨 富 隨 貧 且 隨 喜, 不 開 口 笑 是 癡 人

Sui fu sui p'in ch'ien sui hsi, pu k'ai k'ou hsiao shih ch'ih jen.

> Whether rich or poor be pleased with your lot, for he is a fool who cannot laugh (under all circumstances.)

日 度 三 餐, 夜 眠 一 宿

Jih tu san ts'an yeh mien i su.

> Three meals per day, one sleep per night.

一 兩 黃 金 四 兩 福 氣

I liang huang chin ssu liang fu ch'i.

> For one ounce of gold you must have four ounces of happiness. Note.—This is to enable you to avail yourself of the possession of the gold.

曲 高 必 賤，棋 高 必 貴

Ch'u kao pi chien, ch'i kao pi kuei.

> A good singer will only secure a low position in life; a good chess-player a high one.

久 賭 無 勝 家

Chiu tu wu sheng chia.

No gambler wins in the long run.

常 賭 神 仙 輸

Ch'ang tu shen hsien shu.

> At regular gambling even the gods and genii lose.

Chapter. 3.   Reputation.

有 麝 自 然 香，莫 在 當 風 颺

Yu shê tzǔ jan hsiang, mo tsai tang feng yang.

> Where there is musk the perfume will manifest itself; there is no need to wave it about in the wind.

人 間 富 貴 花 間 露，世 上 功 名 水 上 漚

Jen chien fu kuei hua chien lu, shih shang kung ming shui shang ou.

> Riches and honour amongst men are like dew upon flowers; fame and reputation are like froth upon water.

豹 死 留 皮，人 死 留 名

Pao ssǔ liu p'i, jên ssǔ liu ming

> A dying leopard leaves his skin; a dying man his name.

鴈 過 留 聲 人 去 留 名

Ying kuo liu sheng jên ch'ü liu ming

> As the scream of the eagle is heard when she has passed over, so a man's name remains after his death.

聲 名 大 如 雷 貫 耳

Sheng ming ta ju lei kuan erh

> His fame is great, like thunder in one's ear.

功 名 不 上 懶 人 頭

Kung ming pu shang lan jen t'ou.

> Merit and fame never crown the lazy.

高 山 打 鼓，聲 名 在 外

Kao shan ta ku, sheng ming tsai wai.

The sound of a drum on a lofty hill is heard far and wide.

揚 名 顯 親

Yang ming hsien ch'in

Whoever gains fame dignifies his parents.

扯 旗 放 砲，聲 名 浩 蕩

Ch'ê ch'i fang p'ao, sheng ming hao tang.

Wide-spread his fame, who comes with waving flags and roaring cannon.

虎 死 雄 心 在

Hu ssǔ hsiung hsin tsai.

The tiger is terrible even when dead.

大 丈 夫 旣 不 能 流 芳 百 世 便 遺 臭 萬 年

Ta chang fu chi pu neng liu fang pai shih pien i ch'ou wan nien.

A great man who fails to leave a good name for a hundred generations will leave a bad one for a myriad years.

一 筲 箒 掃 得 乾 淨

t'iao chou sao tê kan ching.

To sweep clean at a stroke. Note.—This is said of a reputation suddenly forfeited from any cause.

好 事 不 出 門，惡 事 傳 千 里

Hao shih pu ch'u men, ô shih ch'uan ch'ien li.

One's good deeds are not known outside the home; one's evil deeds are made known far and wide.

十 年 窓 下 無 人 問，一 舉 成 名 天 下 知

Shih nien ch'uang hsia wu jen wen, i chü ch'eng ming t'ien hsia chih.

During his ten years of study no one asked after him; but by a single effort he made his name and all the empire knew.

樹 老 根 還 在，人 死 兩 丟 開
Shu lao ken huan tsai jên ssū liang tiu k'ai.

> When a tree is old its roots are still living, when a man is dead he is cut off from his kind. Note.—Living persons and disembodied spirits are in two different categories.

黃 泉 路 上 無 老 少
Huang ch'üan lu shang wu lao shao.

> On the road to Hades no account is taken of old or young.

蟲 蟻 也 貪 生 怕 死
Ch'ung i yeh t'an sheng p'a ssū.

> Insects of every kind desire life and fear death.

人 生 在 世 如 風 前 燭 如 瓦 上 霜
Jên shêng tsai shih ju fêng ch'ien chu ju wa shang shuang.

> Man's life is like a candle in the wind, or hoar-frost on the tiles.

人 生 在 世 如 春 夢，靈 魂 一 走 萬 事 休
Jên shêng tsai shih ju ch'ün mêng ling hun i tsou wan shih hsiu.

> Man's life is like a spring dream; when the soul has gone, it is the end of all things.

人 活 百 歲 也 是 死，早 死 早 些 脫 了 身
Jên huo pai sui yeh shih ssu tsao ssū tsao hsieh t'o liao shên.

> Though a man live a hundred years, still he must die: the sooner we die, the sooner we have done with the body.

人 生 修 短 有 數
Jên shêng hsiu tuan yu shu.

> The days of man's life are all numbered, i. e. it is a matter of destiny. Note.— 修 equals. 長

在 家 好 在 外 好 在 數 難 逃
Tsai chia hao tsai wai hao tsai shu nan t'ao.

> You may be equally well at home or abroad, but you cannot escape your fate.

魚 遊 釜 中 雖 生 不 久
Yü yu fu chung sui shêng pu chiu.

> The fish which jumps about in the pan has but a short
> time to live.

人 生 在 世，無 非 是 戲
Jên shêng tsai shih wu fei shih hsi.

> Man's life is but a play.

不 覺 又 是 白 頭 翁
Pu chiao yu shih pai t'ou wêng.

> Before a man knows it he has grown white-headed.

長 江 後 浪 催 前 浪·世 上 新 人 換 舊 人
Ch'ang chiang hou lang ts'ui ch'ien lang, shih shang hsin jên huan-
chiu jên.

> On the Yangtze River, preceding waves are driven
> onward by those which follow; so in the world,
> newcomers take the places of the older men.

古 人 不 見 今 時 月，今 月 曾 經 照 古 人
Ku jên pu chien chin shih yüeh chin yüeh ts'eng ching chao ku jên.

> The ancients see not the present moon, but the present
> moon shone on the ancients.

山 中 也 有 千 年 樹·世 上 難 逢 百 歲 人
Shan chung yeh yu ch'ien nien shu shih shang nan fêng pai sui jên.

> There are trees on the mountains a thousand years old;
> but a centenarian amongst men it is hard to find.

人 見 白 頭 嗔·我 見 白 頭 喜·多 少 少 年 亡 不 見 白 頭 死
Jên chien pai t'ou ch'en, wo chien pai t'ou hsi, to shao shao nien
wang pu chien pai t'ou ssu.

> Some men rail at a hoary head, I delight to see one; for
> so many young men die, before their hair is grey.

人 生 一 世·草 生 一 春
Jên shêng i shih ts'ao sh'eng i ch'ün.

> Man lives a generation as plants a spring.

月 過 十 五 光 明 少·人 到 中 年 萬 事 休
Yüeh kuo shih wu kuang ming shao, jên tao chung nien wan shih hsiu.

> After full moon the light diminishes; after middle age
> man's affairs begin to lessen.

乞丐不過朽木

Ch'ih kai pu kuo hsiu mu ch'iao.

A beggar will not cross a rotten bridge.

今朝不保明朝事

Chin chao pu pao ming chao shih.

To-day does not guarantee the affairs of to-morrow.

上床難保下床來

Shang ch'uang nan pao hsia ch'uang lai.

When we go to bed we cannot be sure that we shall rise again.

妒財莫妒食，怨生莫怨死

Tu ts'ai mo tu shih, yüan shêng mo yüan ssŭ.

If you envy a man's wealth, do not envy his food; if you are dissatisfied with life, do not be so with death.

一世如白駒過隙

I shih ju pai chü kuo ch'i.

A generation is like a white colt passing a crevice, i.e., gone in a moment.

死生有命·富貴在天

Ssu shêng yu ming, fu kuei tsai t'ien.

Life and death are decreed; riches and honour are at the disposal of heaven.

早上勿知晚上事

Tsao shang wu chih wan shang shih.

You can't tell in the morning what will happen at night.

做千日鬼勿如做一日人

Tso ch'ien jih kuei wu ju tso i jih jên.

One day's life as a man is better than a thousand as a disembodied spirit.

千年世界跌駁主

Ch'ien nien shih chieh tieh po chu.

The world, though lasting a thousand years is constantly changing masters.

蓋世英雄難免無常二字，一身事業猶如春夢一塲

Kai shih ying hsiung nan mien wu ch'ang erh tzŭ, I sheng shih yeh yu ju ch'ün mēng i ch'ang.

> The world's greatest man cannot escape from the two words "no continuance"; the business of a lifetime is but a spring dream. Note.—In popular parlance 無常 "No Continuance" is the name of the demon who comes to take man to the realms of Yen Wang 閻王 the Ruler of Hades. He is therefore equivalent to the skeleton figure "Death".

無常一到，性命難逃

Wu ch'ang i tao, hsing ming nan t'ao.

> When Death comes you can't escape him.

無常一到萬事休

Wu ch'ang i tao wan shih hsiu.

> When Death comes all things cease :

世事如山齊處少

Shih shih ju shan ch'i ch'ü shao.

> Human affairs are like the hills, the even places are rare.

人之渡生如客渡海

Jēn chih tu shēng ju k'o tu hai.

> Man goes through life as a traveller crosses the sea.

天有不測風雲，人有旦夕禍福

T'ien yu pu tse fēng yün, jen yu tan hsi huo fu.

> Just as wind and clouds come unexpectedly, so happiness and misery early and late come to man.

人死如燈滅

Jēn ssŭ ju tēng mieh.

> Man dies as a lamp is extinguished, i.e., there's an end of him.

七十三八十四，閻王不叫自己死

Ch'i shih san pa shih ssŭ, Yen Wang pu chiao tzŭ chi ssŭ.

> At seventy-three or eighty-four, if Yen Wang doesn't summon a man, he will die of himself.

遇 急 思 親 戚,臨 危 托 故 人

Yü chi ssŭ ch'in ch'i, lin wei t'o ku jĕn

> In trouble, think of your relations; in danger, depend
> on old friends.

禍 福 無 門,惟 人 所 招

Huo fu wu men, wei jĕn so chao.

> Misfortune and happiness come not of themselves, but
> only at the call of men.

豆 腐 潑 了 架 子 還 在

Tou fu po liao chia tzu huan tsai.

> Though the beancurd is spilt, the stand still remains, i.e.,
> It might have been worse.

人 急 懸 梁,狗 急 跳 牆

Jĕn chi hsüan liang, kou chi t'iao ch'iang.

> The man, when hard pressed hangs himself; the dog
> jumps the wall.

氣 乃 惹 禍 根

Ch'i nai jê huo ken.

> Anger is the cause of misfortune.

啞 巴 吃 黃 連,苦 在 心 裏

Ya pa ch'ih huang lien, k'u tsai hsin li.

> The dumb man who has eaten gentian keeps his troubles
> to himself

獨 木 搭 橋,眞 難 得 過

Tu mu ta ch'iao, chĕn nan tê kuo.

> Extreme danger. *Lit.* A bridge of one pole is difficult to
> cross.

既 墮 釜 甑 反 顧 何 益,反 覆 之 水 收 之 實 難

Chi to fu tseng fan ku ho i, fan fu chih shui shou chih shih nan.

> Since the cooking vessels are broken, why trouble about
> them? Spilt water cannot be gathered up again.

正 離 狼 窩 反 逢 虎 口

Cheng li lang wo fan feng hu k'ou.

> Out of the wolf's covert into the tiger's mouth.

前 門 拒 虎, 後 門 進 狼

Ch'ien men chü hu, hou men chin lang.

> Whilst keeping a tiger from the front door, a wolf enters by the back.

一 葉 旣 動, 百 枝 皆 搖

I yeh chi tung, pai chih chieh yao.

> When one leaf moves all the branches shake.

人 在 家 裏 坐, 禍 從 天 上 來

Jên tsai chia li tso, huo ts'ung t'ien shang lai.

> Whilst men sit at home, Heaven sends calamity upon them.

翻 船 的 幾 時 淹 死 了 扯 縴 的

Fan ch'uan ti chi shih yen ssŭ liao ch'ê ch'ien ti.

> The mischief will fall on your own head. *Lit* Whenever were trackers drowned by those who upset the boat?.

禍 從 天 上 來, 但 求 心 無 愧

Huo ts'ung t'ien shang lai, tan ch'iu hsin wu k'uei

> Misfortunes may come from Heaven, but let us seek to be blameless.

從 苦 中 得 甘

Ts'ung k'u chung tê kan.

> To extract sweetness from what is bitter.

老 鼠 扒 牛 角 越 扒 越 尖 了

Lao shu p'a niu chio yüeh p'a yüeh chien liao.

> Worse and worse. *Lit.* When a rat creeps up the horn of an ox, the higher it mounts the narrower the space.

苦 比 黃 連 勝 十 分

K'u pi huang lien sheng shih fen.

> Suffering is ten times more bitter than gentian.

嗚 呼 哀 哉 人 死 難 猜

Wu hu ai tsai jên ssŭ nan ts'ai.

> Alas! and Alack! The time of a man's death is difficult to guess.

Chapter 6. Injuries: Given and Sustained.

一 搥 一 脚 乾 淨 擊 脫

I ch'ui i chiao kan ching p'ieh t'o.

> Everything destroyed at one blow.   Note.—Said of injury done to anything in one's possession.

大 魚 吃 小 魚, 小 魚 吃 水 蟲, 水 蟲 吃 草 泥

Ta yu ch'ih hsiao yü, hsiao yü ch'ih shui ch'ung, shui ch'ung ch'ih ts'ao ni.

> Big fish eat the small fish, the small fish eat the water insects and the insects eat the weeds and the mud.

吃 得 虧 在 一 堆

Ch'ih tē k'uei tsai i tui.

> Comrades in misfortune.

飛 蛾 撲 燈 自 燒 其 身

Fei ô p'u têng tzŭ shao ch'i shen.

> The moth rushes at the flame of the lamp but only burns itself.

惹 禍 招 災, 問 罪 應 該

Jê huo chao tsai, wen tsui ying kai.

> Those who provoke misfortune and calamity, ought certainly to be condemned.

龍 游 淺 水 遭 蝦 戲, 虎 落 平 垟 被 犬 欺

Lung yu ch'ien shui tsao hsia hsi, hu lo p'ing yang pei ch'üan ch'i.

> A dragon sporting in shallow water is laughed at by the shrimps ; a tiger on the plains is derided by the dogs.

含 血 噴 人 先 污 自 己

Han hsüeh p'en jen, hsien wu tzŭ chi.

> He who spurts blood at another, first defiles himself.

害 人 終 害 己

Hai jen chung hai chi.

> If you injure others you will inevitably injure yourself.

碰 倒 釘 子

P'eng tao ting tzŭ.

> To come into unpleasant contact with hard men. *Lit.* To run against a nail.

鷄 蛋 撞 石 頭, 一 撞 黃 水 流

Chi tan chuang shih t'ou, i chuang huang shui liu.

> At the first stroke of an egg against a stone, the yolk runs out.

暗 藏 甲 兵

An ts'ang chia ping.

> To injure secretly. *Lit.* To hide mailed soldiers.

袖 裏 藏 刀

Hsiu li ts'ang tao.

> The same. *Lit.* To conceal a dagger in one's sleeve.

借 刀 殺 人

Chieh tao sha jen.

> To murder by means of another's sword.

大 船 怕 的 釘 眼 漏

Ta ch'uan p'a ti ting yen lou.

> Great ships fear small leakages.

打 狗 欺 主

Ta kou ch'i chu.

> To beat the dog is to insult his master.

城 門 失 火, 殃 及 池 魚

Ch'eng men shih huo yang chi ch'ih yü.

> Involving others in injury. *Lit.* When the city gate is burning, the fishes in the moat suffer.

拿 得 大 帽 子 來 壓

Na tē ta mao tzǔ lai ya.

> To injure by means of outside authority. *Lit.* To come with the big hat on in order to oppress one.

勿 恃 勢 力 而 凌 逼 孤 寡

Wu shih shih li erh ling pi ku kua.

> Never presume on authority or power to injure orphans or widows.

強 盜 打 死 賣 豬 血 的 饒 命 喝 湯

Ch'iang tao ta ssu mai chu hsüeh ti jao ming ho t'ang.

> As the pigs-blood seller said to the robber,—sup my broth but spare my life.

打虎不着,反被虎傷

Ta hu pu cho, fan pei hu shang.

> If you aim at the tiger and miss, he will certainly injure you.

六月蚊蟲招扇打

Liu yüeh wen ch'ung chao san ta.

> Summer mosquitoes provoke raps with a fan.

解衣抱火自惹其災

Chieh i pao huo, tzu jê ch'i tsai.

> When a man unloosens his coat and takes fire into his bosom, he is provoking misfortune to fall upon him.

自己搬磚打自己的脚

Tzŭ chi pan chuan ta tzŭ chi ti chiao.

> To drop the bricks one is carrying on one's own foot.

叫化子背不起自討的

Chiao hua tzŭ pei pu ch'i tzŭ t'ao ti.

> The beggar cannot carry what he has begged himself.

紙筆殺人不用刀

Chih pi sha jen pu yung tao.

> Paper and pen may take a man's life, without the use of a sword.

嬌鳥被籠

Chiao niao pei lung.

> It is the beautiful bird which gets encaged.

一龍阻住千江水

I lung tsu chu ch'ien chiang shui.

> One may hinder many. *Lit.* One dragon may stop the water of a thousand rivers

一馬不行,百馬憂

I ma pu hsing, pai ma yu.

> When one horse will not go, a hundred have to suffer.

冷水入口,點點在心

Leng shui ju k'ou, tien tien tsai hsin.

> Cold water entering the mouth, goes drop by drop into the heart. Note.—Said of slights or injuries, which are not soon forgotten.

水 缸 裏 搬 罾 寃 綱

Shui kang li pan tseng yuau wang.

> To put the big fishing net into a water jar.   Note.—This
> is another specimen of the innuendo, the meaning
> being in the last two words which indicate suffering
> unjustly. 寃 綱 equals 寃 枉 to wrong.

平 生 莫 作 皺 眉 事, 世 上 應 勿 切 齒 人

P'ing sheng mo tso chou mei shih, shih shang ying wu ch'ieh
ch'ih jen.

> Don't do anything to cause men to frown at you, and
> there will not be a man to grind his teeth at you.

牽 羊 入 虎 群

Ch'ien yang ju hu ch'ün.

> To entice a sheep into a drove of tigers.

打 死 人 要 填 命, 哄 死 人 不 填 命

Ta ssū jên yao t'ien ming, hung ssū jên pu t'ien ming.

> Strike a man dead and you must forfeit your life; kill
> him by craft and you need not.

把 烟 筒 我 鑽

Pa yen t'ung wo tsuan.

> To mislead. *Lit.* To give one a chimney to climb.

瞎 子 害 火 眼 又 很 又 利 害

Hsia tzǔ hai huo yen yu hen yu li hai.

> Aggravated injury. *Lit.* A blind man with inflamed
> eyes, suffers more and more injury.

直 巷 趕 豬 回 頭 一 口

Chih hsiang kan chu hui t'ou i k'ou.

> If you chase a pig in a passage he will turn again and
> rend you.

落 井 下 石

Lo chiu hsia shih.

> To throw stones on a man in a well.

虧 人 是 禍 饒 人 是 福

K'uei jên shih huo jao jen shih fu.

> To injure men is misery; to pity men is happiness.

助 桀 爲 虐
Chu chieh wei nio.

> To help the tyrant Chieh to tyrannize. Note.—Chieh, the last sovereign of the Hsia Dynasty, destroyed by Ta'ng on account of his tyranny and oppression.

心 堅 勿 怕 逼 邪
Hsin chien wu p'a pi hsieh.

> The man of steadfast heart fears not the oppression of evil men.

人 欺 天 勿 欺，吃 虧 就 是 便 宜
Jen ch'i t'ien wu ch'i, ch'ih k'uei chiu shih pien i.

> Although men despise one, if Heaven does not, injury is advantageous.

自 投 羅 綱 別 怨 人
Tzŭ t'ou lo wang pieh yüan jên.

> If you fall into the net don't blame others.

打 人 休 打 臉，罵 人 休 揭 短
Ta jên hsiu ta lien, ma jên hsiu chieh tuan.

> If you strike a man don't strike his face; if you curse him don't remind him of his defects.

奔 石 頭 扎 脚 面
Pen shih t'ou cha chiao mien.

> To run against a stone to wound one's foot. Comp. To cut off one's nose to spite one's face.

狡 蚤 做 事 累 虱 母
Chiao tsao tso shih lei shih mu.

> What the flea does the louse suffers for. Used figuratively for being left in the lurch.

———

Chapter 7. Mourning and Burial.

處 處 黃 土 好 埋 人
Ch'ü ch'ü huang t'u hao mai jên.

> Any soil will do to bury in.

兒 子 哭 娘 驚 天 動 地

Erh tzŭ k'u niang ching t'ien tung ti.

> A son's mourning for his mother startles Heaven and moves Earth.

女 兒 哭 娘 眞 心 實 意

Nü erh k'u niang chen hsin shih i.

> A daughter's mourning for her mother is true and sincere.

媳 婦 哭 婆 婆 假 情 假 意

Hsi fu k'u p'o p'o chia ch'ing chia i.

A daughter-in-law's mourning for her mother-in-law is false and feigned.

兎 死 狐 悲 傷 其 類

T'u ssŭ hu pei shang ch'i lei.

> The hare dies and the fox mourns   Note.—This proverb indicates sympathy, as the fox and hare are supposed to be animals of similar disposition.

只 在 陽 間 渴 碗 茶, 莫 在 陰 間 吃 口 湯

Chih tsai yang chien ho wan ch'a, mo tsai yin chien ch'ih k'ou t'ang.

> It is better to drink a cup of tea on earth, than have a taste of soup in Hades.

貓 兒 哭 老 鼠 假 慈 悲

Mao erh k'u lao shu chia tz'ŭ pei.

> When the cat mourns for the rat it is merely sham pity.

夫 人 死 百 客 臨 門, 將 軍 亡 一 卒 不 至

Fu jên ssŭ pai k'o lin men, chiang chun wang i tsu pu chih.

> When his lady dies, a hundred visitors come to condole; but when the general himself dies, not a single soldier arrives.

夫 死 三 年 妻 大 孝, 妻 死 無 過 百 日 思

Fu ssŭ san nien ch'i ta hsiao, ch'i ssŭ wu kuo pai jih ssŭ

> When the husband dies, the wife will be in deep mourning for three years; when the wife dies, she won't be remembered more than a hundred days.

在 生 不 孝，死 祭 無 益

Tsai sheng pu hsiao, ssŭ chi wu i.

> The sacrifice of an unfilial son at his father's death is of no avail.

在 生 不 把 父 母 敬，死 後 何 必 哭 靈 魂

Tsai sheng pu pa fu mu ching, ssu hou ho pi k'u ling hun.

> Why should he, who does not honour his parents when living, mourn for them when dead.

牀 頭 一 倉 穀，死 了 有 人 哭

Ch'uang t'ou i ts'ang ku, ssŭ liao yu jên k'u.

> Men mourn for those who leave fortunes behind them. Note.—Fortune. *Lit.* A granary at the bedhead.

死 的 顧 死 的·活 的 顧 活 的

Ssŭ ti ku ssŭ ti, huo ti ku huo ti.

> Don't distress yourself for the dead. *Lit.* Let the dead care for the dead, and the living for the living.

哭 則 不 歌，歌 則 不 哭

K'u tsê pu ko, ko tsê pu k'u.

> If a mourner, you cannot sing; if you sing, you cannot mourn.

SECTION XIV. LANGUAGE.

Chapter 1. Conversation.

遇文王施禮樂，遇霸王動干戈

Yü Wen Wang shih li yo, yü Pa Wang tung kan ko.

Meeting Wen Wang, display your politeness and music; meeting Pa Wang, rattle your arms. Note.—Wen Wang was the King Alfred of Chinese history, and Pa Wang, or Huan Kung, a powerful chieftain of the 6th century B. C. The term Pa Wang can be applied to any great military leader.

傳言過話，多討人罵

Ch'uan yen kuo hua, to t'ao jên ma.

Gossip and tittle-tattle provoke the curses of men.

嘴尖毛長說話荒唐

Tsui chien mao ch'ang shuo hua huang t'ang.

The talk of a lantern-jawed, long haired man is wild and incoherent.

看人說話，看事打卦

K'an jên shuo hua, k'an shih ta kua.

You can tell what a man is like by talking to him, you can know what any affair will be by divining.

一言不中，萬言無用

I yen pu chung, wan yen wu yung.

If one word fails in its object, a thousand are of no use.

靜坐常思己過，閒談莫論人非

Ching tso ch'ang ssǔ chi kuo, hsien t'an mo lun jen fei.

Sitting alone, meditate on your own faults; in conversation, talk not of other men's.

紅白喜事難答白

Hung pai hsi shih nan ta pai.

It is difficult to requite the gifts received at weddings and burials. This proverb, (a specimen of the innuendo) is commonly used in the sense of ''mind your own business''. The last three characters having the double meaning of requiting or answering clearly.

順 情 說 好 話，幹 直 惹 人 嫌

Shun ch'ing shuo hao hua, kan chih je jên hsien.

> Say what will please ; straight-forward words provoke dislike.

人 多 舌 頭 多

Jên to shê t'ou to.

> Many men, many tongues.

知 者 不 言，言 者 不 知

Chih chê pu yen, yen chê pu chih.

> Those who know, do not talk ; those who talk, do not know.

罈 口 封 得 住，人 口 封 不 住

T'an k'ou fêng tê chu, jên k'ou fêng pu chu.

> A jar's mouth may be stopped ; a man's mouth cannot.

話 說 三 遍 是 閑 言

Hua shuo san pien shih hsien yen

> It is a waste of words to repeat a thing three times over.

說 話 囉 唆 難 免 無 錯

Shuo hua lo so nan mien wu ts'o.

> A chatterbox is sure to make mistakes.

君 前 無 戲 言

Chün ch'ien wu hsi yen.

> Never joke in the presence of a prince.

言 不 妄 發 筆 不 妄 動

Yen pu wang fa pi pu wang tung.

> Neither let tongue or pen wag as they list.

開 口 獅 子 閉 口 象 不 可 亂 言

K'ai kou ssǔ tzǔ pi k'ou hsiang, pu k'o luan yen.

> An open mouth for a lion, a closed mouth for an elephant. Don't talk too much. Note.—The above which is a rule in drawing, is applied figuratively to talkative people.

逢 人 說 好 話 那 有 不 對
Fēng jên shuo hao hua, na yu pu tui.

> If you compliment everybody, who is there who would
> be your enemy.

鴉 鵲 打 破 蛋
Ya ch'iao ta p'o tan.

> Ceaseless chatter. *Lit.* Magpies and a broken egg.

謹 開 口, 慢 開 言
Chin k'ai k'ou, man k'ai yen.

> Be careful when you open your mouth; speak slowly.
> Comp. Jas. 1.19.

東 打 葫 蘆 西 打 瓢
Tung ta hu lu, hsi ta p'iao.

> Double-tongued. *Lit.* To beat a gourd in the east, a
> calabash in the west.

不 提 不 醒
Pu t'i pu hsing.

> If there is no discussion no one will be aroused.

善 問 者 如 撞 鐘
Shan wen chê ju chuang chung.

> A good questioner is like one striking a bell.

逢 人 且 說 三 分 話, 未 可 全 抛 一 片 心
Fêng jen ch'ieh shuo san fen hua, wei k'o ch'üan p'ao i p'ien hsin.

> When you meet anyone say but few words; don't tell out
> all that is in your heart.

牆 有 縫 壁 有 耳
Ch'iang yu feng pi yu erh.

> Beware of being overheard. *Lit.* Partitions have chinks,
> and walls have ears.

言 多 必 失, 不 言 為 高
Yen to pi shih, pu yen wei kao.

> He who talks much must err; he excels who says
> nothing.

路上說話,草裏有人

Lu shang shuo hua, ts'ao li yu jên.

> When you talk on the road, remember there may be men in the grass.

遇人說人話,遇鬼說鬼話

Yü jên shuo jên hua, yü kuei shuo kuei hua.

> Meeting men or spirits, talk as they do.

見得到,說得出

Chien tê tao, shuo tê ch'u.

> A man may tell what he has seen.

可爲知者道,難與俗人言

K'o wei chih chê tao nan yü su jen yen.

> One may discourse with a wise man; it is hard to converse with a clodhopper.

出在你口．入在人耳

Ch'u tsai ni k'ou, ju tsai jen erh.

> Be careful what you say. *Lit.* That which goes out of your mouth, enters other people's ears.

罔談彼短靡恃己長

Wang t'an pi tuan, mi shih chi ch'ang.

> Never converse on the faults of other; nor presume to speak of your own virtues.

開口不如緘口穩

K'ai k'ou pu ju chien k'ou wen.

> It is not so safe to open the mouth as to keep it shut.

說話要留情

Shuo hua yao liu ch'ing.

> In conversation, you must control your feelings.

會說的不如會聽的

Hui shuo ti pü ju hui t'ing ti.

> A good listener is better than a good talker.

練 胳 膊 練 腿 不 如 練 嘴

Lien ko po lien t'ui pu ju lien tsui.

> Exercising the arms and legs is not so useful as exercising the mouth.

腿 勤 不 如 嘴 勤

T'ui ch'in pu ju tsui ch'in.

> Persistent questioning is better than fleet cunning.

一 言 興 邦，一 言 喪 邦

I yen hsing pang, i yen sang pang.

> A single expression may make a country prosperous, or may ruin it.

巧 言 亂 德

Ch'iao yen luan tê.

> Specious words confound virtue.

念 過 詩 經 會 說 話，念 過 易 經 會 算 卦

Nien kuo shih ching hui shuo hua, nien kuo i ching hui suan kua.

> He who has studied the Shih Ching knows how to converse, he who has studied the Yi Ching knows how to divine.

知 音 說 與 知 音 聽，不 是 知 音 不 與 談

Chih yin shuo yü chih yin t'ing, pu shih chih yin pu yü t'an,

> Converse of music only with a musician.

忠 心 安 社 稷，利 口 覆 家 邦

Chung hsin an shê chi, li k'ou fu chia pang.

> A faithful heart tranquilizes the spirits of the land; a sharp tongue overturns a nation.

觀 棋 不 語 眞 君 子

Kuan ch'i pu yü chen chün tzŭ.

> He is truly a superior man who can look upon a game of chess in silence.

行 船 打 罵，住 船 說 話

Hsing ch'uan ta ma, chu ch'uan shuo hua.

> When the boats are in motion the boatmen strike and revile each other; when the boats are anchored they chat pleasantly together.

成 事 莫 說，覆 水 難 收

Ch'eng shih mo shuo, fu shui nan shou.

> When the thing is once done don't talk about it; spilt water cannot be gathered up.

定 口 如 瓶，防 意 如 城

Shou k'ou ju p'ing, fang i ju ch'eng.

> Close your mouth like a bottle; guard your thoughts as though guarding a city.

呐 呐 寡 言 者 未 必 愚，喋 喋 利 口 者 未 必 智

No no kua yen chê wei pi yü, tieh tieh li k'ou chê wei pi chih.

> He who hesitates and is slow of speech need not be a fool; a glib and fluent speaker is not necessarily a sage.

夏 蟲 不 可 以 語 冰，井 蛙 不 可 以 談 天

Hsia ch'ung pu k'o i yü ping, ching wa pu k'o i t'an t'ien.

> The summer insect cannot speak of ice; the frog in the well shouldn't talk about Heaven.

當 着 矬 人 別 說 矮 話

Tang cho ts'o jên pieh shuo ai hua.

> Don't talk about dwarfs to a pigmy.

說 話 爲 空，落 筆 爲 實

Shuo hua wei k'ung, lo pi wei shih.

> What is said is unreliable: what is written down is definite.

說 話 不 明 猶 如 昏 鏡

Shuo hua pu ming yu ju hun ching.

> Speech that is not clear is like a dull mirror.

三 鼻 子 眼 多 出 氣

San pi tzŭ yen to ch'u ch'i.

> A meddlesome person. *Lit.* Three nostrils blow out too much breath.

Chapter 2. Words.

記 得 從 前 話，到 老 不 嗜 罵
Chi tê ts'ung ch'ien hua, tao lao pu shū ma.

> When you remember the words that you once spoke, you will make up your mind never to curse again.

忠 言 逆 耳 利 於 行，良 藥 苦 口 利 於 病
Chung yen ni erh li yä hsing, liang yao k'u k'ou li yü ping.

> Honest advice is unpleasant to the ear, but induces good conduct; good medicine is bitter to the mouth, but will cure disease.

聖 賢 言 語 神 欽 鬼 伏
Sheng hsien yen yü shen ch'in kuei fu.

> The words of the sages are respected by the gods, and dreaded by the demons.

口 是 風 筆 是 踪
K'ou shih fēng, pi shih tsung.

> The written word abides. *Lit.* The mouth is wind, the pencil is a mark or trace.

話 不 投 機 留 半 句
Hua pu t'ou chi liu pan chu.

> If your words are not acceptable, hold back half of them.

附 耳 之 言 聞 於 千 里
Fu erh chih yen wen yü ch'ien li.

> Words whispered in the ear may be heard for a thousand li.

鼓 在 內 打，聲 不 見 外 響
Ku tsai nei ta, sheng pu chien wai hsiang.

> Beat your drum inside the house, and outsiders will not hear.

美 言 不 信，信 言 不 美
Mei yen pu hsin, hsin yen pu mei.

> Complimentary words are not sincere; sincere words are not pleasing.

寡 言 省 謗 寡 慾 保 身
Kua yen sheng pang kua yü pao shen.

> When words are few, slander is avoided: when the desires are few the body does not suffer.

狂 夫 之 言 聖 人 擇 焉

K'uang fu chih yen sheng jen tse yen.

> A wise man will learn something even from the words
> of a fool.

好 話 一 句 三 冬 煖，惡 話 一 句 惱 人 心

Hao hua i chü san tung nuan, ô hua i chü nao jen hsin.

> One good word can warm the three winter months; one
> bad one can make men angry.

有 肉 當 面 切，有 話 當 面 說

Yu jou tang mien ch'ieh, yu hua tang mien shuo.

> If you have meat, mince it openly; if you have anything
> to say, say it before a man's face.

話 有 幾 說，字 有 幾 撇

Hua yu chi shuo, tzŭ yu chi p'ieh.

> Words are variously spoken; characters have various
> strokes.

一 鋸 兩 把 瓢

I chü liang pa p'iao.

> One word of his settles the matter. *Lit.* By one stroke
> of the saw he severs the gourd into a couple of
> ladles.

一 言 勝 千 百

Yi yen sheng ch'ien pai.

> One word may be better than hundreds or thousands.

一 諾 千 金

I no ch'ien chin.

> His promise once given is as good as a thousand taels.

欲 知 心 腹 事，單 聽 口 中 言

Yü chih hsin fu shih, tan t'ing k'ou chung yen.

> Listen to a man's words if you wish to know his mind.

開 口 見 人 肺 腑

K'ai k'ou chien jen fei fu.

> You understand as soon as he speaks. *Lit.* When he
> opens his mouth his lungs and viscera are visible.

開 心 見 誠

K'ai hsin chien ch'eng.

> When a man opens his mind his real meaning becomes evident.

摸 不 清 白，不 要 亂 答 白

Mo pu ch'ing pai, pu yao luan ta pai.

> If you can't find out the reason, don't answer too glibly.

處 世 戒 多 言，言 多 必 失

Ch'ü shih chieh to yen, yen to pi shih.

> In life be careful not to talk too much ; when words are many there are bound to be mistakes.

鼓 不 打 不 響，鐘 不 撞 不 鳴，話 不 說 不 明

Ku pu ta pu hsiang, chung pu chuang pu ming, hua pu shuo pu ming.

> If the drum is not beaten and the bell not struck, they cannot be heard ; words unspoken cannot be understood.

言 滿 天 下 無 口 過，行 滿 天 下 無 怨 惡

Yen man t'ien hsia wu k'ou kuo hsing man t'ien hsia wu yüan ô.

> Everybody has heard me speak and no one accuses me of falsehood ; everybody has seen my actions and no one says I have injured them.

三 個 蠻 人 抬 不 起 一 個 理 字

San ko man jên t'ai pu ch'i i ko li tzu.

> Three boors cannot carry the character *Right*.

苦 言 藥 也，甘 言 疾 也

K'u yen yao yeh, kan yen chi yeh.

> Bitter words are medicine ; honeyed words cause sickness.

聖 賢 千 萬 語，提 醒 夢 中 人

Sheng hsieu ch'ien wan yü, t'i hsing meng chung jên.

> The myriad words of the sages rouse up dreaming men.

人 平 不 語，水 平 不 流

Jên p'ing pu yü, shui p'ing pu liu.

> When a man is calm he says nothing ; when water is level it does not flow.

傷 人 一 語, 利 如 刀 割

Shang jen i yü, li ju tao ko.

> One hurtful word wounds like a sharp sword.

利 刀 割 體 瘡 猶 合, 言 語 傷 人 恨 不 消

Li tao ko t'i ch'uang yu ho, yen yü shang jěn hen pu hsiao.

> The wound of a sharp knife will close up but the hate
> provoked by harmful words will never die.

有 話 明 說, 不 必 隱 瞞

Yu hua ming shuo, pu pi yin man.

> If you have anything to say say it plainly, there is no
> need to conceal anything.

好 語 似 珠 串 一 一

Hao hua ssŭ chu ch'uan i i.

> Good words are like a string of pearls.

小 辯 害 義 小 言 破 道

Hsiao pien hai i, hsiao yen p'o tao.

> Petty distinctions are injurious to rectitude ; quibbling
> words violate reason.

書 不 盡 言, 言 不 盡 意

Shu pu chin yen, yen pu chin i.

> Books do not exhaust words, nor words thoughts.

高 談 闊 論, 沒 有 一 點 實 行

Kao t'an ko lun, mu yu i tien shih hsing.

> He is merely an eloquent talker ; doesn't do the slightest
> thing.

一 星 之 火 能 燒 萬 頃 之 山, 半 句 非 言 誤 損 生 平 之 德

I hsing chih huo neng shao wan ch'ing chih shan, pan chü fei yen
wu sun sheng p'ing chih tê.

> As a great expanse of hill country may be burnt by a
> single spark of fire, so the virtue of a lifetime may
> be injured by a wrong expression. Note.—One
> "ch'ing" equals a hundred "mou" or Chinese acres.

巧 言 不 如 直 道, 明 人 不 用 細 說

Ch'iao yen pu ju chih tao, ming jen pu yung hsi shuo.

> Plausible talk is not equal to honest speech ; and a clever
> man needs but few words.

言 不 妄 發，發 必 當 理

Yen pu wang fa, fa pi tang li.

> Works may not be foolishly spoken ; what you say must accord with reason.

力 賤 得 人 敬，口 賤 得 人 憎

Li chien tê jên ching, k'ou chien tê jen tsêng.

> Who makes his strength cheap obtains men's respect who makes his mouth cheap obtains their dislike.

有 所 言 必 議 之 而 後 言

Yu so yen pi i chih erh hou yen.

> Think before you speak.

少 開 口 多 閉 目

Shao k'ai k'ou to pi mu.

> He who seldom opens his mouth, often shuts his eyes. Note.—''Shuts his eyes'' i.e., meditatively, thinking well before he speaks.

慮 少 夢 自 少，言 稀 過 亦 稀

Lü shao mêng tzu shao yen hsi kuo i hsi.

> When troubles are few dreams are few ; when words are scarce faults are scarce.

筆 情 達 千 里

Pi ch'ing ta ch'ien li.

> The pen can convey one's meaning for a thousand li.

誇 海 口 說 大 話

K'ua hai k'ou shuo ta hua.

> A great boaster. *Lit.* To boast with a mouth as wide as the sea.

那 裏 有 大 一 尺 的 帽 子

Na li yu ta i ch'ih ti mao tzu.

> Exaggeration. *Lit.* Where is there one hat a foot bigger than another.

一 言 憤 事，一 人 定 國

I yen fen shih, i jen ting kuo.

> One word ruins an affair ; one man subdues a state.

好 言 難 得 惡 語 易 施，一 言 旣 出 駟 馬 難 追

Hao yen nan tê ô yü i shih, i yen chi ch'u ssu ma nan chui.

> Good words are hard to get but evil ones are easily said;
> a word once uttered cannot be overtaken by a team
> of four horses.

頭 可 斬 否 不 可 禁

T'ou k'o chan shê pu k'o chin.

> You can behead a man but you can't shut his mouth.

言 語 虛 化 到 老，無 收 成 結 果

Yen yü hsü hua tao lao, wu shou ch'eng chieh kuo.

> If your words are not sincere even to old age you will
> accomplish nothing.

千 金 容 易 得，好 語 實 難 求

Ch'ien chin jung i tê hao yü shih nan ch'iu.

> It is easier to obtain thousands of gold than kind words.

人 間 私 語，天 聞 若 雷

Jên chien ssǔ yü, t'ien wen jo lei.

> Words spoken in secret by men sound like thunder in the
> ears of Heaven.

言 乃 心 之 聲

Yen nai hsin chih sheng.

> Words are the voice of the heart.

罵 人 不 用 打 草 稿

Ma jên pu yung ta ts'ao kao.

> In cursing anybody it is not necessary to make a
> preliminary draft.

話 不 說 不 知，木 不 鑽 不 透

Hua pu shuo pu chih, mu pu tsuan pu t'ou.

> Words unspoken remain unknown; wood not bored
> remains whole.

SECTION XV. ON LAW AND GOVERNMENT.

Chapter 1. Laws and Penalties.

罰 就 不 打，打 就 不 罰

Fa chiu pu ta, ta chiu pu fa.

If you fine, do not give the bamboo; if you give the bamboo, do not fine. Note.—This rule holds good in Chinese police cases.

瞞 關 漏 稅，拿 着 問 罪

Man kuan lou shui, na cho wen tsui.

If you cheat the Customs and evade duty, you will be caught and convicted.

賞 不 論 寃 仇，罰 不 論 骨 肉

Shang pu lun yuan ch'ou, fa pu lun ku jou.

In rewarding, do not make any difference as regards enemies; in punishing do not make any difference as regards relatives.

斬 絞 軍 流 徒 法 不 可 犯

Chan chiao chün liu t'u fa pu k'o fan.

Do not break the laws the punishment for which is decapitation, strangling, banishment, exile and transportation. Note.—The three latter punishments are banishment for life with military service; banishment to a distant province, and banishment to another part of the same province.

懼 法 不 犯 法，畏 刑 可 免 刑

Chü fa pu fan fa, wei hsing k'o mien hsing.

He who fears the law will not break it; he who dreads punishment will escape it.

立 法 不 可 不 嚴，行 法 不 可 不 恕

Li fa pu k'o pu yen, hsing fa pu k'o pu shu.

In making laws, severity is indispensable; in administering them, clemency.

一 字 定 生 死, 筆 莫 亂 動

I tzu ting sheng ssu, pi mo luan tung.

> One word may decide for life or death, therefore be careful how the pen is used.

黑 筆 寫 白 紙, 一 字 定 生 死

Hei pi hsieh pai chih, i tzu ting sheng ssŭ.

> Of that which is written in black and white, a single word may decide for life or death.

鋼 刀 雖 快 不 斬 無 罪 之 人

Kang tao sui k'uai pu chan wu tsui chih jên.

> Though the steel knife is sharp, it does not behead the innocent man.

善 化 不 足, 惡 化 有 餘

Shan hua pu tsu, ô hua yu yü.

> If gentle means fail, harsh means will be more than effective.

案 上 無 刑, 案 下 無 法

An shang wu hsing, an hsia wu fa.

> No punishment on the Bench, no law below it.

犯 法 心 無 主

Fan fa hsin wu chu.

> Breaking the law is owing to want of self-control.

死 不 可 生, 刑 不 可 贖

Ssŭ pu k'o sheng, hsing pu k'o shu.

> A man once dead cannot be brought to life; punishment once inflicted cannot be taken back.

人 隨 王 法, 草 隨 風

Jên sui wang fa, ts'ao sui feng.

> Men yield to the laws like the grass to the wind.

Chapter 2. Litigation.

八 字 衙 門 朝 南 開，有 理 無 錢 莫 進 來

Pa tzu ya men ch'ao nan k'ai, yu li wu ch'ien mo chin lai.

> The spreading doors of the Yamen face the South, but though you are in the right, don't venture in without money. Note.—Pa Tzu Men 八 字 門 are the wide-spreading gates or doors of official buildings like the 八 character in shape.

榜 上 無 名 叫 不 應

Pang shang wu ming chiao pu ying.

> If your name is not on the roll of successful candidates, you can't put it there.

一 家 有 事 連 累 十 家

I chia yu shih lien lei shih chia.

> If one family has a lawsuit, ten families are involved in trouble.

賊 咬 一 口 入 骨 三 分

Tsei yao i k'ou ju ku san fen.

> The bite of a thief goes three inches into the bone. Note.—This proverb refers to the false statements sometimes made by prisoners at the bar, charging others with complicity in their offences.

告 人 一 狀 三 世 冤

Kao jên i chuang san shih yüan.

> Inform against a man once, and three generations of his family will become your enemies.

無 誑 不 成 詞

Wu k'uang pu ch'eng tz'ŭ.

> An indictment cannot be got up without lies.

一 字 入 公 門，九 牛 拖 不 出

I tsŭ ju kung men, chiu niu t'o pu ch'u.

> If but one word of information against a man get into court, nine oxen cannot drag it out again.

居 家 戒 爭 訟, 訟 則 終 凶

Chü chia chieh cheng sung, song tsê chung hsiung.

> Let householders avoid litigation; for once go to law and
> there is nothing but trouble.

贏 了 官 司 輸 了 錢

Ying liao kuan ssŭ shu liao ch'ien,

> Win your lawsuit and lose your money.

贏 了 猫 兒 輸 了 牛

Ying liao mao erh shu liao niu.

> Winning a cat you lose a cow.

十 塲 官 司 九 塲 和

Shih ch'ang kuan ssu chiu ch'ang ho.

> Nine lawsuits out of ten are settled by arbitration.

原 告 一 張 紙, 被 告 就 要 死 被 告 一 張 紙, 兩 下 都 有 理

Yuan kao i chang chih, pei kao chiu yao ssŭ, pei kao i chang chih,
liang hsia tu yu li.

> The plaintiff's charge makes the defendant seem worthy
> of death; but the defendant's answer shows there is
> right on both sides.

筆 如 刀 利

Pi ju tao li.

> His pen is as sharp as a sword.　Note.—Said of one who
> writes indictments.

欲 加 之 罪, 何 患 無 詞

Yü chia chih tsui, ho huan wu tz'u.

> Wishing to criminate, no difficulty will be met in finding
> a pretext.

筆 下 留 情

Pi hsia liu ch'ing.

> To retain some feeling in writing an indictment.

生 不 入 官 門, 死 不 入 地 獄

Sheng pu ju kuan men, ssŭ pu ju ti yü.

> In life beware of yamens; in death beware of hell.

堂 上 一 張 紙，堂 下 一 張 嘴

T'ang shang i chang chih, t'ang hsia i chang tsui.

On the magistrates' table a sheet of paper; at his feet a mouth.

拿 官 先 拿 家 丁

Na kuan hsien na chia ting.

Before you arrest a magistrate, arrest his domestic.

三 六 百，二 四 百，差 費 房 禮

San liu pai erh ssu pai, ch'ai fei fang li.

Three or six hundred cash; two or four hundred cash; expenses for runners and presents for clerks. Note.—A hundred in this connection is said always to mean a thousand.

久 狀 不 離 原 詞

Chiu chuang pu li yuan tz'ŭ.

A lawsuit, however protracted, can never go beyond the original documents.

會 打 官 司 也 要 錢

Hui ta kuan ssu yeh yao ch'ien.

He who is an adept at lawsuits needs a lot of money.

不 能 見 天 子 言 情

Pu neng chien t'ien tzŭ yen ch'ing.

You cannot interview the emperor to tell him your wrongs.

官 斷 十 條 理，九 條 人 不 知

Kuan tuan shih t'iao li, chiu t'iao jên pu chih.

Of ten reasons by which a magistrate may decide a case, nine are unknown to the public.

氣 煞 勿 可 告 狀，餓 煞 勿 可 做 賊

Ch'i sha wu k'o kao chuang, ô sha wu k'o tso tsei.

Though you are very angry do not go to law; though you are very hungry do not be a thief.

官 去 吏 在 吏 去 案 在

Kuan ch'ü li tsai li ch'ü an tsai.

The magistrate may go but the officers remain; the officers may go but the law-case remains.

訟 心 者 祥‧訟 人 者 殃

Sung hsin chê hsiang, sung jên chê yang.

> Happy is he who accuses himself; wretched he who contends with others.

家 有 三 畝 田,不 離 縣 門 前

Chia yu san mou t'ien, pu li hsien men ch'ien,

> Those who have three acres of land, never leave the door of the yamen, i.e., those who have substance can afford to go to law.

能 打 私 鹽 漕 米,不 打 人 命 干 連

Neng ta ssŭ yen ts'ao mi, pu ta jên ming kan lier.

> You may engage in a lawsuit about smuggled salt or tribute rice, but don't get involved in a murder case. Note.—The former may result in temporary and limited punishment; the latter may mean detention for years.

分 爭 辨 訟,非 禮 不 決

Fen chēng pien sung, fei li pu chueh.

> Disputes and lawsuits cannot be settled except in accordance with propriety.

Chapter 3. Civil Officers.

文 官 點 一 筆,武 官 扒 不 急

Wen kuan tien i pi, wu kuan p'a pu chi.

> At one stroke of the civil magistrate's pencil, the military official hastens to obey. Note. 扒 equals 奔 走 to run. 不 急 indecates hesitancy, i.e., he can't run fast enough.

官 府 坐 堂 書 差 衙 役 幫 忙

Kuan fu tso t'ang shu ch'ai ya i pang mang.

> When the magistrate sits on the Bench he is helped by all his underlings.

若 要 安,先 完 官

Jo yao an, hsien wan kuan.

> If you would be at peace, first settle all the magistrate's claims.

文 憑 印 信 武 憑 號 令

Wen p'ing yin hsin, wu p'ing hao ling.

> The civil magistrate's sign of authority is his seal; the military magistrate's sign of authority is the imperial order.

茅 屋 出 公 卿

Mao wu ch'u kung ch'ing.

> Even thatched cottages yield high officials.

官 高 勢 高 不 如 道 之 高

Kuan kao shih kao pu ju tao chih kao

> High office and high authority are both inferior to rectitude in governing.

三 代 做 官 不 可 輕 師 慢 匠

San tai tso kuan pu k'o ch'ing shih man chiang.

> Though an official of the third generation, you may not lightly esteem scholars or despise artizans.

鹽 糧 兩 道 各 管 一 號

Yen liang liang tao ko kuan i hao.

> The Commissioners of salt and grain each manage their own department.

朝 中 有 人 好 爲 官

Ch'ao chung yu jen hao wei kuan.

> With friends at court it is easy to get into office.

瞞 官 莫 欺 官

Man kuan mo ch'i kuan.

> You may deceive, but you must not insult an official.

臣 門 如 市 臣 心 似 水

Ch'en men ju shih ch'en hsin ssŭ shui.

> A good magistrate's door is like a market place; his heart is as pure water. Note.—Surrounding the door would be a great number of people.

官 高 必 險

Kuan kao pi hsien.

> High office is necessarily dangerous.

清官不到頭

Ch'ing kuan pu tao t'ou.

An honest magistrate cannot succeed.

文官把筆安天下

Wen kuan pa pi an t'ien hsia.

The civil magistrate can pacify the empire with his pen.

官高爵顯

Kuan kao chio hsien.

The dignity of high office is widely known.

官不怕你窮，鬼不怕你瘦

Kuan pu p'a ni ch'iung, kuei pu p'a ni shou.

A magistrate will not consider your poverty, nor an evil spirit your leanness. Note.—The meaning of this saying is, that the one will have your money and the other your life.

清官難逃滑吏手

Ch'ing kuan nan t'ao hua li shou.

An honest magistrate cannot avoid having dishonest clerks.

人心似鐵，官法如爐

Jên hsin ssu t'ieh, kuan fa ju lu.

Men's hearts are like iron, and the law is like the furnace.

家無讀書子，官從何處來

Chia wu tu shu tzŭ, kuan ts'ung ho ch'u lai.

If the homes of the people have no scholarly sons, where are the magistrates to come from.

爲官須作相及第早爭先

Wei kuan hsü tso hsiang chi ti tsao cheng hsien.

A mandarin must aim at being Prime Minister, and so must begin early to contend for the first rank.

官有正條，民有私約

Kuan yu cheng t'iao, ming yu ssŭ yo.

The magistrate has his proper laws, and the people their private agreements.

為 官 不 與 民 作 主，枉 受 朝 延 爵 祿 高

Wei kuan pu yü min tso chu, wang shou ch'ao t'ing chio lu kao.

> A magistrate who is not first among his people, has received the emperor's high distinction and pay in vain.

好 漢 見 官 三 聲 啞

Hao han chien kuan san sheng ya.

> A wise man before a magistrate will be mute for a little while.

窮 官 當 富 客

Ch'iung kuan tang fu k'o.

> A poor official equals a rich merchant.

千 里 做 官 只 為 嘴

Ch'ien li tso kuan chih wei tsui.

> He who takes office far from home, only does so for a living.

在 上 不 驕，高 而 不 危

Tsai shang pu chiao, kao erh pu wei.

> He who in high station is without pride, is exalted without danger.

有 才 不 在 官 大 小；無 才 枉 受 爵 祿 高

Yu t'sai pu tsai kuan ta hsaio, wu t'sai wang shou chio lu kao.

> A man with ability will display it in any office high or low; a man without ability receives high rank and pay in vain.

滅 門 知 府，抄 家 知 縣

Mieh men chih fu, ch'ao chia chih hsien.

> The Prefect can exterminate families; the County Magistrate can confiscate goods.

一 任 清 知 府，十 萬 雪 花 銀

I jen ch'ing chih fu, shih wan hsüeh hua yin

> Even an honest Prefect may, during a three years term of office save a hundred thousand snow-white taels of silver.

未 做 官 說 千 般, 做 了 官 是 一 般

Wei tso kuan shuo ch'ien pan, tso liao kuan shih i pan.

> Before he comes into office he reproves a thousand faults; after he has come into office he commits the same himself.

當 官 有 三 事 曰 清 曰 愼 曰 勤

Tang kuan yu san shih yüeh ch'ing yueh shen yueh ch'ing.

> A magistrate ought to have three qualifications, honesty, carefulness and diligence.

官 有 大 小, 吏 無 尊 卑

Kuan yu ta hsiao, li wu tsun pei.

> Among magistrates, there are distinctions of rank; among their assistants, none.

官 威 不 如 衙 役 威, 衙 役 不 威 官 就 低

Kuan wei pu ju ya i wei, ya i pu wei kuan chiu ti.

> Better awe-inspiring police than awe-inspiring officials; for if the police be not so, the official will be lightly esteemed.

無 限 朱 門 生 餓 殍, 幾 多 白 屋 出 朝 郎

Wu hsien chu men sheng ô p'iao, chi to pai wu ch'u ch'ao lang.

> Large numbers of the gentry beget sons who die of want; many an ordinary family yields one who becomes a courtier.

官 情 如 紙 薄

Kuan ch'ing ju chih po.

> The friendship of officials is as thin as paper.

官 清 衙 門 瘦

Kuan ch'ing ya men shou.

> If the magistrate is upright his yamen will be poor.

官 清 民 自 安

Kuan ch'ing ming tzu an.

> If the magistrate is upright the people will be contented.

一 世 爲 官, 七 世 打 磚

I shih wei kuan, ch'i shih ta chuan.

> To be an official for a lifetime means seven re-births into the world as a beggar. Note.—This proverb is based on the popular idea of transmigration, and indicates corrupt officials who for a lifetime of rapacity will suffer as beggars in the future.

只 許 州 官 放 火, 勿 許 百 姓 點 燈

Chih hsü chou kuan fang huo, wu hsü pai hsing tien teng.

> The magistrate can start a fire but the people may not even light a lamp.

四 衙 却 比 二 衙 大, 四 衙 比 二 衙 多 兩 牙

Ssŭ yu ch'io pi erh ya ta, ssu ya pi erh ya to liang ya.

> The Fourth Assistant Magistrate is higher than the Second Assistant Magistrate because he has two teeth more. Note.—This is a play on the word, ya 牙 referring to the grasping character of the lower officials.

賊 使 非 智, 官 動 非 刑

Tsei shih fei chih, kuan tung fei hsing.

> When the thief uses extraordinary cleverness, the official exercises extraordinary severity in punishment.

文 能 安 邦, 武 能 定 國

Wen neng an pang, wu neng ting kuo.

> The civil official pacifies the state; the military official gives it security.

Chapter 4. Military Officers.

將 軍 上 戰 場, 擒 賊 先 擒 王

Chiang chün shang chan ch'ang, ch'in tsei hsien ch'in wang.

> When a general leads his armies to battle against rebels, he must first seize their leader.

好 鐵 不 打 釘, 好 人 不 當 兵

Hao t'ieh pu ta ting, hao jēn pu tang ping.

> Nails are not made out of good iron, and soldiers are not made out of good men.

強 將 手 下 無 弱 兵

Ch'iang chiang shou hsia wu jo ping.

Under a powerful general there are no feeble soldiers.

將 軍 不 怕 出 身 低

Chiang chün pu p'a ch'u shen ti.

The general is not troubled about the meanness of his origin.

殺 人 一 萬，自 損 三 千

Sha jen i wan, tzu sun san ch'ien.

Though you kill ten thousand, you yourself will have lost three thousand.

養 軍 千 日，用 在 一 朝

Yang chün ch'ien jih, yung tsai i chao.

An army is kept for a thousand days to be used on one single morning.

衝 鋒 破 敵 眞 個 大 膽，掀 天 揭 地 方 是 奇 才

Ch'ung feng p'o ti chen ko ta tan, hsien t'ien chieh ti fang shih ch'i ts'ai.

To rush on the spearpoint and break the enemy's ranks is great courage; to be able to open up heaven and earth shows wonderful talent.

大 將 軍 八 面 威 風

Ta chiang chün pa mien wei fêng.

A great general has everywhere an awe-inspiring reputation.

將 軍 不 下 馬，各 自 奔 前 程

Chiang chün pu hsia ma, ko tzŭ pen ch'ien ch'eng.

A (defeated) general never dismounts, but each soldier flees where he pleases.

千 兵 易 得，一 將 難 求

Ch'ien ping i te, i chiang nan ch'iu.

A thousand soldiers are easily obtained; it is difficult to find one general.

武 官 提 刀 定 干 戈

Wu kuan t'i tao ting kan ko.

> The military magistrate draws his sword and puts down rebellion.

Chapter 5. Yamens and Yamen-Runners.

錢 落 差 手 , 羊 落 虎 口

Ch'ien lo ch'ai shou, yang lo hu k'ou.

> Money falls into the yamen-runner's hands, as the sheep falls into the tiger's jaws.

官 差 不 自 由 , 那 怕 雨 淋 頭

Kuan ch'ai ɔu tzŭ yu, na p'a yü lin t'ou.

> A yamen-runner cannot please himself; what matter if his head gets wet with the rain.

衙 門 雖 小 , 法 度 一 例

Ya men sui hsiao, fa tu i li.

> Though the yamen be small the law is the same.

衙 門 深 似 海 , 弊 病 大 如 天

Ya men shen ssu hai, pi ping ta ju t'ien

> Yamens are deep as the sea and their corruptions lofty as heaven.

公 人 見 錢 如 蒼 蠅 見 血

Kung jen chien ch'ien ju ts'ang ying chien hsüeh.

> Official underlings see money as a fly sees blood.

哄 嚇 騙 詐 差 膽 大

Hung ho p'ien cha ch'ai tan ta.

> Yamen-runners must be brave for they deceive, frighten, defraud, and extort.

有 麼 衙 門 田 , 有 麼 衙 門 地

Yu mo ya men t'ien, yu mo ya men ti.

> What paddy-fields and corn fields belong to the yamen?
> Note.—This is the yamen-runner's answer to the preceding proverb, meaning he has no other method of earning money.

官差吏差,來人不差

Kuan ch'a li ch'a, lai jên pu ch'a.

> However wrong the magistrate and his assistants may be, their messenger is not to be blamed.

跟官人吃官人

K'en kuan jên ch'ih kuan jen.

> Those who follow officials eat the officials' rice.

國課早完卽囊橐無餘,自得至樂

Kuo k'o tsao wan chi nang to wu yü, tzǔ tê chih lê.

> Pay your taxes quickly even if it should empty your purse; then you will be happy indeed.

公門中好修行

Kung men chung hao hsiu hsing.

> An inmate of a yamen may easily acquire merit.

種田財主萬萬年,衙門銅錢一蓬烟

Chung t'ien ts'ai chu wan wan nien, ya men t'ung ch'ien i p'eng yen.

> Husbandry makes men wealthy for countless years; yamen-runners' earnings are but a puff of smoke.

武職的衙門沒有枷

Wu chih ti ya men mu yu chia.

> There are no cangues in military yamens, i.e., the punishments are more severe.

當差由不了自己

Tang ch'ai yu pu liao tzu chi.

> On public service one is not his own master.

爲人別當差,當差不自在,
風裏也得去雨裏也得來

Wei jên pieh tang ch'ai, tang ch'ai pu tzǔ tsai,
Fêng li yeh tê ch'ü yü li yeh tê lai.

> Don't be a public servant, for you can't be your own master; in wind and rain you are bound to come and go.

酒肉灌皮袋,官司仍舊在

Chiu jou kuan p'i tai, kuan ssǔ jên chiu tsai.

> You pour wine and put meat into the leather bag but the suit is still before the court, i.e., the yamen-runners must be fed.

SECTION XVI. ON TIMES AND SEASONS

Chapter 1. Time.

明 鏡 可 以 察 形，往 古 可 以 知 今

Ming ching k'o i ch'a hsing, wang ku k'o i chih chin.

> As you may examine your likeness in a looking-glass, so from past ages you may know what the present is.

一 寸 光 陰 一 寸 金，寸 金 難 買 寸 光 陰，
失 去 寸 金 有 尋 處，失 去 光 陰 無 處 尋

I ts'un kuang yin i ts'un chin, ts'un chin nan mai ts'un kuang yin,
Shih ch'ü ts'un chin yu hsin ch'ü, shih ch'ü kuang yin wu ch'ü hsing.

> An inch of time is as valuable as an inch of gold, but an inch of gold cannot buy an inch of time. If you lose an inch of gold it may be sought for, but it is vain to seek for a lost inch of time.

光 陰 似 箭，日 月 如 梭

Kuang yin ssu chien, jih yüeh ju so.

> Time is like an arrow; days and months like a weaver's shuttle. Comp. Job 7 : 6

過 去 事 明 如 鏡，未 來 事 暗 如 漆

Kuo ch'ü shih ming ju ching, wei lai shih an ju ch'i.

> Past events are clear as a mirror; future events are as dark as lacquer.

觀 今 宜 鑑 古，無 古 不 成 今

Kuan chin i chien ku, pu ch'eng chin.

> Regarding the present, we should be guided by the past; without the past, there had been no present.

工 夫 容 易 過

Kung fu jung i ko.

> Time easily passes.

驗 其 前 便 知 其 後

Yen ch'i ch'ien pien chih ch'i hou.

> By examining the past you may know what is in the future.

相 思 之 甚，寸 陰 若 歲

Hsiang ssu chih shen, ts'un yin jo sui.

To one full of expectation, a moment seems a year.

虛 度 歲 月，就 擱 一 生

Hsü tu sui yüeh, tan ko i sheng.

Idly spent months and years hinder a man for life.

今 朝 不 知 今 晚 事

Chin chao pu chih chin wan shih.

This morning has no knowledge of what will be in the evening.

一 刻 千 金

I k'o ch'ien chin.

One quarter of an hour is worth a thousand pieces of gold.

需 者 事 之 賊

Hsü chê shih chih tsei.

Procrastination is the thief of time.

靜 裏 乾 坤 大，閑 中 日 月 長

Ching li ch'ien k'un ta, hsien chung jih yueh ch'ang.

In peaceful repose, heaven and earth seem vast; in leisure, days and months are very long.

紅 顏 比 春 樹，流 年 一 擲 梭

Hung yen pi ch'ün shu, liu nien i chih so.

A fresh rosy face is like a tree in spring; the flowing years are but a throw of the shuttle.

光 陰 不 可 錯 過

Kuang yin pu k'o ts'o kuo.

Never waste time.

日 出 而 作，日 入 而 息

Jih ch'u erh tso, jih ju erh hsi.

Work with the rising, rest with the setting sun.

尺 璧 非 寶，寸 陰 是 競

Ch'ih pi fei pao, ts'un yin shih ching.

> An inch of time (on the sun-dial) is of greater worth than a foot of jade.

未 來 休 指 望，過 去 莫 思 量

Wei lai hsiu chih wang, kuo ch'ü mo ssŭ liang.

> Do not anticipate the future or regret the past.

今 海 不 及 古 海 之 廣

Chin hai pu chi ku hai chih kuang.

> The sea of to-day is not as broad as the sea of ancient times. Note.—Used ironically of those who are always praising the "old days"

日 久 見 人 心

Jih chiu chien jên hsin.

> Time reveals a man's heart

種 花 一 年，看 花 十 日

Chung hua i nien, k'an hua shih jih.

> You grow flowers for a year, only to see them for ten days.

鐵 樹 開 花，驢 子 年

T'ieh shu k'ai hua, lü tzŭ nien.

> "At the Greek Calends"—Never. *Lit.* In the donkey year when iron trees bear flowers. Note.—The donkey does not occur amongst the twelve animals of the Chinese Cycle.

要 知 將 來，但 看 已 往

Yao chih chiang lai, tan k'an i wang.

> To know the future you have only to look at the past.

Chapter 2. Seasons.

四 月 八 莧 菜 掐，四 鄉 人 家 把 秧 揷

Ssŭ yueh pa hsien ts'ai ch'ia, ssu hsiang jên chia pa yang ch'a.

> On the eighth of the fourth month spinach is pulled, and the farmers all begin to plant out the young rice.

年年三月二十八，家家戶戶吃甘蔗

Nien nien san yüeh erh shih pa, chia chia hu hu ch'ih kan chê.

Each year on the twenty-eighth of the third month, every family eats sugar-cane. Note.—A Wuchang proverb, which takes its rise from the fact that the feast of the Taoist temple outside the East Gate begins on that day.

冬至日長添線

Tung chih jih ch'ang t'ien hsien.

After the winter solstice the days lengthen as though adding thread by thread.

人不知春，草知春

Jên pu chih ch'ün, ts'ao chih ch'ün.

Spring is sooner recognised by plants than by men.

萬紫千紅總是春

Wan tzŭ ch'ien hung tsung shih ch'ün.

It is spring when the gayest colours abound.

秋至滿山多秀色，春來無處不花香

Ch'iu chih man shan to hsiu sê, ch'ün lai wu ch'ü pu hua hsiang.

When autumn comes the hills are covered with beauty; when spring arrives every spot is perfumed with flowers.

鶯花猶怕春光老，豈可敎人枉度春

Ying hua yu p'a ch'un kuang lao, ch'i k'o chiao jên wang tu ch'un.

Orioles and flowers fear the passing away of spring; how then can you teach men to spend it carelessly!

柑子看不得燈，蘿蔔打不得春

Kan tzu k'an pu tê têng, lo po ta pu te ch'ün.

Everything in season. The mandarin orange is over by the time of the Feast of Lanterns; and turnips by the coming of spring.

梧桐一葉落，天下盡知秋

Wu t'ung i yeh lo t'ien hsia chih ch'iu.

When the first leaf of the Wu T'ung tree falls the whole empire knows it is autumn.

年怕中秋,月怕牛

Nien p'a chung ch'iu, yueh p'a pan.

> The year fears mid-autumn, as the month the full moon
> Note.—This proverb indicates that after the times
> mentioned both year and month hasten to their close.

春不退田,冬不退屋

Ch'ün pu t'ui t'ien, tung pu t'ui wu.

> Never leave your fields in spring or your house in winter.

寒極而春

Han chi erh ch'un.

> After the extreme of cold comes spring.

不行春風難望夏雨

Pu hsing ch'ün fêng nan wang hsia yü.

> If there is no wind in spring, you can't expect rain in
> summer.

八月八,蚊子嘴開了花

Pa yüeh pa, wen tzŭ tsui k'ai liao hua.

> On the eighth of the eighth month the mosquito's mouth
> bears flowers. Note.—Chinese observers state that a
> change takes place in the mosquito's mouth similar
> to a flower budding. This hinders them from biting.

八月十五一聲雷,普天之下皆是賊

Pa yüeh shih wu i sheng lei, p'u t'ien chih hsia chieh shih tsei.

> If thunder is heard on the fifteenth of the eighth month
> everybody in the empire will become a thief.

端午不插艾,難喫新小麥

Tuan wu pu ch'a ai, nan ch'ih hsin hsiao mai.

> If at the summer solstice you do not stick up
> artemisia, you will not get any new wheat to eat.
> Note.—The feast of the summer solstice is known
> as 端陽 or 端午 held on the fifth of the fifth
> month. The proverb refers to an incident in the
> career of Huang Ch'ao a noted rebel during the T'ang
> Dynasty. See Smith's Proverbs, p. 108 Mayer's
> Manual No. 213

天 河 吊 角 要 穿 棉 襖

T'ien ho tiao chio yao ch'uan mien ao.

When one end of the Milky Way droops it is time to put on wadded clothes.

斗 柄 北 指,天 午 皆 冬

Tou ping pei chih, t'ien hsia chieh tung.

When the tail of the Great Bear points to the north, there is winter all over the empire.

人 情 莫 道 春 光 好,只 怕 秋 來 有 冷 時

Jen ch'ing mo tao ch'un kuang hao, chih p'a ch'iu lai yu leng shih.

Don't speak too well of the spring-time (of friendliness); rather fear the coming of the bleak autumn (of adversity).

天 上 無 晝 夜,地 下 無 五 穀

T'ien shang wu chou yeh, ti hsia wu wu ku.

If there is no night nor day there will be no harvest.

無 冷 無 熱,五 穀 勿 結

Wu leng wu jo, wu ku wu chieh.

If there is neither cold nor heat there will be no harvest.

草 抽 新 綠 漸 知 春

Ts'ao ch'ou hsin lu chien chih ch'ün.

When plants put forth their new green buds it is a sign that spring is near.

Chapter 3. Weather.

雨 灑 五 更 頭,行 人 永 無 憂

Yü sa wu keng t'ou, hsing jen yung wu yu.

If it rains at the break of day the traveller need not have the slightest anxiety.

東 閃 日 頭 紅,西 閃 雨 重 重,南 閃 長 流 水,北 閃 猛 南 風

Tung shan jih t'ou hung, hsi shan yü ch'ung ch'ung, nan shan ch'ang liu shui, pei shan meng nan fêng.

When it lightens in the east the sun will be red; when it lightens in the west there will be showers of rain; when it lighten's in the south there will be heavy rain; and when it lightens in the north the fierce south wind will blow.

昨 日 商 量 大 不 同 , 半 夜 起 了 老 北 風

Tso jih shang liang ta pu t'ung, pan yeh ch'ih liao lao pei fêng.

> What we arranged yesterday is now all altered, for during the night the north wind has risen.

七 月 中 八 月 偏 , 九 月 十 月 看 不 見

Ch'i yueh chung pa yueh p'ien, chiu yueh shih yueh k'an pu chien.

> In the seventh month it is vertical; in the eighth month oblique; in the ninth and tenth months it can't be seen. Note.—This is said of the Dipper or Seven Stars in the Great Bear constellation.

七 姑 星 七 支 角 , 東 邊 起 西 邊 落

Ch'i ku hsing ch'i chih chio tung pien ch'i hsi pien lo.

> The seven-cornered constellation of the Seven Sisters, rises in the east and sets in the west. Note.—This refers to the seven stars of the Great Bear.

天 熱 難 當 , 趕 風 乘 涼

T'ien jo nan tang kan feng ch'eng liang.

> When the weather is unbearably hot, we try to get into a breeze for coolness.

三 月 三 , 路 上 行 人 脫 衣 單

San yüeh san lu shang hsing jen t'o i tan.

> On the third of the third month travellers cast off their thick clothes and wear thin ones.

九 月 九 行 人 莫 向 湖 邊 走

Chiu yueh chiu hsing jen mo hsiang hu pien tsou.

> On the ninth of the ninth month travellers should not go by the lake side. Note.—There are likely to be storms.

二 月 清 明 不 要 忙 , 三 月 清 明 早 下 秧

Erh yueh ch'ing ming pu yao mang, san yueh ch'ing ming tsao hsia yang.

> When the Ching Ming Festival is in the second month don't be in a hurry; if in the third month, plant your rice early.

九 月 重 陽 抱 火 進 房

Chiu yueh ch'ung yang pao huo chin fang.

> At the Ch'ung Yang Festival in the ninth month, it is the time to enter the house and gather round the fire. Note.—The Ch'ung Yang Feast is held on the ninth day of the ninth month. The figures 1.3.5 7.9., are supposed to belong to the Yang principle in nature, and in this case the figure nine is doubled hence the name of the feast.

關 門 起 開 門 息

Kuan men ch'i k'ai men hsi.

> If it rises in the evening, it will cease in the morning.

六 月 下 連 陰，遍 地 是 黃 金

Liu yüeh hsia lien yin p'ien ti shih huang chin.

> Continuous rain in the sixth month, covers the whole ground with yellow gold.

過 了 七 月 半 方 是 鐵 羅 漢

Kuo liao ch'i yueh pan fang shih t'ien lo han.

> Those who have survived to the middle of the seventh month are iron Lohans. See Section, Temples and Worship

但 得 立 春 晴 一 日，農 夫 不 用 力 耕 田

Tan tê li ch'un ch'ing i jih, nung fu pu yung li keng ti'en.

> If there be one fine day at the coming in of spring, the farmer need not labour hard at ploughing.

春 乾 滿 倉，秋 乾 絕 糧

Ch'ün kan man ts'ang, ch'iu kan chüeh liang.

> A dry spring and a full granary; a dry autumn and no grain.

夏 至 吹 西 風 屋 簷 溝 裏 抹 蝦 公

Hsia chih ch'ui hsi fêng wu yen kou li mo hsia kung.

> When the west wind blows at the summer solstice, you will be able to catch shrimps in the gutters under the eaves of the house. Note.—This indicates a great flood

夜 裡 起 風 日 裏 息

Yeh li ch'i fêng jih li hsi.

A calm day follows a windy night.

耕 田 望 落 雨，做 客 望 天 晴

Kēng t'ien wang lo yü, tso k'o wang t'ien ch'ing.

The farmer hopes for rain, the traveller for fine weather.

朝 看 東 南，晚 看 西 北

Chao k'an tung nan, wan k'an hsi pei.

In the morning, look towards the south-east; in the evening, look toward the north-west. Note.—If the eastern sky be bright in the morning, the day will be fine; if the western sky be bright in the evening, the next day will be fine.

月 暈 而 風

Yüeh yün erh fēng.

A halo round the moon is a sign of wind.

冬 甲 子 雨 牛 羊 凍 死，夏 甲 子 雨 撐 船 就 市 秋
甲 子 雨 禾 生 兩 耳，春 甲 子 雨 赤 地 千 里

Tung chia tzu yü niu yang tung ssŭ, hsia chia tzŭ yü ch'eng ch'uan chiu shih, ch'iu chia tzu yü ho sheng liang erh, ch'ün chia tzŭ yü ch'ih ti ch'ien li.

If it rains during the winter cycle, the cattle and sheep will die of cold; if it rains in the summer cycle, you may row to market in a boat, if it rains in the autumn cycle, the rice stalks will produce two ears (both useless), if it rains in the spring cycle, there will be bare parched land for a thousand li. Note.— The cycle refers to the sixty combinations of characters by which time is reckoned in China, and denotes a term of sixty days. It corresponds to our St. Swithin's, the superstition being that if it rains on the first day of each of these cycles, it will be wet weather for the whole of the period.

東 風 解 凍

Tung fêng chieh tung.

The east wind breaks up the frost.

平 風 息 浪，水 裏 寫 得 字

P'ing feng hsi lang, shui li hsieh tê tzŭ.

It is so calm and smooth, one might write on the water.

東 虹 日 頭, 西 虹 雨

Tung hung jih t'ou hsi hung yü.

> A rainbow in the east will be followed by a fine day;
> in the west, by a rainy day.

五 月 三 八 都 要 雨, 頭 八 無 雨 二 八 休, 三 八 無 雨 種 菉 豆

Wu yüeh san pa tu yao yü, t'ou pa wu yü erh pa hsiu, san pa wu
yü chung lu tou.

> On the eighth, eighteenth, and twenty-eighth of the fifth
> month, it should rain; if it does not rain on the
> eighth, it will not on the eighteenth; if it does not rain
> on the twenty-eighth, sow lentils. Note.—Lentils
> are to be sown because the season will be too dry for
> corn.

熱 極 生 風

Jo chi sheng fêng.

> Great heat brings wind.

雪 花 飛 六 出 先 兆 豐 年

Hsueh hua fei liu ch'u hsien chao feng nien.

> When the big snow-flakes fly it is a good omen of a
> prosperous year. Note.—"Big snow-flakes" literally,
> six-petalled snow flowers.

天 晴 無 人 怨, 久 雨 令 人 愁

T'ien ch'ing wu jen yuan chiu yü ling jen ch'ou.

> Nobody grumbles at fine weather; incessant rains make
> men depressed.

五 風 十 雨 皆 爲 瑞

Wu fêng shih yü chieh wei jui.

> Five days, rain, ten days, wind, are both good omens.

百 里 不 同 天

Pai li pu t'ung t'ien.

> Weather varies every hundred li.

心 定 自 然 涼

Hsin ting tzŭ jan liang.

> If the mind is at rest you will be able to keep cool.

冬 晴 百 日 無 怨

Tung ch'ing pai jih wu yüan.

Nobody complains over a hundred fine days in winter.

雲 掩 中 秋 月, 雨 灑 上 元 燈

Yün yen chung ch'iu yueh, yü sa shang yuan têng.

When the mid-autumn moon is beclouded, there will be rain on the next Feast of Lanterns.

無 雨 四 下 亮, 有 雨 頂 頭 光

Wu yü ssŭ hsia liang, yu yü ting t'ou kuang.

When it is bright all round it will not rain; when it is bright only overhead, it will.

月 到 中 秋 分 外 明

Yüeh tao chung ch'iu fen wai ming.

The moon of mid-autumn is exceedingly bright.

夏 至 一 陰 生, 冬 至 一 陽 生

Hsia chih i yin sheng, tung chih i yang sheng.

From the summer solstice, days begin to shorten; from the winter solstice, they begin to lengthen.

礎 潤 而 雨

Sang jun erh yü.

When the plinths of the pillars are damp there will be rain.

開 門 雨, 關 門 晴

K'ai men yü, kuan men ch'ing.

When it rains in the morning it will be fine at night.

因 寒 向 火, 怕 熱 乘 涼

Yin han hsiang huo, p'a jo ch'eng liang.

Cold sends us to the fire; heat sends us into the shade.

早 霞 暮 雨, 晚 霞 晴

Tsao hsia mu yü, wan hsia ch'ing.

A red sky in the morning means rain in the evening; a red sky in the evening means fine weather.

旱 來 東 風 不 下 雨

Han lai tung fēng pu hsia yü.

An east wind in time of drought brings no rain.

澇 來 北 風 不 晴 天

Lao lai pei fēng pu ch'ing t'ien.

A north wind in time of flood does not bring fine weather.

小 雪 不 耕 地, 大 雪 不 行 船

Hsiao hsüeh pu keng ti, ta hsüeh pu hsing ch'uan.

Ploughing stops at the season of the Small Snow; navigation at the Great Snow.

陰 雲 密 雨 養 天 花

Yin yün mi yü yang ti'en hua.

Dark clouds and fine rain nourish the flowers of Heaven, i.e., the blue skies.

立 春 未 到 雷 先 發, 四 十 九 日 不 成 天

Li ch'ün wei tao lei hsien fa, ssu shih chiu jih pu ch'eng t'ien.

If thunder is heard before the season of "The Beginning of Spring" there will be forty-nine days of bad weather.

SECTION XVII. ON TRAVEL.

Chapter 1, Travelling.

千漿萬篙比不得破篷撐腰

Ch'ien chiang wan kao pi pu tê p'o p'eng ch'eng yao.

> A thousand strokes with the oar and ten thousand pushes with the pole, are not equal to a fully set ragged sail.

不怕走得慢,只怕路上站

Pu p'a tsou tê man, chih p'a lu shang chan.

> Don't be afraid of walking slowly, but of stoppages on the way.

出門十分苦,衣破無人補

Ch'u men shih fen k'u, i p'o wu jên pu.

> Travelling is perfect misery; you tear your clothes and have no one to repair them.

手穩嘴穩到處好安身

Shou wen tsui wen tao ch'ü hao an shen.

> He who does not covet and who can control his words, will be comfortable wherever he goes.

路行站口船灣碼頭

Lu hsing chan k'ou ch'uan wan ma t'ou.

> On land, you go to the end of the stage; on water, you tie up at the jetty.

敲船三日坐,敲碗三日餓

Ch'iao ch'uan san jih tso ch'iao wan san jih ô.

> If you drum on a boat you will have three days delay; if you drum on your rice-bowl you will go hungry for three days.

三人上路,小的吃虧

San jeh shang lu, hsiao ti ch'ih k'uei.

> Of three men on a road, the youngest has to suffer.

未 晚 先 投 宿, 雞 鳴 早 看 天

Wei wan hsien t'ou su, chi ming tsao k'an t'ien.

> Find your lodging before it is dark; and when the cock
> crows take a look at the weather.

一 路 福 星

I lu fu hsing.

> May the star of happiness shine on all your journey.

一 路 平 安 一 路 安 穩

I lu p'ing an i lu an wen.

> May all your journey be in peace.

一 路 順 風

I lu shun fêng.

> May you have a fair wind all the way.

順 風 相 送

Shun fêng hsiang sung.

> May fair winds attend you.

別 時 容 易 見 時 難

Pieh shih jung i chien shih nan.

> To separate is easy, to meet again is more difficult.

路 在 口 裏 一 問 就 知

Lu tsai k'ou li i wen chiu chih.

> He who can use his tongue can find out any road.

篷 高 一 尺, 風 高 一 丈

P'eng kao i ch'ih, fêng kao i chang.

> Raise your sail one foot and you get ten feet of wind.

出 門 如 修 行, 船 底 不 漏 針

Ch'u men ju hsiu hsing, ch'uan t' pu lou chen.

> Travellers are like cultivators of virtue; on board a boat
> you will not lose so much as a needle.

春 雨 不 沾 路

Ch'un yü pu chan lu.

> Spring rain scarcely wets the road.

出 入 平 安

Ch'u ju p'ing an.

> May your going out and coming in be in peace.

在 家 尊 貴，出 門 賤

Tsai chia tsun kuei, ch'u men chien.

> Honoured at home, despised abroad.

離 家 一 里 不 如 屋 裏

Li chia i li pu ju wu li.

> Better at home than a mile from it.

在 家 千 日 好，出 外 一 時 難

Tsai chia ch'ien jih hao, ch'u wai i shih nan.

> A thousand days at home are better than the shortest time abroad.

天 乾 三 年，出 門 一 日 都 望 晴

T'ien kan san nien, ch'u men i jih tu wang ch'ing.

> After three years of drought, all who go out for a day hope for fine weather.

男 兒 五 湖 四 海 爲 朋 友，人 到 何 處 不 相 逢

Nan erh wu hu ssu hai wei p'eng yu, jen tao ho ch'ü pu hsiang fêng.

> If a man makes himself friendly wherever he travels where can he go and not find a friend?

隔 山 容 易 走，隔 水 最 難 行

Ke shan jung i tsou, ke shui tsui nan hsing.

> Mountains do not hinder a journey so much as rivers.

一 擔 金 和 寶，交 與 老 艄 公

I tan chin ho pao, chiao yü lao shao kung.

> On board, everything is in the captain's care.

相 逢 不 下 馬，各 自 奔 前 程

Hsiang fêng pu hsia ma, ko tzu pen ch'ien ch'eng.

> On a journey each pursues his way without alighting to greet every one he meets.

行 船 跑 馬 三 分 險

Hsing ch'uan p'ao ma san fen hsien.

> Whether travelling by boat or on horseback, there is a certain amount of danger.

同 路 無 梭 伴

T'ung lu wu so pan.

> Fellow-travellers must not desert each other.

少 年 子 弟 江 湖 老

Shao nien tzŭ ti chiang hu lao.

> Travel makes a young man old in experience.

急 行 慢 行 前 程 只 有 許 多 路

Chi hsing man hsing ch'ien ch'eng chih yu hsü to lu.

> Whether you hurry on or take it easy, the road before you has only a certain length.

前 車 覆, 後 車 戒

Ch'ien ch'ē fu hou ch'e chieh.

> When the vehicle in front upsets, the one following takes more heed.

長 安 雖 好 不 是 久 留 之 家

Ch'ang An sui hao pu shih chiu liu chih chia.

> There is no place like home. *Lit.* Ch'ang An may be a fine city, but it won't do for a permanent home. Note.—Cha'ng An, the name of one of the old capitals of China.

洛 陽 雖 好 不 如 家

Lo Yang sui hao pu ju chia.

> Same as above. *Lit.* Though Lo Yang be pleasant, it is not like home. Note.—Lo Yang, was also capital of China.

寸 步 脚 錢, 千 里 船 錢

Ts'un pu chiao ch'ien ch'ien li ch'uan ch'ien.

> Remove but an inch and you must pay porterage; travel a thousand li and you only have your boat fare to pay.

有 路 莫 登 舟

Yu lu mo teng chou.

If there is a road don't go by water.

騎 馬 的 不 知 步 行 的 苦

Ch'i ma ti pu chih pu hsing ti k'u.

The rider on horseback knows nothing of the toil of those who travel on foot.

出 門 不 惹 三 子 老 子 小 子 瞎 子

Ch'u men pu jê san tzu lao tzu hsiao tzu hsia tzu.

When you travel do not provoke the old, the young or the blind.

三 年 造 出 一 個 舉 子, 十 年 學 不 到 一 個 江 湖

San nien chao ch'u i ko chü tzŭ, shih nien hsüeh pu tao i ko chiang hu.

You may become a Master of Arts in three years; but you cannot become an accomplished traveller in ten.

坐 船 跑 馬 不 問 路

Tso ch'uan p'ao ma pu wen lu.

Whether travelling by boat or on horseback, never ask about the road.

逢 橋 須 下 馬, 過 渡 勿 爭 船

Fêng ch'iao hsü hsia ma, kuo tu wu cheng ch'uan.

Get of your horse to cross a bridge, and never wrangle at a ferry.

百 里 不 同 風, 千 里 不 同 俗

Pai li pu t'ung fêng, ch'ien li pu t'ung su.

Customs vary in every place. *Lit.* Within a hundred or a thousand li.

Chapter 2. Scenery.

上 說 天 堂, 下 說 蘇 杭

Shang shuo t'ien t'ang, hsia shuo Su Hang.

What Heaven is above, so is Soochow and Hangchow on earth.

流 水 下 灘 非 有 意，白 雲 出 岫 本 無 心

Liu shui hsia t'an fei yu i, pai yün ch'u hsiu pen wu hsin.

> Water rushes down the rapids without any design; and the white cloud rises from the mountain peak without any special intention.

深 山 畢 竟 藏 猛 虎，大 海 終 須 納 細 流

Shen shan pi ching ts'ang meng hu, ta hai chung hsü na hsi liu.

> The mountain ranges inevitably hide the fierce tigers, as the great sea must receive every small stream.

海 無 邊 江 無 底

Hai wu pien chiang wu ti.

> The sea is boundless, the river has no bottom.

萬 川 歸 海 而 海 不 盈

Wan ch'uan kuei hai erh hai pu ying.

> All the rivers flow into the sea, and yet the sea is not full. Comp. Eccles. 1: 7.

名 川 三 百，支 川 三 千

Ming ch'uan san pai, chih ch'uan san ch'ien.

> Of noted rivers there are three hundred; of tributaries, three thousand

江 淮 草 木 亦 知 爾 名

Chiang Huai ts'ao mu i chih erh ming.

> The Yangtse and the Huai, every flower and every tree, each has its own peculiar name.

遠 望 一 叢 林，不 是 屋 就 是 墳

Yuan wang i ch'ung lin, pu shih wu chiu shih fen.

> The distant grove you see either encloses a house or a grave.

SECTION XVIII. ON MEDICINE.

Chapter 1. Disease.

藕 絲 繫 得 鹽 船 住，災 殃 已 滿 病 自 愈
Ou ssu chi tê yen ch'uan chu, tsai yang i man ping tzǔ yü.

As a salt-junk may be held fast by a single filament of
lotus root, so when a disease has reached its climax,
there is a chance of recovery.

少 喫 多 餐，病 好 自 安
Shao ch'ih to ts'an ping hao tzǔ an.

A little food and often will result in recovery and health.

痰 癆 氣 蠱 隔，神 仙 醫 不 得
T'an lao ch'i ku ke, shen hsien i pu tê.

Asthma, consumption, wind, worms, and obstruction, are
maladies that neither gods nor fairies can cure.

服 藥 因 療 病，煎 湯 爲 保 身
Fu yao yin liao ping, chien t'ang wei pao shen.

You take medicine to heal sickness; you make soup to
nourish the body.

說 的 是 眞 方，賣 的 是 假 藥
Shuo ti shih chen fang, mai ti shih chia yao.

The prescription was good but the medicine was of
no use.

藥 灌 滿 腸，口 吞 莫 嘗
Yao kuan man ch'ang, k'ou t'un mo ch'ang.

Though you drink your fill of medicine, avoid the taste
in swallowing it.

服 藥 有 靈，其 效 如 神
Fu yao yu ling, ch'i hsiao ju shen.

Your medicines are as effective as divine assistance.

藥 醫 有 緣 人
Yao i yu yuan jên.

Medicine cures the patient for whom it has an affinity.

反 病 無 藥 醫

Fan ping wu yao i.

> When a disease returns, no medicine can cure it.

黃 金 無 假 阿 魏 無 眞

Hnang chin wu chia a wei wu chên.

> There is no such thing as spurious gold, or genuine asafoetida.

投 以 金 丹 病 魔 立 退

T'ou i chin tan ping mo li t'ui.

> Give a man the true elixir and the evil spirit of his disease will depart at once.

土 性 不 同

T'u hsing pu t'ung.

> Men's constitutions differ in different localities.

病 入 膏 肓 不 可 救 藥

Ping ju kao huang pu k'o chiu yao.

> When the disease enters the region of the heart, no medicine can effect a cure.

耳 不 看 不 聾 眼 不 洗 不 瞎

Erh pu k'an pu lung, yen pu hsi pu hsia.

> Your ears won't go deaf if you don't have them examined; your eyes won't go blind if you don't use eye-wash.

妙 藥 難 醫 冤 孽 病

Miao yao nan i yuan nieh ping.

> The most wonderful medicine cannot cure the desire for vengeance.

攻 之 不 可 , 達 之 不 能

Kung chih pu k'o, ta chih pu neng.

> It is a disease which neither medicine nor needle can reach.

竈 門 栽 楊 柳 , 有 死 無 生

Tsao men tsai yang liu, yu ssŭ wu sheng.

> A willow planted before a cook-house door will die, not live.

千 方 易 得，一 效 難 求

Ch'ien fang i tê, i hsiao nan ch'iu.

> It is easy to get a thousand prescriptions, but hard to obtain one good result.

秋 賣 菓 子，春 賣 藥

Ch'iu mai ko tzŭ, ch'ün mai yao.

> Fruit is sold in the autumn ; medicine in the spring.

冬 不 藏 精，春 必 温 病

Tung pu ts'ang ching, ch'ün pi wen ping.

> If one does not store up vital force in the winter, he will suffer from an epidemic in the spring.

肚 子 裏 沒 病 死 不 了 人

Tu tzŭ li mu ping ssŭ pu liao jen.

> If there is no disease in the abdomen the patient won't die.

日 輕 夜 重，不 早 治 沒 命

Pai ch'ing yeh chung pu tsao chih mu ming.

> Light during the day, but severe at night; (such a disease) if not cured speedily will result in death.

乾 勞 氣 臌 噎，閻 王 請 的 客

Kan lao ch'i ku yeh, Yen Wang ch'ing ti k'o.

> Those who have consumption, dropsy and throat disease are the invited guests of Yen Wang, i.e., doomed to death.

手 脚 無 善 症

Shou chiao wu shan cheng.

> Diseases of the hands and feet are the result of evil practices

春 搗 秋 凍，到 老 沒 病

Ch'ün wu ch'iu tung, tao lao mu ping.

> Keep well-covered in Spring, don't wear too many clothes in the Autumn, and you will never be ill.

老 怕 傷 寒，少 怕 痢 疾

Lao p'a shang han, shao p'a li chi.

> A cold is to be dreaded by the aged; dysentery, by the young.

要 求 南 風 須 開 北 牖

Yao ch'iu nan fêng hsü k'ai pei yu.

> If you want to get the south wind you must open the north window, i.e., to secure health you must pay attention to the necessities of the body.

Chapter 2. Doctors.

問 症 發 藥 與 病 相 合

Wen cheng fa yao yü ping hsiang ho.

> After diagnosing a disease, you must give suitable medicine.

醫 生 坐 轎，窮 家 不 到

I sheng tso chiao, ch'iung chia pu tao.

> The doctor that rides in a chair doesn't come to the home of the poor.

醫 生 出 名 家 家 接 不 贏

I sheng ch'u ming chia chia chieh pu ying.

> A doctor who has made his name has more patients than he can attend to.

道 他 功 高 扁 鵲，誰 知 他 催 命 閻 羅

Tao t'a kung kao Pien Ch'iao, shui chih t'a ts'ui ming Yen Lo.

> He talks of his skill as superior to that of Pien Chi'ao; but after all he is Yen Lo, the one who seeks after your life. Note.—Pien Chiao was one of China's famous doctors. Yen Lo or Yen Wang is the Chinese Pluto.

風 寒 暑 熱 醫 要 曉 得

Fêng han shu jo i yao hsiao tê.

> Whether the sickness is from cold or heat, the doctor ought to know.

包 好 受 謝，人 疑 莫 決

Pao hao shou hsieh, jen i mo chüeh.

> After he has guaranteed a cure and received his fee, his patient is still not sure of recovery.

熟 讀 王 叔 和，不 如 看 症 多

Shu tu Wang Shu Ho, pu ju k'an cheng to.

> Constant practice in treating disease is much better than the profoundest study of the works of Wang Shu Ho. Note.—This worthy was court physician during the Western Tsin dynasty.

急 病 請 三 師

Chi ping ch'ing san shih.

> In a dangerous illness call in three doctors.

良 醫 不 自 醫

Liang i pu tzŭ i.

> A clever doctor does not treat himself.

師 不 談 師，醫 不 談 醫

Shih pu t'an shih, i pu t'an i.

> A teacher will not speak against a teacher, nor a doctor against a doctor.

病 好 不 謝 醫，下 次 無 人 醫

Ping hao pu hsieh i, hsia tz'u wu jen i.

> If you do not remunerate a doctor for curing you once, you will get no one to do so a second time.

趁 我 十 年 運，有 病 早 來 醫

Ch'en wo shih nien yün, yu ping tsao lai i.

> Avail yourself of my ten years' good fortune, and come at once to be healed.

醫 有 割 股 之 心，並 無 虛 假 之 意

I yu ko ku chih hsin, ping wu hsü chia chih i.

> A doctor has the heart to cut flesh off his thigh to give to his patient, but never the mind to deceive him.

打 針 貼 膏 藥，賣 藥 的 用 假 藥

Ta chen t'ieh kao yao, mai yao ti yung chia yao.

> Quacks puncture and plaster, but only use spurious drugs.

學 醫 不 明 暗 刀 殺 人

Hsüeh i pu ming an tao sha jen.

> An unskilful doctor kills men as with a secret dagger.

運 去 先 生 醫 病 頭，時 來 先 生 醫 病 尾

Yün ch'ü hsien sheng i ping t'ou, shih lai hsien sheng i ping wei.

> The unlucky doctor cures the head of a disease; the lucky doctor, its tail.

行 醫 有 十 年 大 運

Hsing i yu shih nien ta yün.

> Doctors have a run of ten years' luck.

醫 不 叩 門，有 請 纔 行

I pu k'ou men, yu ch'ing ts'ai hsing.

> Doctors knock at no doors; they only come when invited·

庸 醫 殺 人 不 用 刀

Yung i sha jen pu yung tao.

> A quack doctor kills a man without using a sword.

半 積 陰 功 半 藏 身

Pan chi yin kung pan ts'ang shên.

> You are at the same time laying up secret merit, and taking care of yourself.

良 巫 之 子 多 死 於 鬼，良 醫 之 子 多 死 於 病

Liang wu chih tzŭ to ssŭ yü kuei, liang i chih tzŭ to ssŭ yü ping.

> Many children of clever sorcerers are killed by evil spirits; and many children of clever doctors die of disease.

不 吃 藥 當 中 醫

Pu ch'ih yao tang chung i.

> To take no medicine is as good as having a middling doctor.

藥 到 回 春，先 生 眞 歧 黃 手 段

Yao tao hui ch'ün, hsien sheng chen Ch'i Huang shou tuan.

> When medicine restores a man to health, the doctor truly has the ability of Chi and Huang. Note.—Chi Pai 歧 伯 was medical tutor to the Yellow Emperor, 黃 帝 and the reputed founder of medicine. The combination of the two characters Chi and Huang, denotes medical skill.

三 指 活 人 性 命．不 爲 良 相 便 爲 良 醫

San chih huo jên hsing ming, pu wei liang hsiang pien wei liang i.

> He who with three fingers on the pulse can restore a man to health, may not be a good statesman, but he is a good doctor.

誇 嘴 的 大 夫 沒 好 藥

K'ua tsui ti ta fu mu hao yao.

> The boastful physician never has good medicine.

吃 藥 不 忌 口，枉 費 大 夫 的 手

Ch'ih yao pu chi k'ou, wang fei ta fu ti shou.

> He who takes medicine and does not diet himself, wastes the skill of the doctor.

內 科 不 治 喘，外 科 不 治 癬，治 時 討 傷 臉

Nei k'o pu chih ch'uan, wai k'o pu chih hsien, chih shih t'ao shang lien'

> Internal practitioners do not try to cure asthma; external practitioners do not try to cure ringworm; if they do attempt it, their reputation is likely to suffer. Note. 內 科 and 外 科 indicate inward and outward treatment; the two great sub-divisions of Chinese medical science.

名 醫 何 必 多 識 字

Ming i ho pi to shih tzŭ.

> A famous doctor need not be a good scholar.

醫 生 治 病 治 死 不 抵 償

I sheng chih ping chih ssŭ pu ti shang.

> A doctor may kill his patient but he will not have to pay life for life.

有 病 亂 投 醫

Yu ping luan t'ou i.

> When you are ill call in any doctor.

良 醫 之 門 下 多 病 人

Liang i chih men hsia to ping jên.

> There are many sick people at a clever doctor's door.

SECTION XIX. FACETIAE.

Chapter 1. Absurd Mistakes, Etc.

老 鴉 笑 猪 黑，自 醜 不 覺 得

Lao ya hsiao chu hei, tzŭ ch'ou pu chiao tê.

> The crow laughs at the pig for being black, and doesn't realize its own ugliness.

麻 鵲 跟 到 鶴 子 飛

Ma ch'iao ken tao yao tzŭ fei.

> Ridiculous ambition. *Lit.* The sparrow flying after the hawk.

跳 過 魚 籃 吃 豆 腐

T'iao kuo yü lan ch'ih tou fu.

> He jumps over the fish-basket to eat the bean-curd, i.e., neglects the valuable for the worthless.

猴 子 戴 鬼 臉 好 大 面 孔

Hou tzŭ tai kuei lien hao tai mien k'ung.

> To make ridiculous assumptions. *Lit.* When the monkey puts on the devil's mask, what a big face he has.

班 門 弄 斧

Pan men lung fu.

> Foolish presumption. *Lit.* To wield the axe before Pan's door. Note.—Pan or Lu Pan, 魯 班 the God of carpenters, was originally a skilful worker in wood in the State of Lu.

看 戲 的 流 眼 淚，替 古 人 耽 憂

K'an hsi ti liu yen lei, t'i ku jên tan yu.

> He who weeps at a play distresses himself for the ancients.

踹 脚 坑 的 憐 憫 打 絲 綱 的

Ch'uai chiao k'eng ti lien min ta ssŭ wang ti.

> The fisherman in the water groping for fish, pities the one in a boat fishing with a net.

撞 木 鐘 的

Chuang mu chung ti.

> To make a vain attempt. *Lit.* To try to ring a wooden bell.

大 哥 莫 笑 二 哥

Ta ko mo hsiao erh ko.

> The elder brother should not laugh at the second.

鬍 子 頭 髮 一 把 梳

Hu tzŭ t'ou fa i pa shu.

> To confound distinctions. *Lit.* To comb the beard and hair together.

揭 開 頂 瓜 皮, 把 飯 倒 進 去

Chieh k'ai ting kua p'i, pa fan tao chin ch'ü.

> To eat greedily. *Lit.* To take off the top of the skull and pour in food.

茅 屋 安 獸 頭

Mao wu an shou t'ou.

> Incongruity. To fix up an ornamental wild beast's head on a thatched hut.

癡 雞 母 觃 鴨 娃, 癡 家 婆 疼 外 孫

Ch'ih chi mu pao ya, wa ch'ih chia p'o t'eng wai sun.

> She is a silly hen that sits on duck's eggs; and she is a silly grandmother that pets her daughter's child.

只 望 葫 蘆 天 樣 大

Chih wang hu lu t'ien yang ta.

> Vain expectations. *Lit.* He only hopes that his calabash will grow as large as heaven.

落 得 河 水 不 洗 船

Lo tē ho shui pu hsi ch'uan.

> Though his boat is in the river he doesn't wash it.

吞 了 怕 是 骨 頭, 吐 了 怕 是 肉

T'un liao p'a shih ku t'ou, t'u liao p'a shih jou.

> He dare not swallow it for fear of bone; he dare not spit it out for fear it is flesh.

瞎 子 上 山 看 景 緻

Hsia tzu shang shan k'an ching chih.

　A blind man ascending a mountain to view the landscape.

蝦 蟆 想 食 天 鵝 肉

Hsia ma hsiang shih t'ien ô jou.

　　Lofty ambition. *Lit.* The toad plans to eat the flesh of the wild swan.

木 匠 做 枷 自 枷 自

Mu chiang tso chia tzǔ chia tzǔ.

　　The carpenter makes a cangue, and wears it himself Comp. Hoist with his own petard.

聽 錯 話 嗜 錯 罵

T'ing ts'o hua shê ts'o ma.

　Cursing the wrong person through misunderstanding.

以 小 人 之 心，度 君 子 之 腹

hsiao jen chih hsin, tu chün tzu chih fu.

　To measure a superior man's mind by a mean man's heart.

抓 沙 抵 水

Chua sha ti shui.

　　To dam water with sand.

望 梅 止 渴，畫 餅 充 饑

Wang mei chih k'o, hua ping ch'ung chi.

　　To feed on fancies. *Lit.* To look up at plums to quench one's thirst; to sketch a loaf to satisfy one's hunger.

抱 薪 救 火

Pao hsin chiu huo.

　　To put out a fire whilst holding fuel.

挑 雪 塡 井

T'iao hsüeh t'ien ching.

　　To fill up a well with snow.

抱 着 燈 臺 鬭 住 亮

Pao Cho teng t'ai tou chu liang.

　　Holding the lampstand he dazzles himself with the light.

得魚忘筌

Tê yü wang ch'uan.

> When the fish is caught the trap may be ignored.

開門揖盜

K'ai men i tao.

> To open one's door and bow in a thief.

砍倒樹捉八哥

K'an tao shu cho pa ko.

> To fell a tree to catch a starling.

買乾魚放生不知死活

Mai kan yü fang sheng pu chih ssŭ huo.

> To buy a dried fish in order to spare its life and set it free, is to recognise no difference between life and death.

着簑衣救火惹禍上身

Cho so i chiu huo je huo shang shen.

> To put on a grass rain coat when extinguishing a fire, is to provoke calamity on one's self.

家懶外勤

Chia lan wai ch'in.

> To be idle at home, diligent abroad.

紅蘿葡炒大蒜亂炒菜

Hung lo po ch'ao ta shan luan ch'ao ts'ai.

> To cook carrots and garlic together is a sad blunder in cookery.

孔子門前賣孝經

K'ung tzŭ men ch'ien mai Hsiao Ching.

> To offer the Filial Classic for sale at the door of Confucius.

關得罎子裏養烏龜

Kuan tê t'an tzŭ li yang wu kuei.

> To rear a tortoise shut up in a jar.

問 道 於 盲

Wen tao yü mang.

> To ask a blind man the way.

求 敎 於 愚 人

Ch'iu chiao yü yü jen.

> To seek instruction from a fool.

抱 琵 琶 進 磨 坊 對 牛 彈 琴

Pao p'i pa chin mo fang tui niu t'an ch'in.

> To carry a guitar into a mill, and play to the ox.

過 後 興 兵 悔 太 遲

Kuo hou hsing ping hui t'ai ch'ih.

> To raise soldiers when the trouble is over, and regret
> one's lateness.

水 裏 撈 明 月

Shui li lao ming yüeh.

> To drag for the moon in the water.

銀 匠 舖 裏 打 鋤 頭

Yin chiang p'u li ta ch'u t'ou.

> To make a mattock in a silversmith's shop.

鐵 匠 舖 裏 打 金 鎖

T'ieh chiang p'u li ta chin so.

> To make gold locks in a blacksmith's shop.

蔴 子 攪 豆 子

Ma tzu chiao tou tzŭ.

> Incongruity. *Lit.* To mix beans with hemp-seed.

雞 蛋 裏 頭 挑 骨 頭

Chi tan li t'ou t'iao ku t'ou.

> To try to pick bones out of an egg.

落 水 擒 水 泡

Lo shui ch'in shui p'ao.

> To drop into water to grasp the foam.

大 炮 打 麻 雀

Ta p'ao ta ma ch'iao.

> To shoot a sparrow with a cannon.

隔 靴 子 抓 癢

Ke hsüeh tzu chua yang.

> To scratch one's calf through top-boots.

不 曉 得 頭 尾 做 事

Pu hsiao tê t'ou wei tso shih.

> To act in ignorance of the beginning or consequences of anything.

強 盜 過 後 殺 壁 子

Chi'ang tao kuo hou sha pi tzǔ.

> To punish the wall after the thief has gone.

扇 子 本 姓 搖，搖 起 就 跑

Shan tzǔ pen hsing yao yao ch'i chiu p'ao.

> A fan's real name is Shake, and with one shake it is gone. Note —This is an allusion to the constant borrowing of fans one from another, and forgetfulness to return them.

鼓 兒 星 東 邊 起 西 邊 落，你 念 七 遍 過，我 念 七 遍 過

Ku erh hsing tung pien ch'i hsi pien lo, ni nien ch'i pien kuo, wo nien ch'i pien kuo.

> The Little Drum Star rises in the east and sets in the west. If you can recite this seven times in one breath, so can I. Note —Besides meaning "what you can do I can," this ditty is used playfully for a test of length of breath and power of utterance.

人 多 好 做 活，人 少 好 吃 喝

Jên to hao tso huo, jen shao hao ch'ih ho.

> When there is work to do the more people the better; the fewer the better, when it is a question of eating.

貓 兒 去 老 鼠 出 來 伸 腰

Mao erh ch'u laó shu ch'u lai shen yao.

> When the cat is away the rats come out to stretch their loins.

瘌瘰頭上打蒼蠅一打一個

La li t'ou shang ta ts'ang ying i ta i ko.

> As easy as for a scabbed-headed person to kill flies on his head; each time he strikes he hits one.

你看我我看你，好看不好看

Ni k'an wo wo k'an ni, hao k'an pu hao k'an.

> We have eyed each other well; now, are we good-looking or not,?

癡漢等丫頭

Ch'ih han teng ya t'ou.

> He is a fool who waits for a servant maid. Note.—She won't come, and so he will be made a fool of.

巡司打公館，熱鬧衙門

Hsün ssŭ ta kung kuan, jo nao ya men.

> Great cry and little wool. *Lit.* A deputy-magistrate in official lodgings—a very busy yamen.

徙宅忘妻

Hsi chai wang ch'i.

> To remove and forget to take one's wife.

包袱雨傘我

Pao fu yü san wo.

> Bundle, umbrella, and I. Note.—Used to banter men with bad memories. It is a remark of the absent-minded traveller, who though possessing his bundle and gamp, thought he had lost himself.

六月天穿皮襖

Liu yüeh t'ien ch'uan p'i ao.

> To wear a fur coat in the summer.

穿冬衣拿夏扇，冷熱不知

Ch'uan tung i na hsia shan, leng jo pu chih.

> He who puts on winter dress, and uses a summer fan, doesn't know the difference between hot and cold.

和尙寺借篦梳行錯路

Ho shang ssŭ chieh pi shu hsing ts'o lu.

> Trying to borrow a comb in a Buddhist monastery, you are on the wrong road.

千鈞之弩不爲鼷鼠發機

Ch'ien chün chih nu pu wei hsi shu fa chi.

> Don't use a ballista of thirty thousand catties to kill a mouse.

蚍蜉撼樹可笑不自量

P'i fou han shu k'o hsiao pu tzŭ liang.

> An ant shaking a tree; how funny not to be able to estimate its own strength.

SECTION XX. ON ANIMALS.

Chapter 1, Beasts.

狗 相 咬 易 得 好

Kou hsiang yao i tê hao.

Dogs fight one minute and are reconciled the next.

狗 通 人 性

Kou t'ung len hsing.

The dog understands his master's mood.

狗 不 嫌 家 貧

Kou pu hsien chia p'in.

Dogs show no aversion to poor families.

狗 有 義 人 不 知

Kou yu i jên pu chih.

Dogs have more good in them than men think they have.

犬 守 夜 鷄 司 晨

Ch'uan shou yeh chi ssu ch'en.

The dog guards the night, the cock rules the morn.

馬 不 背 主

Ma pu pei chu.

The horse never turns its back on its master.

征 馬 戀 鬬 戰

Cheng ma lien tou chan.

Cavalry horses delight in battle.

良 馬 比 君 子

Liang ma pi chün tzŭ.

A good horse resembles a superior man.

人 畜 一 般

Jên hsiu i pan.

Men and beasts are all alike. Note.—This saying is used to dissuade men from killing for food, and also to prevent cruelty.

風 馬 牛 不 相 及

Fêng ma niu pu hsiang chi.

The direction of a wind does not suit horses and oxen alike.

馬 能 識 主

Ma neng shih chu.

The horse knows his owner.

麟 鳳 龜 龍 謂 之 四 靈

Lin fêng kuei lung wei chih ssŭ ling.

The unicorn, phoenix, tortoise and dragon are called the four supernatural creatures.

迅 馬 遊 疆 不 必 守 防

Hsün ma yu chiang pu pi shou fang.

The impetuous steed won't brook restraint.

老 虎 也 有 睡 困 時

Lao hu yeh yu shui k'un shih.

Even the tiger takes a nap.

狗 拿 耗 子 多 管 閒 事

Kou na hao tzŭ to kuan hsien shih.

A busybody. *Lit.* A dog catching rats; minding other folks' business.

來 猫 去 狗，不 賺 白 有

Lai mao ch'ü kou, pu chuan tzŭ yu.

If the dog comes when the cat goes, you will get money without earning it.

狡 兔 有 三 窟

Chiao t'u yu san k'u.

The wily rabbit has three holes to his burrow.

兔 不 喫 窩 邊 草

T'u pu ch'ih wo pien ts'ao.

The hare doesn't eat the grass near its own covert.

Chapter 2. Birds.

燕 子 啣 泥 一 塲 空

Yen tzŭ hsien ni i ch'ang k'ung.

> The swallow's plastering up its nest is labour lost.
> Note.—This saying rests on the migratory character of the bird for its justification.

黃 鶯 不 打 窩 下 食

Huang ying pu ta wo hsia shih.

> The yellow hawk does not rob nests for food.

麻 鵲 雖 小 肝 膽 俱 全

Ma ch'iao sui hsiao kan tan chü ch'uan.

> Although the sparrow is so small yet it has liver and gall all complete.

寒 雞 半 夜 啼

Han chi pan yeh t'i.

> In cold weather cocks crow at midnight.

處 處 老 鴉 一 般 黑

Ch'ü ch'ü lao ya i pan hei.

> Crows are black all the world over.

老 鴉 不 吃 雞 該 鷹 的

Lao ya pu ch'ih chi kai ying ti.

> The crow does not devour fowls; they are the prey of the eagle.

新 秋 鴈 帶 來

Hsin ch'iu yen tai lai.

> The wild goose brings the beginning of autumn.

鷺 鷥 不 吃 鷺 鷥 肉

Lu ssŭ pu ch'ih lu ssŭ jou.

> The egret does not prey on its own kind.

燕 雀 豈 知 鴻 鵠 志

Yen ch'iao ch'i chih hung ku chih.

> What can the swallow know of the wild swan's intentions.
> Note.—This is to indicate the difference between narrow and wider spheres.

燕 子 養 兒 空 勞 力

Yen tzŭ yang erh k'ung lao li.

> The swallow nourishes its young but its toil is in vain,
> i.e., they fly away as soon as possible.

鳳 凰 落 架 不 如 鷄

Fêng huang lo chia pu ju chi.

> The phoenix is not so good at roosting as a chicken, i.e.,
> commonplace people can adapt themselves to
> circumstances better than the high-born.

鷦 鷯 巢 於 深 林 不 過 一 枝

Chiao liao ch'ao yü shen lin pu kuo i chih.

> The tailor-bird weaving its nest in the depths of the
> forest occupies but a single branch.

家 雀 子 過 海 沒 有 落 兒

Chia ch'iao tzŭ kuo hai mu yu lo êrh.

> Without resource. *Lit*. A sparrow crossing the sea
> with no place to rest.

粉 洗 烏 鴉 白 不 久

Fen hsi wu ya pai pu chiu.

> A white-washed crow will not long remain white.

烏 鴉 不 與 鳳 凰 棲

Wu ya pu yü feng huang ch'i.

> Crows do not roost with phoenixes.

白 鴿 只 認 屋 脊 頭

Pai ko chih jên wu chi t'ou.

> The white pigeon only recognises the ridge pole of its
> own home.

黃 鼠 狼 單 咬 病 鴨 子

Huang shu lang tan yao ping ya tzu.

> It is the sick duck alone that is worried by the weasel.

CORRIGENDA.

Page	Proverb No.	
4	7	chieh alter to chien.
59	2	hsien ,, ,, hsieh.
61	3	add chieh.
62	8	jao alter to jo.
67	5	delete s from books.
92	3	ju alter to jo.
97	8	chu ,, ,, shu.
100	8	lou ,, ,, lan.
104	1	kou ,, ,, kuo.
105	1	i ,, ,, tao.
115	6	pu ,, ,, yu.
122	4	t'ien ,, ,, nien.
124	5	add s to character.
135	5	disseminate alter to discriminate.
142	2	ch'ieh alter to ch'ien.
143	7	liu ,, ,, hsi.
161	8	t'an ,, ,, hui.
177	5	pu ,, ,, fu.
193	6	t'ai ,, ,, t'ang.
194	3	chih ,, ,, ch'i.
214	8	add kua fu hao pi.
215	9	add s to keep.
220	2	shoi alter to shui.
220	6	capital Y for yüeh.
221	5	oi alter to of.
250	2	reach alter to reached.
251	6	ts'u ,, ,, ch'u.
294	1	tu ,, ,, to.
295	8	does't ,, ,, doesn't.
298	2	evant ,, ,, event.
303	6	hien ,, ,, chien.
304	9	ehu ,, ,, chu.
324	2	shou ,, ,, ting.
329	1	works ,, ,, words.
341	3	yu ,, ,, ya.
351	1	ch'ih ,, ,, ch'i.
352	4	t'ien ,, ,, t'ieh.
365	5	pai ,, ,, jih.

CORRIGENDA.

―

Page	Proverb No.			
8	2	巳 alter to 己
45	6	之 ,, ,, 子
135	7	點 ,, ,, 占
143	2	add 得 after 不
161	7	鍔 alter to 鐔
170	3	飽 ,, ,, 鮑
187	6	全 ,, ,, 擒
188	4	透 ,, ,, 達
199	7	由 ,, ,, 有
252	8	去 ,, ,, 丟
280	2	詛 ,, ,, 祖
299	7	合 ,, ,, 和
317	5	渴 ,, ,, 喝
350	2	午 ,, ,, 下

INDEX

The figures refer to pages. The figures in parentheses refer to the Sections under which the topic is treated.